A Peerage for Trade

A History of the Royal Warrant

Paul Rowell,
with best wishes,

Tim Heald

Published by

in association with
SINCLAIR-STEVENSON

First published in Great Britain by
The Royal Warrant Holders Association
in association with Sinclair-Stevenson

Nº1 Buckingham Place, London SW1E 6HR

British Library Cataloguing in Publication Data
ACIP catalogue record for this book is available
from the British Library

ISBN 0 9540476 0 5

Main text set in Monotype Adobe Garamond 11pt

Picture Researcher: Deborah Pownall

Studio Photography: A C Cooper (Colour) Limited

Indexer: Jill Ford

Designed and Printed in England by
Barnard & Westwood Limited
9 Railway Street London N1
By Appointment to
Her Majesty The Queen
Printers and Stationers

Acknowledgements **4**

Prologue **7**

CHAPTER ONE   *The First Five Hundred Years* **11**

CHAPTER TWO   *The Victorian Warrant* **25**

CHAPTER THREE   *The Edwardian and Georgian Warrant* **41**

CHAPTER FOUR   *The Elizabethan Warrant* **59**

CHAPTER FIVE   *1979 ~ 1995* **67**

CHAPTER SIX   *1996 to the Present* **81**

The Local Associations **97**

Windsor **99**

Aberdeen **109**

Edinburgh **119**

Sandringham **125**

Appendices **130**

Index **237**

I am not a great believer in the long lists of acknowledgements which so often clutter up the beginnings of non-fiction books and even, these days, of novels. Most of those who helped in the preparation of this book are clearly identified and, at least implicitly, thanked in the text.

All the same there are one or two people whose assistance should be recorded separately. Alan Britten, the Warrant-holding former Vice-President of Mobil, has acted as what, in the commercial publishing world, would be the commissioning editor. In fact, he has done far more than most modern commercial publishers, taking a keen interest in every aspect of the book's research, writing and production and being a tower of supportive strength throughout.

Alan suggested that a professional historical researcher might be useful and recommended Dr Edward Bujak, Visiting Research Fellow at the University of East Anglia. Edward has been an assiduous mole, burrowing away in the Royal Archives at Windsor, the Public Record Office at Kew and in the recently catalogued and organised archive at the Royal Warrant Holders Association office in London. I know that Edward joins with me in expressing his gratitude to Oliver Everett and Lady de Bellaigue, Keeper and Deputy Keeper of the Royal Archives and to Christopher Pickup, Pippa Dutton, Jill Hurdman and Rosie Cox at the Royal Warrant Holders Association for not only making his researches possible but also pleasurable. I am also extremely grateful to Pat Smee, Alan's assistant at Mobil, whose logistical staff work has been impeccable.

We have, throughout, received the encouragement and support of the Royal Household, from Sir Malcolm Ross, from Elizabeth Buchanan at The Prince of Wales's office and particularly from Sir Michael Peat, Keeper of the Privy Purse.

Dr Ann Saunders and Dr Matthew Davies were recommended to us by Michael Skinner and David Peck of the Merchant Taylors' Company. They provided invaluable consultancy over the early history of the Warrant, and I am most grateful to them for their expert knowledge and suggestions for further reading. Finally, we could never have produced the sections on the four regional Associations without the willing help of the four Secretaries of those Associations, Douglas Hill of Windsor, Eton & District, John Storrs of Sandringham, George Alpine of Aberdeen and Willie Munro of Edinburgh.

Between us we have come up with new material but, inevitably, some of the best material has already appeared elsewhere. Betty Whittington who wrote a short but fascinating history of the Royal Warrant in 1961, turned up information which it would be ridiculous to omit. By the same token when I was researching my earlier book, *By Appointment,* I too discovered things that not only bear repeating but actually *have* to be repeated.

By Appointment was commissioned by the Royal Warrant Holders Association to mark the 150th anniversary of their formation. It was published in 1990 and was, essentially, a celebration of the contemporary scene, a lavish production beautifully illustrated. It contained some history but it was primarily designed to give a comprehensive picture of the extraordinary diversity and skills of those who held Royal Warrants towards the end of the twentieth century.

This book, commissioned to mark the Jubilee year in which Her Majesty The Queen celebrates the fiftieth anniversary of her accession on 6th February 1952, is designed to tell the story of Warrant holding, from mediaeval times to the present day. It documents the gradual evolution of the way in which the Monarchy recognised and honoured the tradespeople who served them, and the massive changes in the type of trades and services that they required. In the years after its formation in 1840, it inevitably also becomes a history of the Royal Warrant Holders Association.

Generally, the nearer we get to the present day the more coherent and well-documented the records become. There *are* moments in mediaeval times when the level of documentation almost defies belief. The costumes and regalia of some fourteenth- and fifteenth-century coronations, for instance, are detailed down to the last ermine ruff and golden ring. However rigorous the procedures introduced into the modern accounting systems at Buckingham Palace, twentieth-century court officials would be hard pressed to match the attention to detail of some of their mediaeval predecessors. But, understandably, we don't have such blow-by-blow accounts of what went on between the high and holy days. If the meticulousness of some fourteenth- and fifteenth-century accounts were consistent and we knew as much about the day-to-day organisation of royal life as we do about such great state ceremonials as christenings, weddings, coronations and funerals, we could be a lot less speculative about what happened during the routine of ordinary life.

Often, however, the records just aren't there. Basically there is too little for the early years and conversely there is sometimes almost too much for the later periods. Once you get to the Victorians those interminable banquets with their endless toasts and ballads and entrees all listed chapter and verse, giblet and goblet, induce as much nausea in the researcher and writer as they must surely have done in the original consumer.

Some evidence does not exist because it was deliberately not created in the first place. For centuries it was a characteristic of British business that 'my word is my bond'. A handshake could be at least as binding as a written communication. Understandings, even important financial understandings, were often verbal and contracts were sealed with a nod and a wink rather than pen and ink. We know of hundreds of Royal Warrants ratified with heavy stamped wax endorsements but there are other arrangements about which we will never know.

This suspicion of ancient secrets has made the writing of some of this book tantalising but what has made it such fun is the knowledge that between us we have been digging in hitherto unmined fields of historical gold. There are boxes and envelopes in the archives which have lain unopened since they were deposited there many years ago. It has been a rare privilege to be involved in their reopening.

The Royal Arms above the Secretary's door in Buckingham Place,
first authorised in 1910, by King George V

The most usual meaning of the word 'warrant' and the one that most people would recognise immediately is the sort that is issued for someone's arrest. Anyone who has ever watched a movie involving cops and robbers, or who has read a whodunnit, knows that the first thing a suspect asks an inquisitive or assertive police officer is whether or not he has a warrant. It is a usage which seems to have entered the English language in the mid-fourteenth century from German or ancient French.

Before long, however, 'warrant' assumed a more general meaning based on the fact that the word was a dialect or corrupt form of 'guarantee'. A warrant came to mean any writing authorising what the Oxford Dictionary describes as 'those to whom it is addressed to perform some act'. The nature of the 'act' was vague but when it comes to 'warrant holder' the Dictionary suddenly becomes much more precise. 'A Warrant Holder', it says, is 'a tradesman who has written authority to supply goods to the household of the King or Queen or a member of The Royal Family'.

'Tradesman' would seem to exclude the professions. A doctor might be the royal physician or the royal surgeon but he could not be a Warrant Holder. The same would apply to the royal barrister or solicitor, the Poet Laureate or the Master of the King's (or Queen's) Musick. They might all hold written authorities from the Monarch but unless they were engaged in 'trade' they could not, technically, be 'Warrant Holders'.

The 'authority' must be written. Of that there is no question. A verbal authority is insufficient. Even if you supply endless 'goods' to the King or Queen, or a member of their family, you could not describe yourself as a 'Warrant Holder' unless you had some written proof that you were indeed purveyor of the royal marmalade or the royal piece of bread. And, if the Dictionary is to be believed, the granting of Warrants in the United Kingdom is a purely royal prerogative. The Archbishop of Canterbury or the Lord Chief Justice or the Prime Minister might all take it upon

themselves to issue 'Warrants' to their favoured tradesmen but that would not entitle the recipients to describe themselves as 'Warrant Holders'.

So much for the dictionary definition.

The first known example in England of a formal royal document involving Royalty and 'Trade' was between Henry II and the Weavers Company in 1155. This took the form of a Royal Charter and over the years it was followed by numerous others. The Drapers were granted their charter by Edward III and the Mercers by Richard II. These charters are related to later Royal Warrants in that they formalise a relationship between the Royal Family and those who work in trade. The granting of a Royal Charter to a livery company or guild, however, was not the singling out of one person but the acknowledgement of a group of specialists. The idea was not in itself to ensure special service to the Crown but rather to acknowledge an organisation of experts and allow them to regulate their affairs, maintain and raise standards, and generally promote the excellence of their craft. The Weavers existed not for the benefit of the Monarch but to promote the cause of fine weaving throughout the country. The same applied to the Drapers, the Mercers, the Merchant Taylors, the Skinners and all the rest.

The formal royal recognition of individuals comes later, even though in practice all monarchs would have had particular favourites who would supply everything from crown jewellery to 'beeves and muttons'.

In today's Britain this recognition of individuals has evolved to a point at which it is far more complicated than a mere dictionary could explain. By the beginning of the twenty-first century the conventions of ancient history had become codified and governed by well-established rules. By and large these were laid down and interpreted by a Royal Household Tradesmen's Warrants Committee headed by the Lord Chamberlain. As head of the Royal Household, it was part of the Lord Chamberlain's task to advise the four Grantors – The Queen, The Duke of Edinburgh, The Queen Mother and The Prince of Wales – as to whether the conditions of supply and service had been met, and who therefore should receive their Warrants.

The Royal Warrant Holders Association was, in effect, the other side of the coin. Since its original foundation early in the nineteenth century the Association has been a fascinating and very British combination of trades association and social club. Almost all who held the Warrant belonged to the Association and could rely on the Association's advice and assistance in time of trouble. The Association also acted as a policeman on behalf of the monarchy, making sure that its name and its Coats of Arms were never taken in vain. The Association's office in London employed a Secretary and a small salaried staff overseen by a Council of non-executive, unpaid members. This consisted of a President – a Warrant Holder who served for one year in that office – as well as representatives of the four constituent Associations in other parts of the United Kingdom and all the surviving Presidents.

The Warrant itself was an impressive document

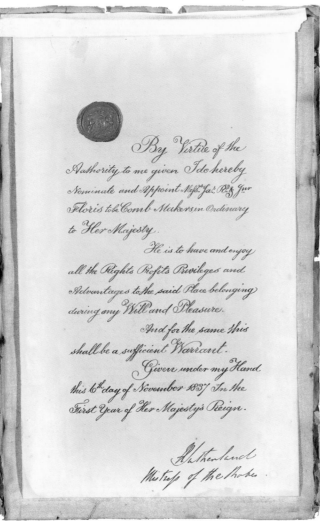

filled out in immaculate copperplate writing and signed by the Lord Chamberlain. The Warrant was 'By Command' of the Grantor and it announced simply that the grantee was 'appointed into the place and quality' of butcher, baker, candlestick-maker or whatever the relevant trade might be. The Warrants were given to individuals rather than companies and as such were a source of great personal pride.

However, it was the grantees' companies which were allowed to display the Royal Coat of Arms in the outward and visible form which is familiar to the public at large. The Royal Arms might be displayed on company premises, delivery vans, writing paper and elsewhere, but the Arms must never be flaunted and their use had always to be governed by dignity and good taste.

In return the obligations and duties of the Warrant Holder were implicit and never spelled out. The unwritten requirement was, quite simply, that the services and goods provided were of a consistently high standard. If this ceased to be the case, the Warrant would be removed. In the event of bankruptcy, sale or death the Warrant would also be

Warrant granted to Floris in the first year of Queen Victoria's reign. The first official Warrant to Floris was granted in 1820, as 'Smooth Pointed Comb-makers' to the new King George IV. Since then, Floris has held the Warrant of every succeeding British Monarch.
J. Floris Ltd.

revoked. But provided standards were maintained, loyalty was rewarded with loyalty. Many Warrant-holding companies have been proud to hold their Warrants for generation after generation. Many would endorse the ringing words of Capt T. Simpson Jay in 1896 that to hold a Royal Warrant was 'a species of peerage for trade'.

After fifty years of the reign of Queen Elizabeth II the essentials seemed unlikely to change dramatically.

This is not to say there will be no change, for the rules and the philosophy have been evolving for hundreds of years and will continue to do so. The essentials, however, have always remained constant.

As long as there is a Royal Family there must be loyal tradesmen to serve and supply them.

The Royal Warrant is the formal recognition of that trust.

The Weavers' Charter, granted by Henry II c. 1155, attested by Thomas à Becket.
The earliest surviving Livery Company Charter.
Weavers Company

King Richard II dining with the Dukes of York, Gloucester and Ireland. Taken from the Chronique d'Angleterre, Volume III, "from the Coronation of Richard II to 1387", by Jean de Batard Wavrin.
British Library/Bridgeman Art Library

Right: *King Edward I investing his son, the future Edward II, as Prince of Wales. Reproduced from Commendatio Lamentabilis in the British Library.* Bridgeman Art Library

Below: *The Queen Eleanor's Cross at Geddington, near Kettering. Erected by Edward I to mark the resting places of his Queen on her journey to London after her death in Lincoln.* John D Beldam/ Collections Photo Library

In 1300 Reginald de Thunderley, an immigrant London citizen, supplied fourteen striped 'clothes' to be used to make special uniforms for the valets of Queen Margaret, the second wife of King Edward I.

De Thunderley was 'Purveyor of Cloth to the Wardrobe' and his striped material appears in an indenture prepared by a man called Perrot, the junior of the Queen's two tailors. Perrot was paid fourpence a day, whereas his boss Thomasin was on a daily wage of sevenpence. In the same document Thomasin is recorded, under item twenty-nine, as having supplied three furs and a rabbit-skin coverlet for an infant's cradle. A week or so earlier The Queen's apothecary purchased pomegranates, cordials and other medicines in York, while in the same city John, her fruiterer, bought apples and pears for the royal table.

John the fruiterer, The Queen's apothecary, her two tailors – a position later described as 'Serjeant tailor' – and Reginald de Thunderley are some of the earliest recorded ancestors of today's Royal Warrant Holders. They are the precursors of such modern tradesmen as Boots the Chemist and Hardy Amies of Savile Row.

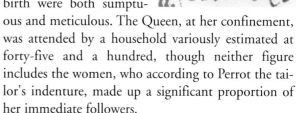

We know about these mediaeval servants of the Crown because they were all involved with the birth of Thomas of Brotherton, later Earl of Norfolk and Earl Marshal of England. His father Edward I had had fifteen children with his first wife, Eleanor of Castile, but ten of those were already dead. So was Eleanor, for whom Edward had erected the famous chain of Eleanor crosses beginning at her death place, Lincoln, and ending at London's Charing Cross. The only male heir prior to Thomas's birth was Prince Edward, subsequently the disastrous King Edward II who fell under the homosexual spell of Piers Gaveston and was disgustingly murdered with a red-hot poker at Berkeley Castle in 1327. He was born in 1284 and was only sixteen at the time of his stepbrother's birth. So the royal birth of 1300 was eagerly awaited.

Thomas of Brotherton was the new Queen's first-born and he made the line of succession doubly secure. No wonder, then, that preparations for his birth were both sumptuous and meticulous. The Queen, at her confinement, was attended by a household variously estimated at forty-five and a hundred, though neither figure includes the women, who according to Perrot the tailor's indenture, made up a significant proportion of her immediate followers.

Reginald de Thunderley was not among them. Unlike the two tailors, he was not a salaried member of staff but rather a valued independent tradesman, much like those who hold the Royal Warrant in modern times. He lived in London and supplied cloth to any client who could pay his price. The fact that the Royal Wardrobe was one of these would obviously have worked to his advantage. The smart set in early fourteenth-century London would know that if the royal tailors wanted thirteen ells of the best scarlett of Lincoln then the man they would go to would be

Reg de Thunderley. If you wanted to dress like Royalty then you would buy your miniver, your pople, your stranling, your samite and your rabbit skin from Thunderley. He purveyed to the Wardrobe. He therefore purveyed to the King. Ergo he must be the best purveyor of cloth in London town.

The document which mentions de Thunderley, a single membrane of parchment discovered by chance in the Public Record Office, is the oldest known such record. Before the late Middle Ages, what the historian Kay Staniland describes as 'records of the domestic arrangements of the royal household' are rare. In earlier times such orders were more often issued verbally. Or records have been lost. Or eaten by mice. So even if there were earlier Thunderleys we don't know about them.

The idea behind the modern 'Royal Warrant' is as old as the institution of monarchy itself. It is founded on the twin pillars of excellence and of service – concepts which have survived through centuries of change.

Even primitive crowns and courts required a support system. From the very beginning the King had to be clothed and adorned, and this had to be done in a way that emphasised his majesty. Being King was a competitive business with threats in every quarter and it was important that kings, their nearest and dearest, their servants, their guards, their whole entourage should be appropriately caparisoned. A King who looked less magnificent than one of his subjects gave rise to doubt. It was also important to appear at least as majestic as the kings of other countries. It is all very well, in these democratic times, for rival heads of state to appear at conferences in identical dark suits. In earlier times such meetings were sartorially and stylistically competitive. The most ostentatious of all was at the Field of the Cloth of Gold when, in 1520, Henry VIII humiliated François I of France in what was, essentially, a mediaeval fashion contest. The Field of the Cloth of Gold was one of many.

But there has always been more to supporting court life than the provision of orbs, sceptres, crowns and ermine robes. Even kings and queens had to have dwelling places with roofs and walls that could withstand the elements. They needed plumbers as well as jewellers, chimney sweeps as well as goldsmiths.

Monarchs dined and drank in style and certainly did not live by bread alone. Nevertheless A. A. Milne was not being entirely facetious when, in his poem, 'The King's Breakfast', he wrote:

Left: *Henry VIII arrives at the Field of the Cloth of Gold, near Guines in France on 7th June, 1520. Copy by Friedrich Bouterwek of an anonymous painting at Hampton Court.*
Dagli Orti/Art Archive

> The King asked
> The Queen, and
> The Queen asked
> The Dairymaid:
> 'Could we have some butter for
> The Royal slice of bread.'

Royalty needed bread and butter. The difference was – and is – that the royal slice of bread should be

the best in the land. Likewise the royal pat of butter. Royal Warrant Holders and their ancestors have to provide for all the royal needs from the mundane to the magnificent and therefore they have always ranged from the everyday to the exotic.

We know about these royal servants from the incredibly detailed and well-preserved accounts of 'The Great Wardrobe'. In the thirteenth century all royal household administration came under the heading of an organisation called 'The Wardrobe'. Around 1236, the 'Great' Wardrobe began to expand dramatically and to develop its own separate identity. It was essentially the commissariat responsible for 'buying and storing non-perishable commodities for the King's use' and it was the quantity of these goods, furniture, hangings, cloth, furs, wax and groceries (from spices to saltpetre) that gave the department its title of 'great''.

Later its scope increased to take in jewels, plate, armour, tents and horse gear. Before long it became a serious 'manufactory' as well. In 1253 it was turning over a stunning £2000 a year and by the end of the century it was in the charge of its own 'Keeper', appointed by letters patent. In the fourteenth century the Great Wardrobe and its Keeper moved out of 'court' and into their own London premises, ending up in a house just north of the city church of St Andrew Castle Baynard. It was bought for them by Edward III from Sir John Beauchamp in 1360.

The Keepers of the Great Wardrobe did not just keep a great wardrobe, they also kept the most meticulous accounts on such great occasions as births, marriages, coronations and deaths. These are the earliest records of transactions between the Royal Household, represented by the Great Wardrobe, and the craftsmen

and traders who today form the bulk of the modern Royal Warrant Holders Association.

The precise functions and duties of different parts of the Royal Household have changed constantly and have always been subject to confusion and misunderstanding. By the time of Richard III's Coronation in 1483 all armour and weapons came under the auspices of the King's Armoury at the Tower and yet it was the Keeper of the Great Wardrobe who was instructed to provide the four swords at the centre of the Coronation ceremony. Why did swords come from the Wardrobe and not the Armoury? A similar confusion arose in fruit and veg. Even before the 1483 Coronation, responsibility for spices, fruit and wax had been removed from the Great Wardrobe and vested in the Great Spicery, which in turn delegated their purchase to the departments of confectionery and chandlery. Yet in the reign of Henry VII immediately afterwards the Keeper of the Great Wardrobe was still buying wax and possibly even spices as well as recording a weekly 'fee' of eleven and a half pounds of wax. One can only guess at the ill feeling and jealousy generated by such poaching.

All the Great Wardrobe accounts were composed in Latin until the reign of Edward IV. By 1480 they were being rendered in English, although there was a brief return to Latin during the reign of Henry VII. At one point in the reign of Edward I the Great Wardrobe was employing 669 officials.

One of the most significant forerunners of the modern Royal Warrant Holder was the Paris-born George Lovekyn. By Lovekyn's day the office of 'Serjeant tailor' was apparently less important than it had been in the reign of Henry III but Lovekyn was unusual because he was tailor to no less than three kings – Edward IV, Richard III and Henry VII. Unlike some of his predecessors, Lovekyn seems to have continued in private practice. Earlier tailors appear also to have been responsible for binding the royal books but Lovekyn passed these duties on to a stationer – surely a more appropriate person.

As a mere 'yeoman of the wardrobe' Lovekyn made robes for Edward IV, the Prince of Wales, the Dukes of Gloucester and Clarence, and Lord Hastings. All these commissions were at the express instruction of the King. Indeed the King often used 'his' tailor to make clothes for those he favoured, including one or two distinguished foreigners.

In 1475 Lovekyn was appointed 'Serjeant tailor' and made the King's clothes from then on. In 1483 he made Richard III's Coronation robes but then lost his 'serjeanty' only to regain it after the accession of Henry VII. On his death in 1504 he was succeeded by his apprentice, Stephen Jasper. His son George served in the King's stables along with his uncle William Pawne who was servant to John Cheyne, Master of the Horse. Another son, Arthur, worked as Pawne's clerk. The Lovekyns were therefore something of an 'Artisan Dynasty'. Theirs was not exactly a 'family business' but being a relation of George Lovekyn seems to have been a definite advantage, particularly if you aspired to work for the Crown. George's situation was obviously not exactly the same as that of a modern Warrant Holder but in his ability to move from the service of one Monarch to another, in his combination of dedicated service with independence of action as well as a comfortable level of economic and social status, he does quite closely resemble the sort of tai-

lors and cutters who are responsible for the apparel of the House of Windsor five hundred years later. It is not too fanciful to imagine George Lovekyn having a mutually interesting conversation with one or two of the Presidents of the Royal Warrant Holders Association in the 1990s and 2000s. He and Robert Gieve of Gieves & Hawkes or Michael Skinner, Chairman of the Savile Row tailors Dege & Skinner, would have a lot in common.

Royal patronage has often been more innovative than critics allow. The first King's Printer was William Caxton, father of British printing. He actually printed the statutes of King Henry VII. Henry VIII, too, had a printer, Thomas Berthelet, who was also the King's Binder and the man responsible for introducing gold tooling to England. Today there is no longer a Royal Printer as such but a Royal Warrant is held by Austen Kopley and it is his company, Barnard & Westwood, which is responsible for the printing of this book.

It was Henry VIII's printer, Thomas Berthelet, who printed out the Statutes of Eltham which were drawn up for 'the good order of his household'. These provide valuable evidence about those who served the needs of the court. As Betty Whittington tells us in her brief 1961 history of the Warrant, there was a man called Thomas Hewytt who

> 'hath bound himself by his deede obligatory to serve the Court with Swannes and Cranes, price the piece two shillings. The said Hewytt shall serve the King with all kindes of Wildfoule, in every degree according to the articles specified. It is ordeyned that the said Purveyor shall have authority by the King's Commission to make his provision of Poultry within this Realm.'

Henry VIII also had a 'Laundresse' called Anne Harris who was appointed by the Comptroller of Green

Left: Anonymous portrait of King Richard III who reigned for two years until he was defeated and killed at the Battle of Bosworth Field, 1485, by Henry, Duke of Richmond, founder of the Tudor dynasty.
Syon House/ Bridgeman Art Library

Below: A modern business card, displaying the Royal Warrant.

Right: *William Caxton showing his first Specimen of Printing to King Edward IV.*
Thomas Ross Ltd

Cloth and who was responsible for 'the washing of the napery which shall serve the King's Own Table'. In return for washing whatever was required she received £1 10s a year and free wood, sope (sic) as well as 'any other thing'.

An interesting sidelight on sixteenth-century hygiene is provided by the additional information that Ms Harris was asked to provide two chests. The first of these was for 'cleane Stuff' and the second for 'the stuff that hath been occupied'. This was presumably the Tudor equivalent of the dirty-clothes basket and to prevent noxious fumes the Laundresse had to 'further provide as much sweet Powder and Sweet Herbes as shall be necessary for the sweet keeping of the said stuff'.

Henry's daughter, Queen Elizabeth I, had a Household Book, which also provides revealing detail regarding the people we would now call butchers and fishmongers but who were then described as 'Yeomen Purveyors of Veales; Beeves and Muttons; Sea and Fresh Water Fish'. These yeomen were evidently paid and rewarded on a regular basis. Thus, 'Purveyors of Beeves and Muttons to have £13 13s 4d a yeare and all riding charges. The Purveyor of Veales 100 shillings a yeare, and 20 pence per diem Board Lodging. Purveyor of Fish £10 a yeare entertainment and £22 11s 8d a yeare for losses and necessaries.'

Elizabeth I had a vast and elaborate wardrobe, which was looked after by a small department within the Great Wardrobe known as the Wardrobe of Robes. Clothes were an integral part of her 'Gloriana' image and accordingly they had to be sumptuous. She had so much in the way of gowns, robes and jewels that she was in the habit not only of losing clothing and jewellery but also of giving much away. One of her 'daybooks' deals almost exclusively with items that she gave away to servants and courtiers such as tailors and laundresses who might today come under the heading of Warrant Holders. So, for example, in 1564 The Queen gave Mrs Marbery, one of her 'Chamberers', some some single-linen hose in February and some double-linen hose in April. Her tailors, Walter Fyshe and, later, William Jones, simply made too many clothes for her to store, let alone wear, and the result was that she gave much away.

The historian Janet Arnold observes that the amount of clothing The Queen gave away puts a corrective gloss on her supposed extravagance and adds that her daybook 'conjures up a fascinating picture of Elizabeth shedding jewels on her Progresses like some perambulating Christmas tree. Among them were gold and blue enamelled buttons lost at Chartley, gold pansies at Deptford, a small gold acorn and an oakleaf at Westminster and pearls at Richmond. Occasionally the jewels were recovered, but they must often have been kept as souvenirs by the lucky finders, "lost from her majesties back"'.

Elizabeth's gifts, some ordered by Warrant, such as one to George Brideman on 28th March 1572 for a 'Night gowne' for the Earl of Leicester, ranged from robes for the most noble Order of the Garter for foreign Royalty to russet satin for a doublet for the Steward to the Cardinal of Chatillon, which was almost certainly a payment from the state for spying on his master.

There is often a problem with ascertaining the precise nature of a relationship between the Monarch and others. Discretion and deference make bad history. Even in modern times there is, for instance, still speculation about the relationship between Her Majesty Queen Elizabeth II and her prime minister Mrs Thatcher. So-called 'experts' have jumped to all manner of conclusions but no one *knows* because neither The Queen nor Mrs Thatcher has ever discussed it in public. This discretion is a tradition sanctified by the weight of centuries and it applies – or is supposed to – even more to royal servants than to prime ministers. Think of the opprobrium heaped on the royal nanny, Mrs Crawford or 'Crawfie' who spilled some really quite innocuous beans when talking about her time in the royal nursery with the Princesses Elizabeth and Margaret. Or the royal reaction to the publication of a kiss-and-tell book by the former private secretary to Diana Princess of Wales. In earlier times such revelations would have led to the block or the scaffold by way of the rack and the Tower.

Although Oliver Cromwell preferred the title of 'Protector' to that of King, he persisted with a number of politically incorrect regal practices. According to Roy Sherwood in his study, 'The Court of Oliver Cromwell', the Protector employed a timber merchant, a master carpenter, a master mason, an ironmonger, a master joiner, a master carver, two bricklayers, a painter, two smiths, a carpenter, two plasterers, a paviour, a glazier, a man responsible for the 'lashing of ropes', a mattlayer and three others 'of unspecified occupation'. All these were described as servants of 'His Highness' and assigned to one of the two 'Protectoral Palaces' at Whitehall and Hampton Court. In addition to these 'below stairs' artisans Cromwell also employed a personal hatter, tailor, upholsterer and three measurers of cloth.

The Board of Green Cloth, which traditionally dealt with Royal Warrants of Appointment was, like

Left: The "Armada" portrait of Queen Elizabeth I, attributed to George Gower, circa 1588, now at Woburn Abbey.
Bridgeman Art Library

Above: *Equestrian engraving of Oliver Cromwell, c.1655, by Albert Haelwegh. Cromwell's crest is featured at the bottom.*
Stapleton Collection/ Bridgeman Art Library

Right: *King Charles II, painted by Pieter Nason, or one of his circle, wearing the lace traditional to that period.*
Bridgeman Art Library

the Crown itself, technically in abeyance for most of Cromwell's reign. However it was reconstituted a year before his death. The Protector was also keen on displaying his Coat of Arms, which was even worn by his personal bargemen. Such evidence seems to suggest a certain growing vaingloriousness and perhaps an aspiration, in time, for the eventual accession of King Oliver the First.

We know tantalisingly little about the relationship between King Charles the Second and his Lace Drapers. The Lace Drapers clearly had a close relationship with their sovereign but its details were not discussed. Even in the twenty-first century Royal Tradesmen do not go scurrying to the popular papers telling tales out of school. If they did they would certainly not retain their Warrants.

We do know that on 10th March 1674 a petition concerning the Lace Drapers was sent to the Earl of Arlington, the Lord Chamberlain. It said, 'I desire Your Lordship to give Order that Mr William Rutland and Mrs Katherine Eaton may be sworne His Majesty's servants in the quality of Lace Drapers for all things belonging to the Robes in the place of Mr Eaton deceased.'

We know that some years earlier a petition had been sent to Arlington's predecessor, the Earl of Manchester, desiring him to swear in a Mr Eaton 'to serve the King with Lace for all necessarys belonging to the Robes'.

The assumption has to be that Mr Eaton died in 1674 and his business passed to his widow Katherine and William Rutland. This, of course, is a guess and unfortunately the same has to apply to Rutland. We can only guess the nature of his relationship to Mr and Mrs Eaton. It seems most likely that he was Eaton's assistant and inherited a share in the business. But maybe he was the widow Eaton's boyfriend. Or perhaps he was just a new business partner.

In any event their royal service as Lace Drapers was sadly short-lived for in June the following year another petition was addressed to the Lord Chamberlain. This one read, 'I desire your Lordship that you will please give Order for the swearing of Katherine Allen widow, Lace Draper to His Majesty in Ordinary in the place of Katherine Eaton, deceased, to have and enjoy all profitts, perquisites and advantages thereto belonging that she may be admitted into the said place accordingly.' So poor Katherine Eaton survived to enjoy barely a year as the Royal Lace Draper.

An invaluable source, cited by the estimable Betty Whittington, is Dr Edward Chamberlayne, who produced several editions of *The Present State of England* rather in the manner of the twentieth century's several versions of *The Anatomy of Britain* by Anthony Sampson. At first, Chamberlayne seems to have taken a dim view of Royal Tradesmen whom he described as 'those that live by buying and selling, people of the baser sort'. By the end of Charles II's reign, however, he changed his mind and declared that those who supplied the Crown on a regular basis were no longer 'people of the baser sort' but 'Persons of Quality'. In 1684 he identified some of these as 'Mr Wareing, Haberdasher of Hats; Nicholas Eustons, Button Maker; Mr Kinnard, Joyner; William Black, Locksmith; Mr Holder,

KLEY. BERKELEY

Locksmith; John Hargood, Sword Cutter; Robert Seignor, Watchmaker in Reversion; Mr Middleton, Operator for the Teeth; Stephen Wysing, Corn Cutter; and David Gassiers, Goffe-Club Maker'.

The most significant aspect of the surviving seventeenth-century petitions is that they require the swearing in of the petitioners as 'His Majesty's servants' no matter whether they are dealing with the Lord Chamberlain's department or the Lord Steward's department. The Lord Chamberlain's servants are always described as 'tradesmen' whereas the Lord Steward's are 'purveyors'. This distinction persisted until 1854. To a modern onlooker it may seem mere semantics but at the time the difference was clear-cut and significant.

The Lord Chamberlain's department was, essentially, the one that dealt with life 'above stairs' whereas the Lord Steward's looked after 'below stairs'.

According to the Public Record Office this meant that the Lord Chamberlain was responsible for 'The Chambers, Wardrobes, Office of Robes, Ceremonies, Revels, Musicians, Chapels, Housekeepers, Messengers, Yeomen of the Guard, Watermen, Physicians, Artists, Craftsmen and other offices such as Librarian, Latin Secretary, Poet Laureate, Examiner of Plays and Keeper of Lions at the Tower'. The Lord Steward looked after 'The Kitchen offices (Almonry, Ewry, Bakery, Confectionery, Buttery, Spicery, Poultry, Larder, Pantry, Wine Cellar, Scullery), the Counting House, Wood and Coal Yards, the Verge, porters, harbingers, caretakers, waiters, table deckers and other related positions such as Keeper and Repairer of the Buckets, Keeper of Ice and Snow, Trunkmaker, Brewer and Cistern Cleaner'. The Lord

Steward was also in charge of the gardens and the stables.

Whether they are the Lord Chamberlain's 'tradesmen' or the Lord Steward's 'purveyors' the word 'servant' is common to both. This implies that they were not just outside agents supplying goods and services, but rather members of the court itself. One can assume, therefore, that the 'proffitts, perquisites and advantages' would have included a regular salary. We know, for instance, that King James II's clockmaker, Mr Herbert, was granted a Warrant in 1686 which, among other things, awarded him a salary of two hundred (pounds?) per annum.

It is unclear, however, whether the down side of this arrangement was that it prevented one engaging in trade outside court. One of the main 'perquisites and advantages' of those serving the Monarch, whether it is a mediaeval Reginald de Thunderley or a modern manufacturer of marmalade or mothballs, is that the royal favour confers an advantage in one's dealings with the ordinary commercial world. But we don't know whether or not Mr Herbert could make clocks for commoners or whether Mr and Mrs Eaton could supply lace for the robes of the aristocracy.

Dr Chamberlayne's 1700 edition lists a number of 'Purveyors' to the Court of King William and Queen Mary. These included purveyors of bacon, poultry, fish, butcher's meat and oysters as well as a linen draper, a wine merchant and two brewers.

Royal Warrants were much sought after and

Left: Engraving by Stanley Berkeley of golf being played in the early 17th century

Below: Mid-seventeenth century English court kitchen. "The French might produce decorative marvels but when it came to pies, the English were acknowledged masters".
"The Fine Art of Food"

during the eighteenth century it was common practice for fees to be levied on new Warrant Holders by various court officials. This practice was discontinued on a piecemeal basis during the nineteenth century but throughout the 1700s it became generally understood that if you aspired to being a Royal Tradesman you paid for the privilege. In a household divided into a number of autonomous departments with officials dispensing patronage on all sorts of different levels the opportunity for corruption was obviously considerable. Until 1831, for instance, a fee of five guineas was levied by the Clerk of the Stables from every new tradesman appointed to the Royal Mews. This practice was abolished that year by the Master of the Horse acting on the recommendation of the Clerk Marshal. Other departments did not, however, follow suit – a clear indication of the continuing independence of different departments of the Royal Household.

A year after the banning of fees in the Stables the Lord Steward's department made it clear that all new Warrant Holders were still required to pay fees 'upon appointment' to supply

'fish (cured and uncured), oysters, 'turtle', milk, cream, cheese, butter, eggs, vegetables, grocery, ale, beer, wines, spirits, liqueurs, mineral water, soda water, confectionery, chocolate, fruit, butcher's meat, pork, poultry, bacon, lard, flour, yeast, bread, biscuits (including both Swiss and 'fancy' biscuits), tea, maccaroni, salt, vinegar, mustard, 'comestibles', flowers, tobacco and snuff, fishing tackle, hats and caps, stationery, corks, linen, wax, tallow candles, lamp oil, coal, charcoal, braziers, ironmongery, oil lamps and tableware – pewter, cutlery, china and glassware'.

From the earliest days of monarchy different royal officials had often pursued different and sometimes contradictory policies. This led to confusion both for those who had to deal with the situation at the time and also for subsequent historians. The Lord Steward's fees were eventually abolished in the 1850s. But there seems no good reason why they survived so much longer than those in the Master of the Horse's department.

A good example of authority's attempts to stamp out graft and corruption in the Stables at the end of the eighteenth century is provided by a Warrant which also establishes one of the earliest real links with the present day. Signed by the Earl of Westmorland on 17th June 1796 – the thirty-sixth year of the reign of George III – it reads as follows:

'By Virtue of the Powers invested in me by His Majesty, I do hereby constitute and appoint

Philip Douglas Firmin to serve His Majesty's Stables in Quality of Buttonmaker (in the room and place of Samuel Firmin deceased) and as both the Goodness and Price of the Buttons delivered will be strictly examined into, so, for the Encouragement of such Tradesmen as shall have the Honor of serving His Majesty in this Department, it is ordered, that their Bills shall be regularly paid at the End of each Quarter, and that no Poundage, Fee nor Perquisite, shall be given to the Clerk of the Stables, or to any other Person whatsoever.'

The Earl of Westmorland has clearly fingered the Clerk of the Stables as a man on the take, and it sounds as if he has a clear idea of who 'any other Person whatsoever' might be. In its clarity and detail it is an unusual Warrant — more like a contract than our modern idea of a Warrant.

Even more significantly, however, it is one of the first Warrants granted to a company which still, more than two centuries later, is providing goods and services to the Royal Household. Firmins were the royal buttonmakers then and they remain the royal buttonmakers now. Such continuity is rare but from this time on the number of such companies continues to grow. Familiar modern names who held Royal Warrants around the end of the eighteenth century include James Swaine who was whip maker to George III and James Wilkinson who was his gun maker. Richard Wall was The Prince of Wales's pork butcher and, after he became King George IV, George Chubb was his locksmith. Robert Garrard was William IV's goldsmith and Mrs Caley was Queen Charlotte's milliner

and dressmaker. J. Schweppe & Co. were manufacturers of soda water to the Duchess of Kent and her daughter Princess Victoria.

Moreover, the custom of displaying Coats of Arms at one's premises was beginning to become established. Johnson and Justerini – forerunners of today's Justerini & Brooks – displayed the three-feathered crest of The Prince of Wales on their letterhead together with the boast that they were his 'Foreign Cordial Merchants'. This was in 1779. And the Coat of Arms of HRH the Duchess of Gloucester, daughter of King George III, could be seen over the shop front of Mr John Burgess in the Strand.

Towards the end of the eighteenth century the profligacy of The Prince of Wales, later Prince Regent and ultimately King George IV, meant a significant increase in the number of Royal Tradesmen. 'Prinny' is supposed to have spent £10,000 a year on clothes alone. Earlier monarchs were less extravagant and the number of Royal Tradesmen was quite limited. Such a select band could quite easily be incorporated into the servant structure of court life, but by the 1770s this was no longer the case.

Diversification and expansion was not simply the result of extravagance. The world was becoming a more sophisticated place. Mediaeval courts were often grand but they were relatively primitive. The most important hard-core servants were tailors, goldsmiths, skinners, saddlers, cordwainers and others of that ilk. Now, as the eighteenth century turned into the nineteenth, there was far wider variety of artefacts available to the fashionable and wealthy. A medi-

Left: The exterior of Floris' Jermyn Street shop, displaying the Royal Arms of King George IV, dating from 1820. J. Floris Ltd.

Below: *King George IV, after his coronation in 1821, wearing full garter robes, painted by Sir Thomas Lawrence.* Vatican Museum and Galleries/Bridgeman Art Library

Right: *A customer is weighed on the 18th century scales which still stand in the front room of Berry Bros' shop in St. James's Street.*
Berry Bros & Rudd Ltd.

aeval king might have dined off gold or silver plate and drunk from gold or silver goblets. Now it would be china and porcelain, glass and crystal. A far wider range of fabrics and furnishings was also becoming available.

The expansion in international trade meant an increase in imports, many of them exotic. Naturally such luxury items found their way into royal palaces, part of whose function was to demonstrate a lifestyle superior to that of the common or even aristocratic people. Enterprising tradesmen were not backward in promoting their wares. One odd example was provided by King George IV's 'plush manufacturer', a man named James Harris who was reported in the press in 1822 to have 'imported at Liverpool a quantity of fruits exquisitely delicious and hitherto unknown in England'. Harris came from Coventry but moved to Brazil whence, presumably, came these fruits, a box of which he dispatched to His Majesty. Harris obviously had an eye for publicity because news of the gift found its way into the *Eton and Windsor Express* which reported that 'Mr Peter Moore, with becoming attention and respect, conveyed them on Tuesday last to

Carlton Palace to be forwarded to Windsor'.

It was not just that goods and services were becoming more varied and complex. Huge social changes were also taking place. The status of the Crown was much diminished and that of the newly emergent middle class correspondingly enhanced. One entertaining example is the relationship between the Hanoverians and their esteemed wine merchant Mr Berry at 3 St James. Berry had a set of weighing scales – they are still there – in the front room of his shop and most if not all the sons of King George III used to drop in for a drop of something and to have themselves weighed. On one occasion some government jobsworth attempted to remove the scales just as one of the Royal Dukes came in to be weighed. 'Who dares to say that my old friend Berry is guilty of fraud,' cried the (unidentified) Duke. 'Leave those things here and let me be weighed.' The scales stayed. 'Queen Victoria's Wicked Uncles' were an extremely undignified crew, none more so than her immediate predecessor, King William IV – who fathered no less than ten illegitimate children with the actress Mrs Jordan. The 'Sailor King' drank only sherry and was accustomed, even after his accession, to wander over to Berry's for a glass or two, after which he would walk up the street, sometimes arm in arm with a friend, followed by an enthusiastic throng of spectators. On one famous occasion outside White's Club a lady of the night managed to plant a smacking kiss on the royal cheek.

The relationship between the Royal Family and their favourite wine merchant was perhaps uniquely familiar but it was symptomatic. The records of the Windsor and Eton Warrant Holders – of which more in the section of the book devoted exclusively to their Association – demonstrate a tremendously independent and boisterous attitude on the part of the Royal Tradesmen by the early years of the nineteenth century. They were forever holding parties, drinking loyal toasts, illuminating their houses and having a good time.

Masthead of the issue of The Morning Post which reported events at the Thatched House tavern.
RWHA archive

In 1817 there was a royal fête at Frogmore, which was described as 'the most splendid entertainment which has been given at Windsor for many years'. This was an affair in which The Royal Family participated to the full. The local paper reported:

'The assemblage of nobility and persons of distinction, the splendour of the arrangements for the entertainment, the magnificence of the repast provided by Royal liberality, and above all, the freedom and condescension with which The Queen and her august family moved amidst the various classes of glad spectators, altogether constituted a scene which few besides the British Court could display, and which British subjects best know how to appreciate.'

Such jollities became the rule in Windsor at least. There were dinners, aquatic expeditions to Clifden, fireworks and cricket matches.

In London they dined as well. In the last year of the reign of William IV more than fifty of his tradesmen dined together at the Thatched House tavern in St James's Street, an event which was recalled 165 years later at the Royal Warrant Holders Banquet of 2000 by Sir Brian Jenkins, the former Lord Mayor of London and chairman of the Woolwich, in proposing the health of the Association. There is a note of poignancy in the toast to the King, which was accompanied with the hope that 'his Majesty would speedily be restored to the enjoyment of health, and that the country would for many years to come be destined to enjoy the happiness of his paternal sway'.

In the event he died the following year.

At dinner the toast in his honour was, however, greeted with cheers and his health was drunk with 'great cheering' and drunk 'nine times nine and the utmost enthusiasm' – an expression which slightly perplexed 2000's principal guest, The Princess Royal. 'Nine times nine' is not a practice nor a figure of speech that has survived.

In 1837 the Chairman seemed to be forever calling for a 'brimming bumper' with which to lead the company in the drinking of toasts. After the King came the Queen ('Loud cheering'), Princess Victoria and the rest of the Royal Family ('loud applause'), the Army and Navy ('Great enthusiasm'), His Majesty's Ministers ('solemn silence'), the Archbishop of Canterbury and the Established Church ('the most rapturous enthusiasm and all the honours'), the Duke of Wellington ('Great and continued cheering'), Sir Robert Peel and the prosperity of the manufacturing interest (most ardent gratification and it was drunk with nine times nine and one cheer more) and Sir George Murray ('Great and continued acclamation . . . greatest possible enthusiasm'). More toasts followed to the Lord Chamberlain and the Lord Steward; the Marquis of Chandos and the Agricultural Interest and others, but the enthusiasm levels for these are, alas, unrecorded. Finally, 'the company separated at a late hour, looking forward to the enjoyment of many anniversary returns of the joyous occasion'.

By the time the young Queen Victoria came to the throne a year later in 1837 certain principles regarding the Warrant were either established or well on the way to being so. The most important regarded the clubbability and self-sufficiency of the now numerous Royal Warrant Holders. They were servants of the Crown. Of course they were. It was this which distinguished them. It was the bond which bound them together and differentiated them from the common run of tradesmen. But they were also persons of substance and standing in their own right.

Now, therefore, was the time to formalise these bonds. For reasons of sociability and self-interest a degree of organisation began to seem essential.

It would certainly be of benefit to the Warrant Holders themselves but whereas some such nineteenth-century associations took on the characteristics of a trade union and treated the employer as an adversary, this was emphatically not the case with the Warrant Holders and Royalty. Their loyalty to the Crown was paramount and unquestioned. Indeed, the original name of the infant organisation they formed in 1840 was not simply 'Society' or 'Union' or even 'Club' but 'The Royal Tradesmen's Association for the Annual Celebration of Her Majesty's Birthday'.

What could be more loyal than that.

Queen Victoria, aged 21, drawn and printed by W. Drummond and W.H. Mote. The portrait, authorised by Her Majesty, was published in November 1842.
Sam Twining

THE

ROYAL BRIDE.

Queen Victoria in the dress she wore for her marriage to Albert on 10th February, 1840.
She continued, throughout her life, to wear pieces of the Honiton lace on ceremonial occasions.
Lithograph by C. Wilson.
Mary Evans Picture Library

Everything changed in the sixty odd years of Victorian Britain and the Royal Warrant was no exception. At the beginning of the reign the essentials of granting and receiving the Royal Warrant were effectively unaltered since the Restoration of the Monarchy under King Charles II. By the time the old Queen died the twentieth century had begun and lawyers, Acts of Parliament, organisation and bureaucracy had brought a semblance of order to a state of affairs which had been, essentially, one of amiable anarchy.

Victoria began issuing her own Royal Warrants about two months after her accession in 1837. They were dated and signed by the Lord Chamberlain and grantees had to take an oath administered by Her Majesty's Gentleman Usher in Daily Waiting. This was a solemn affair. All new Warrant Holders had to swear on the Bible with the exception of Quakers who affirmed and Jews who swore on the Old Testament. They were required to

> solemnly swear that I will be a true and loyal servant to our Sovereign Lady Victoria, of the United Kingdom of Great Britain and Ireland Queen, and that I know nothing that may be hurtful or prejudicial to Her Royal Person, State, Crown or Dignity but I will hinder it all maybe in my Power, and reveal the same to the Lord Chamberlain of the Queen's Household or one of the Most Honourable Privy Councillors. That I will serve The Queen truly and faithfully in the Place and Quality of . . . and will obey the Lord Chamberlain at all times.

So there was more to being a Victorian Warrant Holder than simply supplying or purveying.

Some of Victoria's Warrant Holders are now unfamiliar names pursuing unfamiliar trades and crafts. Mrs Dillon the Worker of Bookmarkers, Mrs Peachey the Modeller of Wax Flowers, Miss Whitfield the Envelope Maker, Mrs Dent the Chronometer Maker, Mrs Mawe the Minerologist and Mrs McGregor the Lapidiary were just a few of a small regiment of women who seem to have produced no Warrant-holding descendants.

Other Victorian Warrant Holders, some from even earlier reigns, are still going strong. John Broadwood & Sons still make the royal pianos; Cadbury Brothers, chocolate; Carr & Co., biscuits, Chubb & Sons, locks and safes; Toye Kenning & Spencer, lace, embroidery and insignia; G. B. Kent & Sons, hairbrushes; Twining & Sons, tea; James Purdey & Sons, shotguns. Selections are always invidious but that is a random sample of names famous then and famous now. Some of those companies are radically different, others seem virtually unchanged, but all of them are still serving the Royal Family.

A relationship between Queen Victoria and what is now known as 'trade and industry', which graphically illustrates the way in which the two can benefit

each other, is that between Her Majesty and the Honiton lacemakers. The old-established lace industry in South Devon relied on the work of skilled female lacemakers in such remote rural communities as Honiton itself, and villages such as Beer and Branscombe. In the early nineteenth century it was in what seemed like terminal decline.

One of the Queen's first acts was to appoint a Beer woman, Miss Jane Bidney, as 'Lace Manufacturer in Ordinary' in August 1837. About a year later Miss Bidney was asked to supervise the making of a truly remarkable piece of lace work, which meant employment for about 200 Devonian women from March to November 1839. A contemporary newspaper account said 'These poor women derive a scanty subsistence from making lace, but the trade has latterly so declined that, had it not been for the kind consideration of her Majesty in ordering this dress, they would have been destitute during the winter.'

Victoria was so determined to have something to wear at her wedding which was as unique as it was beautiful that once the dress and accompanying flounce had been completed she ordered the destruction of the designs.

It was in these designs that the secret of this astonishing piece of work truly lay. By British standards it was revolutionary. Queen Victoria in her diary described it simply as 'Honiton, imitation of old' and Queen Mary later described it as 'Honiton bobbin lace applied to a machine net ground copied from a Brussels design'. Actually the designer was the Pre-Raphaelite painter William Dyce and his concept was unlike anything hitherto done in Britain.

In a letter to Sir Henry Cole dated 18th June 1852 Dyce wrote that it was the 'earliest specimen of the old style of Brussels point lace executed at Honiton. The design was executed at the School of Design which accordingly had the merit of effecting the revolution in Honiton lacemaking which followed the working of the dress.' He added: 'They do much better things now; but for the time the Queen's dress was I think a great effort, though to judge of its merits you ought to see the rubbish that used to be produced at Honiton 12 or 14 years ago.'

Although subsequently best known as a painter, Dyce (1806 – 1864) was always interested in design and had made a study of European design schools for

Left: *William Dyce, designer of Queen Victoria's Honiton lace wedding dress. Dyce is shown in a watercolour portrait by David Scott, sketching in Venice from a gondola in 1832.* Scottish National Portrait Gallery/ Bridgeman Art Library

Below: *Queen Victoria, centre right, wears her own bridal lace when attending the marriage of the Duke of York, later King George V, to Princess Mary of Teck, in the Chapel Royal on 6th July, 1893. On Queen Victoria's left stands the Grand Duke Ernest Louis of Hesse. On her right is the Queen of Denmark, and behind her stand the Prince and Princess of Battenberg. To the left of the picture is the bride's mother, the Duchess of Teck. Picture taken from a watercolour by Amédée Forestier.* Royal Collection Picture Library

the Council of the Government School of Design at Somerset House. In making this study Dyce seems to have been profoundly impressed by the superior skills and designs of the French lace industry. In an astonishingly short time he managed to translate this French artistry and technique into an English environment.

Queen Victoria continued to wear this fabulous wedding lace in various forms throughout her life. One such occasion was the wedding of her grandson, later George V, to Princess Mary of Teck. 'I wore my wedding lace over a light black stuff,' she recorded.

Dyce, the designer, enjoyed only a brief flirtation with lacemaking but Miss Bidney turned the commission to good effect. She opened a shop at 76 St James's Street, Piccadilly and advertised as follows:

Miss Bidney, who has had the honour of making the whole of the Lace for Her Most Gracious Majesty's Bridal Attire, begs to announce to the Nobility and Gentry, that she has prepared for sale an extensive variety of Court Suits, Bridal Dresses, Flounces, Berths [sic], Pelerines, Squares, Veils, Scarfs, Cuffs and Laces of all Widths, as well as Court Costumes of rich and modern patterns, superior to any made in Brussels.

Miss Bidney has spared neither expense nor exertions to render the industrious efforts of her country women worthy of the distinguished patronage which Her Majesty has been graciously pleased to bestow on them.

Alas, Miss Bidney disappeared from view almost as soon as she arrived. In the words of the costume historians Kay Staniland and Santina M. Levey, 'Not only was Miss Bidney too early commercially, but stylistically the lace that she produced was at least a decade in advance of its time.'

A major strand in the history of the Royal Warrant has been the ability of the monarchy to foster the best of British craftsmanship. It is a tradition which is very much alive in the early years of the twenty-first cen-

Right: The Freemason's Hall, Queen Street, by Rowlandson and Pugin. Taken from Ackermann's "Microcosm of London" published in 1808. Victoria and Albert Museum/Bridgeman Art Library

tury when the modern Warrant Holders administer a Trust dedicated to Queen Elizabeth The Queen Mother, the purpose of which is to perpetuate the best of British craftsmanship by providing scholarships to the very best of British. Nevertheless, there are few finer examples of Royalty helping to nurture British craftsmanship than Queen Victoria's wedding dress and lace.

Three years after The Queen's accession her tradesmen decided that the time had come to band together into a formal organisation: 'The Royal

Tradesmen's Association for the Annual Celebration of Her Majesty's Birthday'.

Nowadays the word 'Tradesman' no longer features in the title of the Royal Warrant Holders or any of its constituents, although the Edinburgh Warrant Holders held to the original nomenclature long after it was abolished elsewhere. 'Trade' in Victorian Britain carried social connotations in a strictly regulated social hierarchy.

A typical example of this appeared in a contemporary book of etiquette entitled *Manners and Rules of Good Society*, which purported to be by 'A member of the Aristocracy' (the implicit snobbery coupled with the reluctance to reveal the alleged aristocrat's name strongly suggested that it was by nobody of the kind!). 'At retail trade the line is drawn,' wrote the 'aristocrat', 'and very strictly so. Were a person actually engaged in trade to obtain a presentation, his presentation would be cancelled as soon as the Lord Chamberlain was made aware of the nature of his occupation.'

The original Association of Royal Tradesmen inverted this snobbery by boldly declaring the nature of their occupation and also by excluding from their company people such as lawyers who might have considered themselves socially superior. They were united in their loyalty to the

Crown and their commitment to render good service to the Monarch. If 'aristocrats' chose to condescend to them that was their affair. They were proud to be 'Tradesmen'.

There had obviously been some form of organisation before 1840 because we know that Warrant Holders had been in the habit of meeting at Freemason's Hall, the Thatched Tavern and various places in and around Windsor mainly for the purpose of toasting the sovereign on his or her birthday.

We also know that these dinners were convened by a number of specially appointed Stewards and that official invitations were printed.

The original minute book, carefully preserved in its plum-coloured box with brass clasps, tells us, in exemplary Victorian copperplate, that on 25th May 1840 after the toasts had been drunk with the 'usual honors' the chairman 'begged leave to submit to the company present a proposition he had made to his Brother Stewards and which had met with their concurrence, viz. that of Her Majesty's Birthday, which proposal was agreed to by all present'.

The first chairman was John Hunter, one of Her Majesty's tailors. His company has now been absorbed into the modern Warrant-holding company of Dege & Skinner, bespoke tailors and shirt makers of Savile Row. Their Chairman, Michael Skinner, President of the Association in the year 2000, has in his possession a work book of his original predecessor with some of his exquisite sketches and drawings. Sadly, however, there is no clue as to why exactly he put the proposition about forming an Association nor why his brother Stewards so readily agreed. The old system seemed to work perfectly satisfactorily. The most plausible explanation is probably that the Victorians had a general passion for order and organisation, and Victorian men in particular were keen on male bonding.

Despite the existence of the dozen or so female Warrant Holders already mentioned, the Association was exclusively masculine. Men who supplied goods to any department of the Royal Household or to the department of woods and forests were eligible for membership. For a guinea, a member could attend the annual dinner or, if he wished, send his son

Above: *Sketches by John Hunter, the tailor, first Chairman of the Association.* Michael Skinner

Left: *The opening page from the first Minute Book of the Royal Tradesmen's Association, recording the first anniversary dinner, in honour of Queen Victoria's Birthday, 25th May 1840.* RWHA Archive

instead. A friend could come as a guest but the charge then would be twenty-five shillings. Women were definitely not allowed but lest the Association should be thought to be discriminating there was a special concession whereby if a lady or a firm of ladies held a royal appointment or Warrant they should be allowed to 'appoint a Gentleman to represent them'. There is no evidence of Miss Bidney of Beer nor any other lady Warrant Holder taking advantage of this dubious privilege.

For several years dinners continued to be held at the Freemasons Tavern although in 1844 the Staples Brothers of the Albion Tavern in Aldgate Street offered to hold the dinner at their place. This was turned down by the Stewards 'in consequence of the majority of the members residing at the West End many of whom have signified a wish to dine even nearer than the Freemasons Tavern'. In 1848 the Stewards changed their mind and asked the Staples if they could dine at the Albion, whereupon the brothers replied 'regretfully' that this would not be possible as their 'large room was engaged by the attorney general for entertaining the Gentlemen of the Bar'. So there!

The original membership was only twenty-five but in 1841 it was 'agreed unanimously that Dinner should be ordered for 80', which is where the figure remained for ten years. Loyal members felt this was a poor reflection on those eligible to dine and in 1851 300 letters were sent out to 'the General Body of Gentlemen who held appointments for the Crown, requesting them to belong to the Association'.

From the very beginning the Lord Steward or the Board of Green Cloth sent two bucks, so that the Royal

Tradesmen could dine off royal venison, and those who did belong to the Association clearly believed that this regal munificence made failure to come to dinner an act of serious *lèse-majesté*. Those of the 300 who did not reply were paid a personal call by Mr Scarman, one of the Stewards. The Association was crisp in the wording of its request. The Stewards, they said, 'cannot but feel it only requires their applications to enable you to obey Her Majesty's Commands in celebrating Her Majesty's Birthday by dining together on 31st May, the appointed day'. And 'the stewards beg to assure you they feel they are only performing their duty in calling your attention to the Royal Command. They consider condescension so great on the part of Her Majesty in presenting the Association with venison for the occasion that the tradesmen so greatly favoured can do no other than gratefully accept and do honour to the gift.'

Does the wording of this letter imply that the formation of the Association was not entirely voluntary? When John Hunter and his fellow Stewards originally proposed the idea of an Association it looked as if it *was* entirely voluntary. Now, however, the use of the words 'Her Majesty's Commands' suggests that the idea was not spontaneous but came as the result of an order from on high.

Despite this 'command' (or perhaps because of it!), membership fell far short of the total number eligible. This seems remarkable in view of the close personal interest which The Queen evidently took in the proceedings. In 1861 the Association had a note from the Palace saying that the date they had chosen to dine was not 'consonant with the feelings of Her Majesty'. The 10th July was the day

Right: *Extract from the second Minute Book, recording the anniversary dinner of 13th May 1852.* RWHA Archive

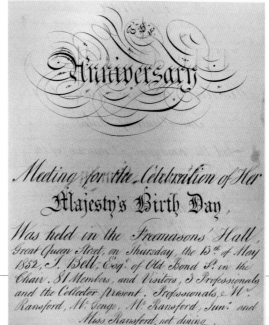

Anniversary

Meeting for the Celebration of Her

Majesty's Birth Day,

Was held in the Freemasons' Hall, Great Queen Street, on Thursday, the 13th of May 1852, J. Bell, Esqᵉ of Old Bond Sᵗ in the Chair. 81 Members, and Visitors, 3 Professionals and the Collector present. Professionals, Wᵐ Ransford, Mᵗ Genge, Mᵗ Ransford, Junᵗ and Miss Ransford, not dining.

'specially appointed for its (The Queen's birthday) celebration' and the dinner was duly moved. The following year the dinner was cancelled 'in consequence of a communication from the Lord Chamberlain's Office'. Prince Albert had died.

Dinner was a guinea in 1840 and it was still a guinea in 1889. In 1840 your guinea got you 'Dinner, Dessert and wine including twice of champagne'. In 1860 a surcharge of a shilling a head was levied for 'Real Turtle and Punch', though it was removed the following year. But in fifty years the price of dinner remained unchanged.

A typical Victorian Royal Tradesmen's dinner menu carried drink on the left of the card and food to the right. The wines in 1884, the year of the earliest extant menu in the Association archive, went: Chablis; Punch; Hock; three different champagnes – Moet et Chandon, Georges Goulet and Wachter; Liqueurs; Port and Claret. On the food front there were seven separate courses *excluding* cheese, salad, fruit and nuts, and coffee with cognac. The menu was written in French and the seven courses began with anchovies, olives and shrimps, and continued with soup, fish (sole, salmon, whitebait), sweetbreads, guinea fowl and

a sorbet named after the Prince of Wales. After that, under the heading *Relevés*, came lamb with mint sauce and new potatoes, York ham braised in champagne, French salad, Her Majesty's haunch of venison, lobster mayonnaise, and then a *rôti*, which was Roast Aylesbury duckling with asparagus, and finally a choice of four different puddings including such apparent exotica as Timbales à l'Impératrice and Pudding Glace Diamond.

The invitation for 1884 specified 'Five for half past five o'clock' – an early start, which was obviously justified by the prodigious amount of food and drink on offer.

But it wasn't just the eating and drinking which is such a contrast with our own relatively parsimonious times. Victorian dinners were extravagant affairs in every respect. In 1884 the company drank no fewer than eleven separate toasts. The minute book refers frequently to the fact that 'The usual loyal and fratristic toasts were given and responded to', so we can be reasonably sure that eleven was more or less the norm. Naturally they drank to The Queen first. Then they drank to the remainder of her family. Then to the Army, Navy and Auxiliary Forces. The Mistress of the Robes then received a toast on her own, followed by the Lord Steward, the Lord Chamberlain and the Master of the Horse who were toasted together. Then they toasted the Chairman; the Association; the Stewards and the Stewards Elect; the Honorary Secretary; the Visitors. Finally they toasted the Ladies who might just as well have been bracketed with 'Absent Friends' for they were, of course, notable chiefly for not being there. Nor, though the men drank to them, were Her Majesty the Queen or the Mistress of the Robes. Presumably if Victoria had expressed a desire to be present an exception would have been made to the all-male ruling and she would have been allowed in under the guise of not being a woman in the accepted sense. It seems unlikely, however, that a similar dispensa-

Left: *Programme cover and menu of the anniversary dinner, 10th November 1890, in honour of the birthday of The Prince of Wales.* RWHA Archive

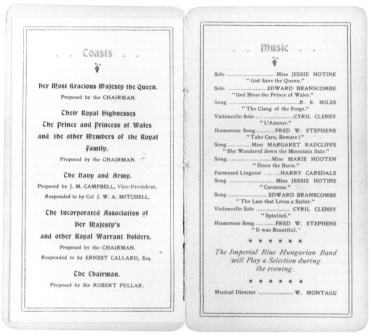

*Above: **Menu and music programme for the 58th anniversary banquet, 21st May 1898.** RWHA Archive*

*Below right: **Menu card for the 57th anniversary banquet, 1897.** RWHA Archive*

tion would have been accorded to the Mistress of the Robes.

Each toast would be proposed at the end of a speech – longish, one would imagine – and the reply would also have been couched in suitably wordy terms.

And, naturally, no such occasion would have been complete without music. Here again the curious nature of male chauvinism in the world of the Victorian middling classes manifests itself in the presence of several lady soloists among the performers. For years the musical direction was in the hands of Mr Henry Chaplin who appears to have made an annual charge of ten guineas which included three or four singers as well as Miss Kate Chaplin (violin) and Miss Nellie Chaplin (pianoforte). It seems reasonable to suppose that the Misses Chaplin were Henry's daughters though it is unclear whether another regular pianist, Mr F. R. Kinkee, was related or not.

There was always a sung grace taken from the 'Laudi Spirituali' of 1545 followed by two verses of 'God Save the Queen'.

The rest of the evening was, in the traditional manner of such affairs, liberally sprinkled with songs. The favoured themes tended to be patriotic or even jingoist as in such favourites as

'Where are the boys of the Old Brigade
Who fought with us side by side,
Shoulder and shoulder and blade by blade
Fought till they fell and died?'

There was humour, too, sometimes mixed in with a gentle xenophobia as in a perplexing song called 'Happy Fatherland', which began,

The Germans are a noble race,
And of that race I'll sing:
They love their Pa's and adore their Ma's
And they idolise their King.

A Scottish song such as 'The Sands of Dee' or 'Charlie is My Darling' seems to have been de rigueur, and the pièce de résistance was the romantic ballad such as 'Friends or Lovers' sung to the company by Miss Henden-Warde.

They stood beneath the beeches
where the sunlight never reaches,
And the road beneath them lay;
There had been some idle chatter
o'er a very little matter,
And what won't people say?
So she drew a ring from her dainty hand
And then fitted it on once more;
'Of course we shall always be friends' said she,
'Tho' our dream of love is o'er.'
'Oh yes! we shall always be friends,' said he;
'The truest and best of Friends,' sighed she,
And the twilight shadows grew dim and grey,
As they stood and talked on each side of the way.

Throughout Queen Victoria's reign this dinner, later dignified by the description 'banquet' which it carries to this day, was the high spot of the Royal Tradesmen's year. The old menu cards, beautifully printed and decked out with royal crests and pictures, ribbons and bows, are extraordinarily evocative. They conjure up a vision of Victorian England which it takes little or no imagination to see, hear or even smell. Well-groomed whiskers, well-starched shirt-fronts, port and cigars, and never a woman in sight unless serving or singing. It is a strange paradox that this ineffably masculine party should be held to celebrate the birthday of the woman who reigned over them and in whose service they took such pride. Odder still that they should evidently have found nothing strange about this aspect of their Association. This was the apogee of the Victorian gentleman at play and for years it was not just the crowning glory but also the principal purpose of the Association of Royal Tradesmen.

Gradually, however, the Association began to become more than simply a dining club. Signs of this became apparent in a number of different ways, some of them, incredibly, invading dinner itself. There were

extraordinary scenes at the Criterion on 10th November 1891 when The Prince of Wales's Tradesmen met to celebrate their royal master's birthday. A man, unnamed, rose during dessert and tried to launch an attack on the Prince. It's difficult to work out from the contemporary reports what exactly he was complaining about, but he was obviously cross and it looks as if he was agitated about the Prince's

relationship with the London stores. In any event the loyal Tradesmen took exception to what he was trying to say or perhaps to the fact that he was trying to say anything at all. The report tells us that 'He was met with cries of "traitor" and other unpleasant noises. . . At length The Prince of Wales's Tradesmen at dinner got tired of simply yelling and commenced throwing at their obnoxious colleague at first champagne corks and then nuts, apples, oranges and bananas.'

This was not the only evidence of discontent among some of the Royal Tradesmen. As early as 1844 the Windsor and Eton Association abandoned their traditional custom of illuminating their homes and business premises in honour of royal birthdays. The reason, apparently, was that an old custom of distributing royal largesse in the form of 'beef, suet, plums, currants etc. to the different members of the establishment on Her Majesty's birthday' was abruptly discontinued. Five years later a wholesale reform of the ancient 'Office of Woods and Forests' led to protests from Windsor that the Board which replaced it was being 'peremptory and cheese-paring' and inviting the local tradesmen to 'cut each other's throats' in their efforts to provide the cheapest possible goods and services. For years the Windsor and Eton tradesmen believed that they were being undercut by city slickers from London and that the shift of power at court from Windsor Castle to Buckingham Palace worked to their commercial disadvantage.

Some tradesmen seem to have been prepared to provide goods or services at well below the going rate – or even completely free of charge – if by doing so they could be assured of a Royal Warrant. And the practice of paying fees on being granted a Warrant at least by the Lord Steward's department continued unabated during the early years of Queen Victoria's reign.

Until 1845 purveyors paid the Master of the Household £1 6s 7d on appointment and a further £1 19s 5d to be divided equally between the three Clerks of the Green Cloth. The Master's fees were abolished

Left: *Queen Victoria and Prince Albert - viewing the Llamas in the House Park, Windsor. Painting by Gourlay Steell (1819-1894).*
Bridgeman Art Library

Right: *Programme cover for the banquet celebrating Queen Victoria's Jubilee, 24th May 1887.*
RWHA Archive

in 1845 and the Clerks' five years later. Between the Queen's accession and 1850, 232 Purveyors were granted Warrants and they paid over fees of £632 18s 11d for the privilege.

It is interesting to note that the final abolition of all such fees was not made by internal Palace ruling but in the form of a letter from the Treasury. On 16th May 1850 the Clerk to the Lord Commissioners of Her Majesty's Treasury wrote in uncompromising terms to the Lord Chamberlain:

> My Lord, I am directed by the Lord Commissioners of Her Majesty's Treasury to acquaint Your Lordship . . . that on considering the Report of the Commissioners appointed for the management and control of the Household feefund . . . My Lords concur in the suggestion that the fees . . . paid by Tradesmen upon appointment to Her Majesty . . . be abolished.

Other precedents and practices which are still part of Royal Warrant procedure were also established or defined in Victoria's reign. For example, we learn from a letter from the Master of the Horse's department dated 23rd December 1870 that traders who went bankrupt would automatically lose the Warrant. This remains true today. The unfortunate offender in 1870 was a Royal Tailoress called Mrs Neighbour who was told: 'The Master of the Horse would have been glad to have continued to give the order for liveries but it is against the custom of all the Departments of Her Majesty's Household to employ tradesmen who have unfortunately become insolvent; and the Master of the Horse has therefore been obliged to make other arrangements for the supply of liveries for stable servants at Windsor.'

The thorny question of transferring Warrants was another which caused problems. Historically, of course, Warrants were granted to individuals because in earlier times that was how trade was conducted. 'Companies' were the great livery companies and the idea of a private company composed of a number of

individuals trading under a single name was one which really only started to become widely established towards the end of the eighteenth century. Despite the growth of such companies Warrants went on being granted to individuals – a practice which is retained to this day. At times, as we shall see, Warrants were granted to more than one name within a company but the idea that Warrant Holders should be real flesh-and-blood people rather than impersonal organisations was always paramount. Warrant-holding – and granting – has always been a family affair and this has been a crucial element in the way the system works. Holding a Warrant is a source of corporate pride but vesting the title in a particular person, be he or she the chief executive or an appropriate company director, gives the practice a human face which would otherwise be lacking.

Some people believed, however, that despite this the Warrant was really granted to the company and that therefore if they acquired the company they should automatically inherit the Warrant. Thus, in the autumn of 1888 Mr E. Baldock Stone bought the firm of C. Smith & Son, gold lace men to Her Majesty's Stables, from the Warrant Holder Mr J. G. Smith. Smith had gone bankrupt and Baldock Stone was his principal creditor. The new owner therefore wrote to the Master of the Horse, the Duke of Portland, requesting that the Warrant 'be transferred into my name'.

It didn't work and eventually, and with reluctance, Stone returned the Warrant – which the firm had held since 1829. However, he then wrote to the Crown Equerry, Colonel Sir George Maude, in January 1889. His tone was somewhat lacking in the necessary humility. Worse still, the letter carried more than a hint of blackmail in its tail. The Crown Equerry did not take kindly to such threats. 'Sir,' wrote Stone,

'It is with the greatest reluctance that I trouble you with this letter . . . but the exigencies of this business compel me, however unwillingly to do so – The Season having practically begun – the first Drawing Room having been gazetted – as it being still uncertain if this firm is to have a re-grant of the Royal Warrant, held by it for the last 60 years, we are quite at a loss to know whether or not to make, at a cost of many pounds, our annual stock of the Royal Livery Laces, and this dilemma is my excuse for troubling you.

I would wish to take this opportunity of expressing my great regret if through ignorance alone, I have caused you annoyance in this matter, for instance it was not my wish to in any way intrude upon you in the Riding School, but I was directed there by a clerk. . . I called because I had received no acknowledgement of the receipt of my written application. . .

I am perfectly willing to accept my present position, at the same time a gentleman who has been on friendly terms with the present Secretary of State for War, has been engaged in cases with the present Lord Chancellor and Home Secretary and other eminent men; and who knows several Members of Parliament who will take up his case in 'The House' if need be, cannot be ranked quite as an ordinary Tradesman.

This firm has served their Majesties faithfully since 1829, and I must use the influence I undoubtedly possess to assist me in retaining/obtaining the appointment.'

Bad move. Colonel Maude was not amused.

Left: *Osborne House, Isle of Wight, painted by Thomas Allom (1804-72).*
Christopher Wood Gallery/Bridgeman Art Library

Three days later he replied as follows:

Sir,

I reply to your letter of the 25th just, I am desired to inform you that it is not the Master of the Horse's intention to give your firm any share of the work of supplying gold-lace to his Department.

All the Masters of the Horse have discouraged the idea of *the Queen's business* being transferred when a firm changes hands and as this point has been urged by you with such persistency, the Master of the Horse finds it necessary to resist it.

The paragraph in your letter, moreover, in which you state several eminent men and Members of Parliament will take up your cause if need be 'in the House' being in the nature of a threat renders it quite impossible for the Master of the Horse to comply with your demand.

Mr Stone did not give up easily. Indeed, he called at the Royal Mews to protest and also 'that my respectability might be tested'. This was not a success. He was met by 'the paid secretary of the department' who greeted him with the 'grossest incivility'. He accordingly wrote one further letter of complaint but this seems to have gone unacknowledged and the luckless claimant finally disappears from the annals of the Association.

These were bad times for trade and Stone's persistence was obviously due in part to the fact that business was not brisk. Possession of a Royal Warrant might have enhanced it; lack of a Warrant, especially for someone dealing in embroidery and lace, was a disadvantage. Worse still was losing a Warrant. Fairly or not, the loss of one's Warrant, for whatever reason, carries a stigma. The occasion almost always attracts adverse publicity. People assume that even if a crime has not been committed, the Warrant Holder who is deprived of his pride has fallen from grace. Better never to have held the Warrant than to have it taken back.

Hard times made some people behave badly. It was not unknown for traders to accuse rivals of going bankrupt and then suggesting that they take their place as Warrant Holders. One who tried this trick was William Coombes, a saddler on the Isle of Wight who wrote to Colonel Maude in 1887 accusing another saddler, Henry Upton, who held the Royal Warrant for work carried out at Osborne House, of becoming bankrupt. On being taxed with the matter Upton said he was 'somewhat surprised'. It was true, he admitted, that 'by reason of the bad times and long credit that I am obliged to give' he had been compelled to apply for a receiving order but after a creditors' meeting all was resolved and the order annulled. 'I therefore hope', he wrote, 'to retain the appointment and continue as heretofore to do what may be required when Her Majesty is at Osborne.'

Other companies went to bizarre lengths to secure Warrants. One was a Liverpool hatter, John Thomson of Satchell & Son who, in 1886, asked The Prince of Wales if he might become his hatter. The only reason for advancing this claim was that more than a quarter of a century earlier he had presented the Prince's father, Prince Albert, with 'a collection of Scotch Glengarry Caps for his own and the young Prince's wear'. Satchell said that the 'late lamented Prince Consort' had been 'graciously pleased to approve' of these hats and Satchell had been awarded his Warrant, so surely the Prince of Wales would like to carry on where his father left off. It was a cheeky effort but it failed. The Prince of Wales did not grant Mr Satchell a Warrant for Glengarries – or for any other kind of hat.

As hard times grew harder, many tradesmen gave up the pretence of even such far-fetched claims to the Warrant and simply put up a set of Royal Arms over their shopfronts without a by-your-leave from anyone. Towards the end of the century members of the Association were becoming increasingly concerned about unauthorised rivals passing themselves off as bona fide Warrant Holders in this cavalier fashion. The only way to prevent such fraud was to pass laws making it illegal. This was duly done and in 1883 the Patents, Designs and Trade Marks Act, the first of a series of such Acts, ruled that

> Any person who without the authority of Her Majesty or any of the Royal Family assumes or uses in connexion with any trade, business, calling or profession, the Royal Arms, or Arms so nearly resembling the same as to be calculated to lead other persons to believe that he is carrying on his trade business, calling or profession by or under such authority shall be liable to a fine not exceeding twenty pounds.

Four years later this seemed to be confirmed in the Merchandise Marks Act of 1887 which said 'Any person who falsely represents that any goods are made by a person holding a Royal Warrant or for the service of Her Majesty or any of the Royal Family shall be

(again) liable to a penalty not exceeding twenty pounds.' The policing of this was formally carried out by the Lord Chamberlain, but in practice it was alert – and jealous – Warrant Holders who were most likely to blow the whistle on the fraudsters.

In 1895 the Warrant Holders were sufficiently exercised and organised to apply to the Lord Chamberlain for permission to form themselves into an incorporated association. This represented a formal move from being simply a social group into an official body and the purpose of the move was to suppress 'a rapidly growing and unfair practice on the part of some unscrupulous tradesmen throughout England, who are guilty of exhibiting over their shopfronts and on their bill-heads and notepaper the Royal Coat of Arms . . . those who can boast of this Royal patronage have formed themselves into a society with the object of protecting their rights'.

The Lord Chamberlain, after consultations with the Lord Steward and the Master of the Horse, had 'no objections' and the Association was duly incorporated. The original wording of the title implied that only those who held the Warrant of The Queen herself were entitled to membership. Two years later, therefore, the words 'and other Royal' were inserted into the title because 'Warrant Holders to their Royal Highnesses the Prince and Princess of Wales, the Duke of Saxe-Coburg and HRH Princess Mary of Teck, are anxious to join our Association but as we are at present constituted we cannot accept them'.

This comparatively small change was approved at the highest level and consent was obtained from the

EDWARDS' "HARLENE" CO., 95 & 96, HIGH HOLBORN, LONDON, W.C.

Right: Haynes Gibbs, first Secretary of the Association, 1896. RWHA Archive

Lord Chamberlain, the President of the Board of Trade, the Home Secretary and The Queen herself.

The incorporation seems to have been widely welcomed. *Vanity Fair* produced a typical reaction. 'I have often wondered how it is that so many tradesmen are able to flaunt the Royal Arms over their places of business and on their note paper,' the magazine wrote,

> and still more have I wondered how it is that the comparatively few tradesmen who are entitled to do these things allow those shameless persons who have no such right to affect it. It is quite certain that the right to show the Royal Arms is a rare privilege, that is conferred and can only be conferred, by Royal Warrant; and as this privilege ought to be and is, of much value, it is an extraordinary thing that tradesmen of the baser sort – and there are many such – who have it not should be allowed to take custom from those who have it by pirating the right. I am therefore glad – as well for the sake of the public and for that of those deserving tradesmen who have won the privilege of a Royal Warrant – to hear that the Warrant-holding tradesmen throughout the kingdom have formed themselves into a Society for the protection of their rights. This is the Incorporated Society of Her Majesty's Warrant-holders; and they seem to me have done well in choosing for their President Mr Tom Simpson Jay, of Regent Street – a man who is well entitled to the office both by virtue of the many Royal Warrants that he holds and of his energy and business capability. Mr Jay will, I understand, answer all inquiries that may be addressed to him on the subject; which piece of information will no doubt interest the many piratical tradesmen who have for so long been decking themselves with Royal feathers.
>
> This Society is well conceived, and not a day too soon.

In 1898 a Bill was introduced which sought to amend these two earlier Acts by extending the abuse of the Royal Arms to include any 'Armorial Bearings or Insignia' as well as any 'word or words' suggesting a Royal patronage. Unfortunately this never became law.

There was disquiet, too, about the granting of Warrants to foreigners. This was an entirely legitimate practice but there was a feeling in Britain that members of the Royal Family, in particular the Prince of Wales, were making rather too free with their favours, notably when on holiday in the South of France. Hence a letter from the Board of Green Cloth signed by its chairman, the Earl of Pembroke, to Fleetwood Edwards, the Keeper of the Privy Purse.

> I think it highly desirable,' wrote Pembroke, that in consequence of a very large number of Royal Warrants already granted to tradesmen in Nice no further applications should be entertained.
>
> In the whole of Ireland there are but 13 Warrants and 10 have already been granted to Nice. This is in my Department alone. There is a rather strong feeling among the tradesmen at home upon the subject which is stirred up on each occasion of a foreign tradesman's name appearing in the *Gazette* as having received a Warrant.

The point was clearly taken for on 2nd July that year Edwards wrote back to Pembroke saying that The Queen had agreed that henceforth 'No more Warrants should be issued in Nice'.

Queen Victoria's reign was a time of great change – not least in the relationship between The Royal Family and the tradesmen who served it. Most local tradesmen who served the Royal Household lived and worked near one or other of the Royal Palaces. This obviously meant that from the earliest times, there were concentrations of Royal Tradesmen around St. James's, Windsor and Edinburgh. When, much later, the Royal Family acquired Balmoral, the same thing happened. Coats of Arms sprung up along the little High Street of Ballater and in nearby Aberdeen, just as they would in the late 20th century around Sandringham, and in Tetbury when The Prince of Wales moved into Highgrove.

At first, any association between these tradesmen seems to have been loose and informal, often limited to the tendering of loyal messages, or meeting to celebrate a Royal Birthday or some other significant occasion. Towards the end of the 19th century however, the prevailing trend towards more structured business and social organisations led them to become more organised. The Edinburgh Association was founded in 1894. In 1896, the National Association became incorporated. Two years later, the Windsor & Eton Association was formally created, having existed in its informal state for three quarters of a century, and in that same year, George Thomson was moved to document the history of the Aberdeen Association.

It had become clear that despite the enormous diversity of Royal Tradesmen, they shared a number of different interests and bonds, and that these could best be nurtured by creating a structure with a constitution, a Secretary, and Committee, and all the apparatus associated with what was something between a social club and a trade association.

As The Queen celebrated her Diamond Jubilee in 1897 after sixty years on the throne, the President of the Aberdeen Association, a whisky distiller named

Left: *George Shirras, President of the Aberdeen Association of Warrant Holders in 1897. Sketch featured in Pillars of Bon Accord, 1892.* Diane Morgan

Below: *Queen Victoria's Diamond Jubilee procession, 1897. The original painting, entitled "Queen and Empire" was presented to Her Majesty to commemorate the event, by the Royal Warrant Holders Association.* The Royal Collection Trust

George Shirras, celebrated her unprecedentedly long reign with a paean to progress. In doing so he showed how, in tune with the times, Warrant-holding had come to encompass a whole new range of modern activities. 'With the accession of The Queen,', he said at a great Scottish banquet,

'the 18th century really came to an end. The opinions and ways of thinking formerly prevalent underwent a rapid change. Then began the greatest revolution the world has ever seen – the revolution of science. Many causes conduced to this end. The development of Watts' splendid invention; the advent and stupendous increase of railway communication; the establishment of lines of ocean steamers; the practical application of electrical phenomena; the facilities afforded for the transmission of letters by post; the admission of the people to a share in the Government of the country; the breaking down of religious disabilities; the opening of the Universities, the dissemination of education, marked a fresh departure, and heralded the approach of a new order of things, which, advancing with mighty strides, leads every thoughtful observer to ask of himself, 'Where will it all end, and what shall be the measure of human attainments fifty years hence?'

In sixty years the population of the United Kingdom had gone from 25 to 40 millions; London had more than doubled from 2 to 4 millions; the National Revenue had more than doubled from 52 millions to 112 millions; foreign trade went from 125 millions to 738 millions. The Queen was now undisputed Empress of India; she was Queen of Burma; in Hong Kong she ruled the most important naval station in the Far East and

'The opening up and partial settlement of vast regions in Africa under British influence, are bringing to the natives of the Dark Continent the blessings of civilisation and providing new and ever-increasing outlets

for the trade of this country'.

At home, said the doughty Aberdonian Warrant Holder, Britain had at The Queen's accession been

'practically without railways and the Atlantic had been crossed only once, experimentally, by a steamship. Now the country is covered with a network of rails and great ocean steamers connecting the Mother Country with India, the Colonies and America.'

And so he went on: the electric telegraph in 1837, the Penny Post in 1840;

'the earth and sea girdled by wires and cables, transmitting words with the speed of thought'; chloroform and antiseptic surgery. In short, 'Of marvels in every phase of knowledge there are no end.'

As Victoria's reign drew to a close her Warrant Holders reflected the innovation, the ingenuity and the diversity which characterised that period. They were a vivid example of the age in which they worked.

Sketch at the Chairman's table at the first banquet of the newly incorporated Royal Warrant Holders Association.
The two Secretaries, Walter and Haynes Gibbs are shown bottom left.
RWHA Archive

Since 1840 the Warrant Holders had been called 'The Royal Tradesmen's Association'. In 1895 the title became 'The Incorporated Association of Her Majesty's and Other Royal Warrant Holders Limited'. Then, in 1902, this was changed to 'The Royal Warrant Holders Association Limited' and finally, after the Royal Charter of Incorporation in 1907, 'The Royal Warrant Holders Association'. This almost represented a return to the simplicity of the original with the single exception that 'Tradesman' became 'Warrant Holder'. It has remained the title of the Association ever since.

The first President of the Royal Warrant Holders to have his name inscribed in gold on the honours board, which still hangs on the wall of the Association's London office, is T. Simpson Jay whose family company, Jay's, traded as silk mercers in Regent Street. He was President in 1896. We know little about him beyond these bare facts but even they give some indication of the sort of man who was at the helm of the Warrant Holders at the turn of the century.

A magazine por-trait done from a photograph by the London Stereoscopic Society in Cheapside after his annual banquet at St James's Hall is captioned 'Capt. Tom Jay'. It shows an almost walrus-moustached figure with receding dark hair and a purposeful expression laced with a hint of humorous twinkle. 'We all of us lay great store on our Warrants,' he said in a speech that year. 'It is a species of peerage for trade; a distinction which we can only attain to when we and our fathers before us have, by industry, perseverance, and integrity, built up a business after years of toil to such a high position as to be rewarded by the grant of Her Majesty's Warrant.'

Jay's premises were in central London. This remained true for all his immediate successors and only gradually did Presidents come first from outside the fashionable West End and then from outside London altogether. The addresses of Jay's eight successors were, respectively: Pall Mall, Old Bond Street, Wigmore Street, Great Marlborough

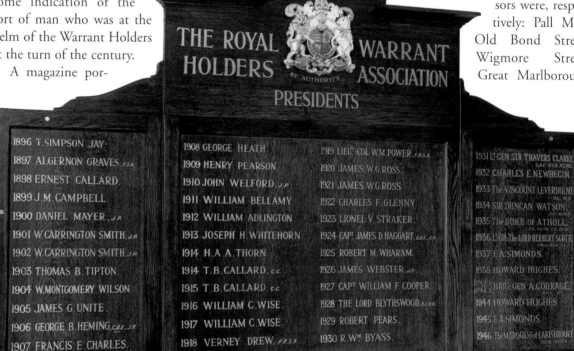

THE ROYAL WARRANT
HOLDERS ASSOCIATION
BY AUTHORITY
PRESIDENTS

1896 T. SIMPSON JAY.	1908 GEORGE HEATH.	1919 LIEUT. COL. W.M. POWER, F.R.S.A.
1897 ALGERNON GRAVES, F.S.A.	1909 HENRY PEARSON.	1920 JAMES W.G. ROSS.
1898 ERNEST CALLARD.	1910 JOHN WELFORD, J.P.	1921 JAMES W.G. ROSS.
1899 J.M. CAMPBELL.	1911 WILLIAM BELLAMY.	1922 CHARLES F. GLENNY.
1900 DANIEL MAYER, J.P.	1912 WILLIAM ADLINGTON.	1923 LIONEL V. STRAKER.
1901 W. CARRINGTON SMITH, J.P.	1913 JOSEPH H. WHITEHORN.	1924 CAPT. JAMES D. HAGGART, O.B.E., J.P.
1902 W. CARRINGTON SMITH, J.P.	1914 H.A.A. THORN.	1925 ROBERT M. WHARAM.
1903 THOMAS B. TIPTON.	1914 T.B. CALLARD, C.C.	1926 JAMES WEBSTER, J.P.
1904 W. MONTGOMERY WILSON.	1915 T.B. CALLARD, C.C.	1927 CAPT. WILLIAM F. COOPER.
1905 JAMES G. UNITE.	1916 WILLIAM C. WISE.	1928 THE LORD BLYTHSWOOD, R.C.V.O.
1906 GEORGE B. HEMING, C.B.E., J.P.	1917 WILLIAM C. WISE.	1929 ROBERT PEARS.
1907 FRANCIS E. CHARLES.	1918 VERNEY DREW, F.R.S.A.	1930 R.W^M BYASS.

1931 L^T-GEN. SIR TRAVERS CLARKE, G.B.E., K.C.B., K.C.M.G.
1932 CHARLES E. NEWBECIN.
1933 The VISCOUNT LEVERHULME, D.L., M.P.
1934 SIR DUNCAN WATSON, J.P., M.INST.
1935 The DUKE OF ATHOLL, K.T., G.C.V.O., C.B., D.S.O.
1936 L^T-COL. The LORD HERBERT SCOTT, C.M.G., D.S.O., M.V.O.
1937 F.A. SIMONDS.
1938 HOWARD HUGHES.
1939/1943 BRIG.-GEN. A. COURAGE, D.S.O., M.C.
1944 HOWARD HUGHES.
1945 F.A. SIMONDS.
1946 The MARQUESS of CARISBROOKE, G.C.B., G.C.V.O.

Left: *Bond Street, 1906.*
Hulton Getty Picture Library

Below: *44 Regent Street, c 1900. The Coats of Arms above Liberty's are clearly visible.*
Hulton Getty Picture Library

Street, Regent Street (twice), Old Bond Street (again) and Mortimer Street. All these were within easy walking distance of each other. Even when the presidency did go further afield it did not go far: the Edgware Road, to be precise. That was in 1905 when James Unite of John Unite Ltd, tentmakers, held office. Then it was back to the centre of town for four years before another excursion to north London, which this time was Elgin Avenue, Maida Vale, where John Welford of Welford & Son, dairymen, was President in 1905. The first President from outside London would appear to be Captain James Haggart of Haggarts the tartan manufacturers, though we don't know for certain that he made his plaid north of the border. After that it was Captain William Cooper of Frank Cooper, the family marmalade makers based in Oxford High Street, who was President in 1927.

So at the beginning of the modern era there was a definite sense of the Association operating in a London which had many of the qualities of a sophisticated and affluent village. The leaders of the Royal Warrant Holders in those years tended to come from a physical area which was quite small and, most significantly, within easy striking distance of Buckingham Palace.

Tom Simpson Jay, the 1896 incumbent, was not only a Londoner. He was also the head of a family business which bore his own name. The same was true of his two immediate successors who were Algernon Graves of Henry Graves & Co. Ltd, printsellers and publishers, and Ernest Callard of the bakers Callard, Stewart & Watt.

After that, eponymity disappeared for a while but the companies had the same flavour of small family businesses. Callard's successor was Mr Campbell of Debenham & Freebody, later, of course, a famous department store with branches all over the country but then just 'furriers and silk mercers'. After him came Daniel Mayer of P. Erard, makers of harps and pianofortes. Then there were W. Carrington Smith of Carrington & Co., jewellers and silversmiths, Thomas Tipton of Scotts, the hatters, and W. Montgomery Wilson of H. D. Rawlings, mineral water manufacturers.

The Great War seems to have produced change. By what one has to assume is a coincidence the President in 1914, the year of the war's outbreak, was Mr Thorn of the Panton Street gunmakers, Charles Lancaster & Co. Ltd. Then, in 1916, the Association welcomed the first President who seemed to represent

a company which belonged entirely to the modern age. This was William Wise who was the President for two years in the middle of the war and held the Warrant on behalf of his company, Paul E. Chappuis, manufacturers of daylight reflectors.

Until 1905 the affairs of the Association seem to have been conducted from the office of the President or one or other of the office holders, but that year a twelve-year lease was acquired on a second-floor office suite at 8 Hanover Square. This highly desirable address was right in the middle of the Warrant-holding West End of London and cost the Warrant Holders £130 a year.

Their landlady was a Miss Emily Rideout who imposed some curious conditions. She insisted that her premises should not be used to carry on any manufacturing, trade or other business nor be used as a hospital, lunatic asylum or place of worship, entertainment or public amusement. Nor were the Warrant Holders allowed to 'hang out any clothes or linen'.

The Warrant Holders seemed happy to comply and, two years after renewing the lease in 1917 for a further eight years at an increased rental of £160 a year, they were offered the chance of buying the entire property outright. Their lawyer, the energetic L. J. Tillett of Norwich, seemed keen on the purchase, urging the Committee not to '"slam, bang, bolt and bar the door" in Mr Winston Churchill's very best style'. He seemed to think that the asking price of between £13,500 and £14,000 could easily be raised, even if it meant borrowing from the bank. A survey carried out by Browett, Taylor & Cordery of Holborn revealed that the property was 'somewhat old but substantially built'. It contained a flat on the top floor, offices on the first and second floors, a large shop and showrooms on the ground floor, and what amounted to another flat in the basement. The surveyors considered the property 'a profitable and very secure investment' but the Association did not feel able to make an offer and continued as tenants. It would be more than eighty years before they finally acquired

a property of their own.

In the 1920s the presidency began to look still more modern. Between 1920 and the outbreak of the Second World War the Presidents represented manufacturers of 'radiator tablets' (Boilerine Ltd) soap (James Webster of John Knight Ltd, and Robert Pears of A. & F. Pears Ltd), milk (Travers Clarke of the Express Dairy), motor cars (Herbert Scott, Rolls-Royce Ltd) and hot drinks (the Duke of Atholl, Bovril).

That last President is an odd juxtaposition, popular meat extracts not being the sort of product you associate with Scottish dukes, nor with The Royal Family, come to that. However, it is noticeable that whereas none of the Presidents of the first thirty years had a title, the following decade provided a duke, a viscount, two lords and two knights. Not that they represented particularly blue-chip or aristocratic companies. They were the Bovril-making duke, a manufacturer of soaps and detergents (Viscount Leverhulme of Lever Bros), a motorcar manufacturer (Lord Herbert Scott of Rolls-Royce) an 'Insurance Provider' (Lord Blythwood of General Accident), a milkman (Lieutenant-General Sir Travers Clarke of the Express Dairy) and an engineer (Sir Duncan

Right: Royal Warrant Holders and their guests at the Banquet held on 3rd June, 1903, in honour of the Prince of Wales's birthday, at the Princes Restaurant, Glasshouse Street.
RWHA archive

Watson, Duncan Watson Ltd, electrical engineers).

The difference between the thirties and the first decade of the twentieth century is that the later period produced more diversity, grander grantees and an increase in the number of large national companies.

It is the diversity which impresses initially. What other organisation could be headed by Robert Wharam of the sanitary engineers, Thomas Crapper one year (1925) and William Byass of the sherry producers, Gonzalez Byass, almost the next (1930)? The monarchy and the community which served it was not afraid to acknowledge the existence of common-

or-garden water closets on the one hand and elegant Spanish fortified wine on the other.

More significant, however, was the arrival on the Warrant-holding scene of really large and important national or even international companies. Firms like Lever Brothers and Rolls-Royce were serious blue-chip players on the world market. The fact that directors of such significant enterprises were prepared to play their part in the Association's affairs alongside the more traditional small family tailors, grocers and 'village'-type stores was a real and significant innovation.

The Royal Warrant Holders have always mixed business with pleasure. The pleasure, as we have already seen, has always involved the ceremonious and convivial with an abundance of banquets and luncheons and the drinking of loyal toasts. This continued throughout the reigns of Edward VII and George V, although the extravagance of the Victorian era slowly but noticeably and regularly declined. This, in part, reflected the character of the pleasure-loving Edward VII and his more sober son. It was characteristic of Edward VII that one of his first warrants was that granted to the champagne house of Lanson. On his succession the King commanded that his stock of Lanson should never fall below 2000 bottles. In order to avoid the jealousy of rival champagne houses he also ordered that the Lanson should always be served from decanters and not from identifiable bottles.

The business side of Warrant holding has taken a number of different forms but at the beginning of the twentieth century 'Policing the Warrant' was unquestionably the most important activity of the Association and its Secretary. This meant protecting the interests of the Warrant Holders and the integrity of the monarchy against abuse by unscrupulous tradesmen. In 1905 and 1907, a Merchandise Marks Act and a Trades Mark Act were passed as part of a general tightening up of company legislation. Unfortunately these did little to resolve the difficulties experienced by the Royal Warrant Holders when it came to policing the Warrant.

Abuse was both flagrant and widespread. There were a lot of crooks and conmen prepared to pretend that they were entitled to the Warrant when they were nothing of the kind. Moreover, a surprising number of people seemed quite indifferent to such deception.

In 1905 Samuel Holman, the Secretary of the Royal Warrant Holders Association, reported to the Select Committee on Trade Marks that he and the Association experienced 'great difficulty' in 'suppressing the improper use of the Royal Coat of Arms'. That very year the Association had been forced to deal with no fewer than 213 cases of such improper use. This was more than double the number of the previous year. If the situation was not exactly out of control, it was very far from satisfactory.

According to Holman one of the problems was that the onus was on the Association to prove that the offending tradesmen were *deliberately* trying to make potential customers believe that they were conducting their business by royal authority. The *intent* was as important as the *effect*. Holman complained that this was 'impossible to prove'.

Whenever an abuse was drawn to the Association's attention Holman wrote an official letter to the offending party, asking them to stop whatever they were doing. This, he said, usually 'has the desired effect'.

If the letter did not have the 'desired effect' the Association went to court. On the whole the courts sided with them but a sympathetic hearing relied, in Holman's words, 'more, I think, with the magistrate than with the Act of Parliament. I think we have been very fortunate; I think most of the London magistrates have been very lenient to us, and I think they

Right: Slade's advertisement opposed by the Association in November 1907. A perpetual injunction, with costs, was granted by Mr Justice Neville on 28th January, 1908.
RWHA Archive

have taken our view of the case and have given us relief in nearly every case.'

One or two magistrates, however, seemed indifferent or even hostile. On one occasion a shop called Glave's in Oxford Street displayed, entirely without authority, no less than *eleven* different Royal Coats of Arms. The magistrate was unmoved and seemed not to understand why the Association was complaining. As far as he was concerned the shopfront belonged to the shopkeeper and he could display upon it whatever he wished. He therefore found for the defendant.

Even distinguished lawyers sometimes seemed as confused as magistrates. In 1907, for instance, a firm of confectioners was prosecuted for displaying the Royal Arms on the labels of

their toffee tins. Counsel for the defence argued that this was not meant to persuade potential toffee buyers that they were buying a product endorsed by the monarchy. Perish the thought! 'The use of the Royal Arms', said my learned friend, 'you will see every day in the common form at the head of the *Daily Mail*, for instance, and at the head of *The Times* and many of these papers, not that anybody imagines there is any Royal Warrant for that. The Royal Arms, by themselves, do not amount to a representation.'

The prosecution replied that *The Times* was a registered trade mark.

The defence said, '*The Times* may be but that does

not apply to the *Daily Mail*.'

Counsel for the prosecution seems to have been stymied by this. 'Well, I don't know,' he said, 'I cannot answer that.'

In 1907 the Royal Warrant Holders Association confronted 300 such cases of abuse; the following year it was 400. It was obvious, at least to the Warrant Holders, that the existing legislation was inadequate.

Legislation to deal with outsiders who caused offence was important, but it was also vital that the Association should exercise proper control within its own house. Shortly after the accession of King George V, in 1910, the Association's Secretary, Algernon Graves, produced a 'Private and Confidential' memorandum to increase the Association's 'usefulness' now that 'The Royal Warrants are all starting afresh'.

One of the main problems at this time was that although there were about 1200 Warrant Holders altogether, only some 600 actually belonged to the Association. This meant that the Association could only exercise control over half the Warrant Holders and didn't even know accurately who they all were. 'It is impossible to keep a complete record of who the Warrant Holders in all departments are,' complained Graves. 'The Lord Chamberlain's office publish their list in the *Gazette* and the Board of Green Cloth, the Master of the Horse and the Mistress of the Robes theirs, but some such as Marlborough House do not, I think, publish any.'

Graves's radical suggestion was that in the granting of new Warrants membership of the Association should be a compulsory condition. That way the Association could publish one definitive alphabetical list and also exercise control over **ALL** Warrant Holders. This idea was never put into effect and even in the early twenty-first century there were still a small number of Warrant Holders who did not belong to the Association.

Graves had particular concerns about the habit, in some quarters, of members of the Royal Family granting 'Verbal Warrants'. The Association had recently lost a case in the police courts when the defendant had claimed that his Warrant had been verbally granted and Graves continued, 'The Association have often had much trouble in their prosecutions by the sudden production of a Warrant they had hitherto no knowledge of – and issued by a Member of the Royal Family who was not, to their knowledge, in the habit of doing so.'

Graves also argued for a strict printed code of conduct to be sent to all Warrant Holders about how they could use their Warrants 'in the Way of Advertising'. Specific edicts he wanted were a total ban on the use of the Royal Arms on omnibuses and in 'the public press'. He also argued that Warrant Holders should not be allowed to describe themselves as 'His Majesty's Butcher or Watchmaker' but only 'Butcher to His Majesty'. This question had already been dealt with by the Lord Chamberlain's office. And, 'Warrant Holders should not be allowed to issue framed notices with Royal Arms – largely displayed to be hung in shops of people who are not Warrant Holders. This form of misuse is much practised by Mineral Water Manufacturers, Cocoa ditto, and Tea ditto.'

In 1914 a new Bill was brought forward to amend

Section 68 of the 1905 Trades Mark Act. 'Section 68' was as evocative an item in its day as 'Catch 22' or 'Clause Five'. As the section stood it only dealt with unauthorised use of the Royal Coat of Arms. Warrant Holders, however, wanted this extended to include what was referred to as 'The Royal Crown' and 'The Prince of Wales's Feathers'. It was important also to make clear what displaying the Arms really *signified*. Neither *The Times* nor the *Daily Mail*, in the case of the toffee tins of 1907, was seriously using the Royal Arms to suggest that they were 'By Appointment' to the Crown. They were not pretending that they were, in any significant sense, 'Royal newspapers'. The toffee makers, however, *were* using it to suggest that the Royal Family ate their sweets and that they were confectioners 'By Appointment'.

Right: Sewing the "tails" for King George V's coronation robe at Messrs Nicholays. The robe consisted of over 400 skins and about 600 tails.
Michael Skinner

Legal language could try to deal with this. The existing Act described the offence as the unauthorised use of the Royal Arms in a manner 'calculated to lead to the belief' that the Royal Coat of Arms was being used with due authority. In other words, the prosecution had to prove that any abuse was deliberate and that the offender was dishonestly abusing the Royal Arms for commercial advantage. The Warrant Holders wanted 'calculated to lead to the belief' changed to simply 'indicating or suggesting'. This would mean that you would no longer have to prove 'malice aforethought' to get a conviction. If the new wording became law, defendants would no longer be able to say 'We made a mistake' and get away with it. Ignorance or incompetence would be no excuse.

Unfortunately for the Warrant Holders, this Bill never became law. By the end of 1914 parliamentarians had other things on their minds.

Fourteen Members of Parliament supported this abortive legislation and nine of them were actively connected with Warrant-holding companies. Two Harmsworths were directors of Perrier water, A. P. du Cros was chairman of the Dunlop tyre company, Sir John Dewar was a director of the eponymous Scotch whisky firm, Dewars. Colonel Gretton and Lieutenant-Colonel Ratcliff were directors of Bass, the brewers; Mr Burgoyne was a director of Burgoyne's, the wine merchants; A. S. Rowntree was a director of the family chocolatiers of York and the Rt Hon. T. H. Ferens was a director of Reckitt's 'Blue', the dye manufacturers. By the end of the century the Warrant Holders would have been hard pressed to put together such an impressive parliamentary lobby, even though they could in the 1980s and '90s boast a Warrant-holding Speaker of the House of

Left: *Lord Weatherill, former Speaker of the House of Commons and Grantee for Bernard Weatherill Ltd., livery tailors, awarding a QEST scholarship to Sharon Smith in November 2000.* RWHA Archive

Commons in the tailor, Sir Bernard (later Lord) Weatherill. Even as Speaker, Sir Bernard always carried a silver thimble in his pocket as a reminder of his trade.

In 1922 another attempt was made to reform the various Merchandise Marks Acts which had become law between 1887 and 1911, and in particular the contentious 'Section 68' of 1905. This Bill failed in 1922, was reintroduced in 1923 and failed again.

In 1925 a new Secretary, Major Brookhouse, was appointed. His starting salary was £41 13 4d a month and he was granted an annual holiday of three weeks. There is no question, in his letter of appointment from the President, Robert Wharam of Crapper the sanitary engineers, of his being a part-time appointment. It was made clear that no other business engagements should be entered into while he was employed by the Warrant Holders and that the office hours were 9.30 a.m. to 6 p.m. Monday to Fridays and 9.30 a.m. to 1 p.m. on Saturdays. In addition, if 'any special service be required' it should have the Major's 'necessary attention'.

A year after Major Brookhouse's appointment, reforming legislation was introduced yet again but this time it was postponed because of 'unforeseen and unavoidable delays on the time of Parliament'. These were unspecified but it sounds like the General Strike of 1926.

Understandably, Major Brookhouse and the Warrant Holders were unhappy about the constant parliamentary rebuffs to their proposed reforms. 'Section 68' survived.

In 1928 Captain Garrow Jones MP, later ennobled as Baron Trefgarne, asked the Home Secretary what steps were being taken to 'restrict the use of the words "Royal" and "Imperial" in the titles of various companies'. The response, delivered by Captain Hacking MP, later Major Sir Douglas Hacking, merely expressed the hope that if and when new legislation was introduced then the provisions of the unsuccessful Bill of 1922 would be included. In view of this Bill's repeated failure this response fell on stony ground.

The Home Office was apparently wary of introducing legislation which seemed to question the basic principle of 'innocent until proved guilty'. But there were many grounds for confusion. It was clear, for example, that a pub calling itself 'The Royal Oak', 'The King's Arms' or even 'The Royal Standard' was not suggesting that members of the Royal Family habitually drank there, any more than the Royal Coat of Arms on the front page of national newspapers suggested that they read them. This was the slightly tongue-in-cheek advice of Louis Tillett, the Norwich lawyer who had unsuccessfully advocated the purchase of the Hanover Square building in 1919. Tillett was a significant figure in the Association's affairs.

There was, at last, some consolation in the Companies Act of 1929, which prohibited the registration of any company with a name including the words 'Royal' or 'Imperial', or which in any way was 'calculated to suggest the patronage of the King or any member of The Royal Family or connection with His Majesty's Government or any department thereof'.

In 1933 the President of the Board of Trade set up a committee to consider the question of trade marks yet again. Representations drafted by Tillett were made complaining that 'defects' in the existing legislation had been causing problems 'extending over 30 years'.

In the event the Warrant Holders had to wait until 1938 before a new Trade Marks Act was passed. This fell far short of what the Association wanted and led the frustrated Tillett to comment that the official response to his ideas was 'pause, hesitate, prepare,

PATEY LONDON

postpone and end by leaving things alone'.

Despite this official inertia and unhelpfulness the Association was ever-vigilant in trying to stamp out the constant abuse of the Royal Arms by unscrupulous tradesmen and businessmen. In doing so they were, of course, protecting the Royal Family but also their own hard-won rights and privileges.

The early years of the twentieth century seem to have been the worst and that startling figure of 400 cases for the year 1908 was never exceeded. The number never again rose above 300 and by the end of the Great War the Association was dealing with fewer than 200 cases a year. During the twenties the figure hovered around the low hundreds with a minimum of exactly a hundred in 1920 and a maximum of 126 in 1927. In 1929 there was a dramatic decrease to just seventy, after which it never again rose above 100.

If anything, the problem was even greater abroad. On the Indian sub continent the Association employed a representative called John Faletti who in 1913 tried to get a Bill through the Indian parliament to prevent the improper use of the Royal Coat of Arms. The government of India were unconvinced and asked for more evidence of abuse. The Royal Warrant Holders in London therefore sent a message to members in India to dig some out: 'Any Warrant Holder in India desiring information in connection with the above-mentioned matter, or in connection with the issuing of the Royal Warrants of Appointment, or the use of the same when granted, should communicate with Mr John Faletti, at Faletti's Hotel Cecil, Simla.'

In 1915, on 21st April, the President of the Board of Trade received the President of the Royal Warrant Holders, T. B. Callard of the Old Bond Street bakers Callard, Steward & Watt, together with James Coleman, the Association's Secretary. Callard and Coleman told him the existing law was too weak and

that the Royal Coat of Arms should be legally registered in foreign countries.

The Board of Trade expressed the hope that after the war something should be done and indeed, by 1920 the Council of the RWHA was able to report to its members that despite a marked increase in the use of the Royal Coat of Arms 'calculated to deceive' they were actively pursuing such abuse. 'These cases', reported the Council, 'are brought to the notice of the Board of Trade, and official action invariably follows in the Country concerned, and usually with successful results.'

Some countries didn't seem fully to understand the issues. Mr Faletti, the Association's man in India, even in 1922 engineered a personal interview with the Viceroy and managed to get the government there to issue an order to eradicate abuse of the Royal Coat of Arms. Unfortunately the government acted overzealously and issued a blanket ban. This meant that no goods bearing the Royal Arms could be imported into India whether the company involved was entitled to

display the Arms or not. The long-suffering Mr Faletti protested and the order was amended so that bona fide Warrant Holders were allowed to display the Royal Arms on any of their goods imported into India.

Sometimes, of course, companies were expected to fend for themselves, either acting individually or in groups. In 1921 several British firms took advertisements in the New York papers after a 'great number of cases of improper use with American firms'. Some of these were the result of 'ignorance of the law and customs in this country' and were easily dealt with. Others, however, 'are not so easily disposed of'.

One particular American abuse surfaced in 1932 when it transpired that it was a 'widespread custom' for German needle manufacturers to place the British Royal Coat of Arms on the packets of needles they exported to the United States. The Association took up the matter and was able to secure a voluntary undertaking from the German Needle Manufacturers' Association to desist. The incident begs a number of questions such as why America was such a big market for German needles and, if so, why the Germans felt it necessary to pass their product off as being given a British royal imprimatur. But the most curious aspect of this odd example of Anglo-German co-operation is that it should have taken place just a year before Hitler became Chancellor.

There was also, in 1932, an interesting edict from Canada where the Governor-General issued a prohibition forbidding 'advertisements, trade literature and displays on the premises of tradesmen, hotel proprietors and others who now supply or have previously supplied goods or services to the Governor-General or to his predecessors'. Companies throughout the Empire had decided that if they enjoyed the patronage of the sovereign's representative, namely the Viceroy or the Governor-General, they should be entitled to display the Royal Coat of Arms. Canada's ruling created a precedent, which the Association circulated to all other dominions. In future situations the personal Arms of the Viceroy or Governor-General were to be 'the correct display', not the Royal Coat of Arms itself. As a result the indefatigable Mr Faletti in India was able to report that he had persuaded no less a person than the Governor of the Punjab to tell his own personal Warrant Holders to cease using the Royal Coat of Arms. This 'put a stop in that part of India to a practice prevalent in many parts the country'.

Foreign abuse was certainly not restricted to the Empire. In the following year, 1933, the Association dealt with cases in France, Spain, Malta, Greece, Cyprus, Uruguay, the Argentine Republic and Belgium. The year after that, abuses were reported as far afield as Egypt, Peru, Sweden and Japan. In 1935 the Association reported that it

> 'continued to exercise a vigilant watch over all foreign trade mark applications advertised in the official Journals published in countries where registration can be effected – a new departure in its activities initiated recently. It is evident there is a tendency in foreign countries to endeavour to obtain registrations containing British Royal Emblems or references to British Royal patronage.'

A year later the Association reported that they were having to be even more vigilant in the face of 'a growing tendency in foreign countries to obtain the advantage of British prestige by embodying in such registrations British Royal Emblems or references to British Royal patronage'. Fighting such abuse was costing a lot of money and although in 1937 'the majority of infringements reported from overseas

Left: 1901 advertisement for Keen's Mustard featured in the programme for the Coronation of King Edward VII.

Michael Skinner

come from English speaking countries and from France', the practice was worldwide. That same year it had spread to Austria, Hungary and Colombia.

It is difficult sometimes to say whether some companies were deliberately trying it on or whether they were genuinely ignorant of the legal implications. Even after legislation was tightened and codified some traders advanced the flimsiest reasons for using coats of arms, apparently in good faith. In 1927, for example, Martin & Company of the Burlington Arcade were ordered to remove the Royal Arms from their premises. The reason the company thought they were entitled to display it was that the father of the present Mr Martin had been 'honoured at the Great Exhibition of 1862' (*sic*). Even the Warrant Holders thought this was carrying the hereditary principle a little far!

One of the oldest Warrant Holders, J. Schweppe & Co,, who started business in the 1780s 'when Mineral Waters were practically unknown' claimed, some time in the reign of King George V: 'The fact that they have held Royal Warrants continuously for so many years (a particularly interesting one being dated Kensington Palace, March 1836, to the late Queen when Princess Victoria) is sufficient proof of the uniform excellence of their products.' Schweppe started with soda water, added lemonade and ginger ale, tonic water and ginger beer and, early in the twentieth century, a lime juice cordial which 'has met with immediate success'.

Alas, imitation proved the most damaging form of flattery and the company was moved to make a public protest:

A firm with such a reputation has naturally many imitators both at home and abroad, and they ask their many patrons in all parts of the world to beware of the fraudulent imitations of their labels. In so short a space it is impossible to give a list of agents in various parts of the world where Schweppes Minerals can be obtained, but the name of the Agent for same

in any place will be sent on communicating with the head office at West Kensington

The Royal Warrant Holders Association was able to assist them if part of their imitators' tactics was to plagiarise the Royal Coat of Arms or claim royal patronage. But not otherwise. Years later, in the 1990s and beyond, some companies were inclined to claim that they were entitled to a Royal Warrant simply because they were important British companies contributing to Britain's reputation, balance of payments and so on. The Palace, however, insisted that such considerations had nothing to do with the Warrant, which was entirely dependent on genuine and regular supply to one of the Grantors.

On the whole the Association stuck to its last and concerned itself entirely with matters to do with the Warrant. In the first half of the twentieth century much of its time was taken up with this policing of the Warrant. It could be time-consuming and tiresome, but it was essential business and over the years the Association won the arguments to such an extent that these abuses dwindled to a point of comparatively little significance.

Very occasionally the Association forgot itself and was guilty of a sort of Pooterish *folie de grandeur*. The most spectacular example of this came at the Council meeting of 29th February 1912, when a motion was passed that 'The government be urgently requested to bring in legislation (with the knowledge and assent of

Right: Trade Mark application by J. Perry & Co., ruled to be unacceptable by Mr Registrar Griffin at the Trade Marks Office in July 1906, after seven statutory declarations of opposition by the Association. RWHA Archive

His Majesty's Opposition) that shall terminate this most disastrous coal strike'. A copy of this resolution was sent to the Prime Minister, Mr Asquith, and another to the Lord Chamberlain to be forwarded to His Majesty the King. There is no evidence that either paid the slightest attention nor that the Royal Warrant Holders on any other occasion departed from a well-defined and understood brief which confined their activities exclusively to matters to do with the Royal Warrant. Terminating strikes did not come within their remit!

One of the most bizarre cases of pre-war 'abuse' came to light in the course of researching the earlier Royal Warrant book, *By Appointment*. In 1988 the Secretary of the day, Commander Hugh Faulkner, discovered a case involving a Parisian company called Old England of 12 Boulevard des Capucines. As the name suggests, the company traded on the Anglophilia of a certain sort of Frenchman. Their motto was 'Quality First' and this claim was bolstered by a widespread and totally unjustified use of the British Royal Coat of Arms.

According to the files this abuse had been drawn to the attention of the British embassy in Paris over fifty years earlier, in 1936. The embassy duly reported the matter to the Royal Warrant Holders Association in London and a letter of remonstrance was despatched asking Old England to stop. Correspondence ensued but nothing seemed to have been resolved before the outbreak of World War Two. Soon afterwards the Germans marched into Paris and, as it turned out, occupied at least part of the Old England premises at 12 Boulevard des Capucines.

There the matter might have rested, gathering dust in the archive. However, by an extraordinary coincidence Commander Faulkner had, while shopping in Paris, recently acquired a particularly chic overcoat and when he opened the old file he suddenly experienced a frisson of déjà vu. Sure enough, when he returned home and looked inside the overcoat he found a label inside the collar of the coat which confirmed that the garment came from Old England of Paris. Moreover, the label carried a coat of arms which looked horribly like a Gallic rendition of the one belonging to the British Queen.

So, almost half a century after the original correspondence was discontinued, Commander Faulkner wrote to number 12 Boulevard des Capucines, drawing attention to the Association's previous letter and to the matter of the label in his overcoat.

The reply from Old England's Managing Director, Monsieur J. M. Henriquet, was swift and courteous. His company had, as requested before the war, amended their official business writing paper along the lines requested by the Royal Warrant Holders Association. The coat of arms used on their products had also been amended and a sample was enclosed. There *was* a stained-glass window at 12 Boulevard des Capucines which contained a Royal Coat of Arms but this had been there since 1886 and was registered as an ancient monument. The Germans had tried to get rid of it during the occupation but had failed. Surely it would be an undesirable irony if the British should now succeed where their enemies had not?

All this was duly considered by the Council and it

ST JAMES'S PALACE, S.W.

January 29th, 1932.

My dear General,

The Prince of Wales desires me to say that he will be very pleased to accept your invitation to attend the Annual Dinner of the Royal Warrant Holders' Association at the Connaught Rooms on Wednesday evening February 17th.

Yours sincerely,

Godfrey Thomas

Lieut-General Sir Travers Clarke, G.B.E., K.C.M.G., K.C.B.,
Royal Warrant Holders' Association,
8 Hanover Square, W. 1.

Left: *Letter from The Prince of Wales, accepting the Association's invitation to the 1932 Banquet.* RWHA Archive

was agreed that on the whole, honour was satisfied. Indeed, the entire business was so amicably resolved that in the year of the 150th anniversary, M. Henriquet attended the annual banquet as the guest of that year's President Barry Reed, himself the head of a distinguished firm of men's outfitters on the opposite side of the Channel.

After the accession of Edward VII all Royal Warrants included in the wording the name of the grantee's firm and company, and until the death of George V it was possible to have three different grantees named in a single Warrant. This sometimes had the effect of prolonging the validity of a single Warrant but it rather belied the origins of the custom which, as we have seen, was to grant Warrants to one particular individual. Conferring it on a group, however small, seemed to diminish the sense of privilege and exclusivity, and the custom was changed by King George VI.

During the inter-war years the social activities of the Association continued undiminished. Members continued to gather in large numbers at prestigious locations for their annual banquet.

One of the Warrant Holders' most ambitious projects of those years was the construction of the 'King's House'. This was conceived as a tribute to mark the twenty-fifth anniversary of the accession of King George V. It was intended to be a 'small residence' and to be used by the Sovereign 'to place at the service of any person whom His Majesty might think worthy of this indication of the royal favour'.

The idea was that it should not only be a Jubilee tribute from the Royal Tradesmen but that it should also be a demonstra-

tion of their various skills. The Warrant Holders' intention was that 'the House shall represent the "last word" in construction, furnishing and equipment, thus setting a standard to which regard would be paid all over the world. All materials and equipment would be of Empire origin and supplied by Royal Warrant Holders.' The intention was that the property be 'vested in The King and his successor Kings of England . . . making it in effect Crown Land'. 'The house could then be included as one of His Majesty's Grace and Favour houses.'

The house would be fully endowed so that it could be maintained 'in perpetuity' and there would be a fund to take care of this administered by a board of trustees.

At a Council meeting in the Hanover Square office on 17th October 1934 it was announced that His Majesty was in favour of the scheme. Two offers of land were received from powerful Warrant Holders. One was from Lord Leverhulme on behalf of Lever Brothers and

Holders, could use a reproduction of the house on a chocolate box provided it was properly attributed.

In the special supplement produced for the Ideal Home Exhibition in the spring of 1935, the architect of the King's House, C. Beresford Marshall, said that the tribute reflected the King's famous phrase, 'The foundations of the National Glory are set in the Homes of the People.'

Many of the Warrant Holders who contributed to the project took the opportunity to draw attention to their goods and services. Jeyes' White Porcelain Toilet Box (with nickel fittings) was 'selected and installed throughout the King's House'; Thomas Potterton's gas water heaters were installed 'for the important duty of Summer Hot Water Supply'; 'The Decorating and the Furnishing of the Drawing Room, the single Guest's Room and the Loggia of this House were all carried out by Hamptons, Pall Mall East, SW1.'; 'Smith's Synchronous Electric Clocks are in the King's House. Why not in yours?'; 'Hoover Ltd are privileged to announce that the King's House presented to His Majesty by the Royal Warrant Holders Association in celebration of His Silver Jubilee is equipped with Hoover electric cleaners'; 'The Architect for the King's House specified STAYBRITE RUSTLESS STEEL EQUIPMENT throughout the kitchen'. The asphalt came from the Limmer & Trinidad Lake Asphalt Co.; the barometer from Newton & Co., and the bidet from Edwin John & Co. The Wilton Royal Carpet Company covered the floors, G. P. & J. Baker curtained the windows and Sanderson papered the walls. Four separate companies provided fires and fireplaces, and Merryweather were responsible for fire extin-

the other from Lord Iveagh on behalf of Guinness and Son. The Guinness offer of a site at Burhill, Surrey, near the golf course just outside Walton-on-Thames, was preferred because 'proposed development was not so close and the site more isolated'. In their advertising the Burhill Estates Company, offering other houses and sites at prices from £1750 upwards, claimed that this was a place 'where your property is protected from depreciation and open spaces are guaranteed for ever'. The King was keen that the first occupants should be the Duke and Duchess of Kent.

As well as being an expression of loyalty to the King, the house was also an opportunity for discreet advertisement and the minutes of the 1934 meeting reported: 'In view of the popular interest it is bound to attract, it has been arranged that, before permanent erection, the complete house should first be exhibited to the public at the Ideal Home Exhibition in March and April next, where it is anticipated well over half a million members of the public would be able to view it.' It was also agreed that Messrs Fry, Warrant

guishers. The piano was from Marshall and Rose ('Upright models from 48 gns, Grand models from 69 gns'). The William and Mary stools in the drawing room were hand-embroidered in tent-stitch by 'a craftswoman who is the only Woman Warrant Holder'. However, restrictions on space in the exhibition hall made it impossible to show the chauffeur's quarters.

Sadly, King George V died before the house could be formally presented and it went instead to King

Edward VIII. The Duke and Duchess of Kent never moved in. Instead, the house was briefly cared for by a Sergeant-Major McKay from the Royal Corps of Commissionaires, before becoming the home of Admiral Sir Reginald Tupper. Tupper was a career naval officer with a distinguished war record, first as Vice-Admiral, Atlantic Blockade, and latterly as Admiral, Northern Patrol. He had retired in 1921, decorated by the French and the Spanish as well as collecting a GBE to add to his KCB.

The Admiral certainly seemed to take a proper

pride in the place. On 18th January 1937 the Association's Secretary, Major Brookhouse, called to discuss 'various matters in connection with the King's House'. As a result the Major wrote to A. M. Woodman, the Warrant Holder at Benjamin Edgington, 'Marquee, Tent, Rick Cloth and Flag Manufacturers, Complete Outfitters and Contractors'. 'Dear Woodman,' he wrote. 'I saw Admiral Sir Reginald Tupper today and he was very much concerned about the flagstaff, and being a sailor, he is very anxious indeed to have one. He expresses a strong preference for having a small one on the roof.'

An earlier offer by the company to supply a flagstaff had been turned down but this time Mr Woodman was able to reply, 'Dear Brookhouse, Many thanks for yours of the 18th re flagstaff for Admiral Sir Reginald Tupper. I think the best thing is for us to do the work for you at cost.' This was done and until the Admiral's death at the end of World War Two a flag was proudly flown from the roof of the King's House. In time, however, the house was to become a glorious failure and an experiment never to be repeated.

Betty Whittington, in her brief but well-researched history of 1961, points out that King Edward VIII issued no Warrants and suggests that because of his 'democratic outlook' he intended to do away with the whole apparatus. 'Democratic outlook' or not, Edward had, as Prince of Wales, granted a number of Warrants but during his brief and disastrous reign he had, on the whole, other things on his

the Warrant was concerned it was almost like the restoration of the monarchy.

The outbreak of the Second World War at the end of the decade produced a hiatus. Whereas no previous President served more than two years Brigadier Courage of White Horse Distillers was President from 1939 until the end of 1943. The two Presidents who followed him, Howard Hughes of Alfred Hughes & Sons, cake and biscuit manufacturers and F. A. Simonds of H. & G. Simonds, brewers, were both drafted in for a second term, having already served a year each in the 1930s.

The President was backed up by a Secretary who during those difficult years of World War Two was the same Robert Pears of Pears Soap who had been one of the youngest ever Presidents in 1929. Pears was the last totally civilian secretary. His successor, R. H. W. Hope, was the holder of the Military Cross and after him each of the four Secretaries who served through the second half of the twentieth century and beyond were retired officers from the Army or the Royal Navy. If one wanted unquestioning loyalty to the Crown coupled with a high level of administrative efficiency it was to

mind. He might indeed have been keen to do away with them but Betty Whittington does not produce any evidence for the idea and his younger brother seemed perfectly happy to continue with them. As in so many other royal matters, the accession of King George VI represented a return to normality. As far as

the Armed Services that one looked.

The Association spent most of the war outside London. On the expiry of the Hanover Square lease the office was moved out to Beaconsfield in Buckinghamshire, where a flat was rented at 2 The Council Chambers. The annual rent was just £200 compared with the £300 they were paying for Hanover Square at the outbreak of war. Beaconsfield was a quiet, mainly residential town with a distinguished eighteenth century high street, nearer to Windsor Castle than to Buckingham Palace, but well away from any concentration of Warrant Holders' business premises. The town was far less likely to fall prey to enemy bombing than the West End of London and was therefore a relatively safe haven for the already significant archive built up during the Association's life so far. Generally speaking the Association, along with the rest of Britain, pulled in its belt, battened down the hatches and prayed for victory for King and Country.

Robert Pears, President in 1929, and Secretary
of the Association from 1937-1946.
RWHA Archive

The President's Badge of office.

The Royal Warrant Holders Association moved back to London from their wartime retreat in Beaconsfield in 1947. Their new home at 7 Buckingham Gate was to be their office for the next half-century. Situated just across the street from Buckingham Palace, opposite the Diplomatic Entrance (to the Royal Mews and the Queen's Gallery), it could not have been nearer the fount of royal power and influence. As an efficient working machine it was mildly eccentric and unreformed. The Secretary worked at one end of the impressive oval boardroom table under the gaze of generations of former Presidents whose black-and-white photographs lined the walls. His assistants occupied a sort of landing half way up the winding iron-railed staircase. This arrangement precluded privacy but also meant that no visitor could ascend to the Secretary's presence without passing the ever-watchful staff on guard below. Buckingham Gate may not have been perfect but it was better than Beaconsfield.

Right: *The Lord Forteviot, MBE, President 1947, Grantee for John Dewar & Sons Ltd., Scotch Whisky Distillers.* RWHA Archive

In 1950 Princess Elizabeth, installed in Clarence House with the Duke of Edinburgh, began to grant her own Warrants for the first time, causing the *Tatler* to remark that 'relations between the Court and Trade have received a fillip'. In the same issue the magazine noted that Walls, 'the sausage people', had just discovered an old Warrant of Queen Victoria's appointing their founder Thomas Wall 'into the place of Pork-in-ordinary'.

The post-war Presidents were predominantly from the world of food and drink. The 1947 President was Lord Forteviot of John Dewar & Sons, the whisky distillers and his immediate successor, Oliver Watney of Watney, Mann, the brewers. Other presidential purveyors of beverages of one kind or another over the next two decades included the Hon. R. Hanning Philipps (1954) of Schweppes, one of the oldest of all Warrant-holding companies; Stephen Twining (1956) of the ancient tea merchants, whose son Sam was to be President in 1972, and an influential Hon. Treasurer thereafter; Sir Harry Hague (1957), whose company, A. Wander Ltd., made Ovaltine; H. M. Braid (1960) of Johnny Walker, the Scotch whisky distillers; E. D. Simonds (1963) of H. & G. Simonds, the brewers; and Keith Stevens (1966) of the wine merchants, Corney & Barrow, whose grantee Adam Brett-Smith was to be President in 2001.

The food-providing Presidents were Sir John Bodinnar (1952), a pork butcher who was also a director of bacon products at the Ministry of Food and Chairman of the Bacon Marketing Board – a latter-day 'Pork-in-ordinary'!; Reginald Palmer (1953) of Huntley & Palmers, the biscuit and cake manufacturers; William Chivers (1955) of Chivers & Sons, purveyors of jams.

The gaps between food and drink were filled by Sir Frederick Wells Bt (1950) of Sanitas & Co. Ltd.; Rupert Carr (1958) of Day & Martin, boot polish manufacturers; Sir Richard Burbidge Bt (1959) of Harrods, outfitters and suppliers of provisions and fancy goods, who were later, under the ownership of the controversial Mohammed Al Fayed, to surrender all four of their Warrants; J. W. Isaac (1961) of Garrard & Co. Ltd., the Crown Jewellers; Sidney Hine (1962) of Day, Son & Hewitt, suppliers of animal medicine; Sir Edward Rayne (1964) of H. & M. Rayne, shoemakers and handbag manufacturers; J. Williamson (1965) of the Army & Navy Stores, suppliers of household and fancy goods.

Throughout most of this period the Secretary of the Royal Warrant Holders Association was Brigadier

Morrison. Morrison succeeded R. H. W. Hope, OBE, MC in 1952, the year of the accession of Queen Elizabeth. He had come to the notice of the Association through the Twining tea family. Morrison was Private Secretary to Stephen Twining's brother – Sam's uncle – when he was Governor of Tanganyika. He seemed just the sort of chap as far as the Twinings were concerned and, indeed, proved to be a popular and respected Secretary for many years.

In 1954 Brigadier Morrison had the unusual task of issuing a Notice of an Extraordinary General Meeting to consider the future of the King's House. After Admiral Sir Reginald Tupper died in 1945 the house was taken over by Marshal of the RAF Lord Trenchard and Lady Trenchard. Now, however, it was proving too difficult and expensive to maintain. It was also said that the environs, so optimistically extolled when it was originally built two decades earlier, had 'so radically altered in recent years' that it was 'becoming increasingly unsuitable for the purpose for which it was originally intended'. The motion was passed and the house was sold for about £50,000. This money was used to buy another 'Grace and Favour' residence. Poor, 'unsuitable' Walton-on-Thames gave way to the more fashionable and convenient north London suburb of Highgate. The Trust Fund of £10,000, which had been used to maintain the King's House at Burhill, Walton-on-Thames, was transferred to help maintain the new property in Highgate.

This was not the end of the King's House story for Highgate proved, in its way, as 'unsuitable' as Walton-on-Thames and the second King's House was sold in its turn, the resulting funds being used to purchase a third house. This was in Pimlico, conveniently situated within walking distance of Buckingham Palace and therefore an eminently suitable residence for Sir Robin Janvrin, who became the Queen's Private Secretary in 1999. This was thoroughly sensible but a sad end to the proud hopes which surrounded the original project back in the 1930s.

Apart from the drama surrounding the King's House, the fifties and sixties were, on the whole, uneventful years in the Association's history. Cases of misuse continued to occur and the Association even retained an American attorney to oversee matters in the United States. His name was Boynton P. Livingston. Bill Palmer remembers Livingston as 'a great character' whose only reward for writing admonitory letters to American companies who were breaking the rules was an invitation to the Association's functions in London. He always sat at the top table, smoking the Havana cigars (after the loyal toast of course) he came to England to buy. At Palmer's banquet in 1976 he arrived wearing full Highland dress! Other notable guests at the banquet during those years included Sir Alec Douglas-Home and the two most celebrated after-dinner speakers of the day, Lord Mancroft, and the surgeon Sir Arthur Dickson-Wright, whose daughter Clarissa was later to attain culinary television fame as one of the 'Two Fat Ladies'. Prime Minister Harold Wilson was once a guest of his notorious friend Joseph Kagan, manufacturer of the 'Gannex' mackintosh, but he left after the reception and did not stay for the meal.

In 1956 His Royal Highness the Duke of Edinburgh became a Grantor for the first time, issuing twenty-nine Warrants in his first list and provoking the *Daily Mirror* into paroxysms of republican rage. 'What utter nonsense,' stormed the *Mirror*. 'It is silly and obsolete. It is Royal Patronage at its most

Left: *The Earl of Airlie, Lord Chamberlain to Queen Elizabeth The Queen Mother, supervising arrangements for the 1953 Coronation. Lord Airlie's son, the 13th Earl, subsequently served as Lord Chamberlain to the Sovereign from 1984-97.*
Hulton Getty Picture Library

undignified.'

Despite the paper's colourful language it was not entirely easy to follow its logic. 'Believe it or not,' the *Mirror* continued,

> the firm which takes in the Duke of Edinburgh's washing may display his Arms, and its name is boosted in a Royal proclamation.
>
> Are working women likely to send their bras and scanties to the White Heather Laundry in the hope that they will pass through the same mangle as the Ducal underpants, or be ironed in close proximity to the Royal undervests?

This tirade may have seemed silly and inconsequential, but it was a salutary reminder that not everyone was in favour of the monarchy or at least of the system of granting Royal Warrants. The *Mirror* sold several million copies every day and was highly influential.

In 1966 Brigadier Morrison died suddenly while still serving as the Association's Secretary. Shortly afterwards the Assistant Keeper of the Privy Purse, Sir Rennie Maudslay, sent a letter of condolence to Sidney Hine as 'the only person I feel I know well in the Association'. After paying tribute to Brigadier Morrison – 'excellent person . . . will be greatly missed . . . always so helpful and understanding' – Sir Rennie moved on to the question of a successor. The man he had in mind was 'a certain Colonel Bill Keown-Boyd, who is well known to a number of us here'. Keown-Boyd was known to be looking for a job because he had been short listed for one at the Palace the previous year. Sir Rennie said 'He is an extremely nice man and very capable.'

The following day Sidney Hine wrote to Keith Stevens of Corney & Barrow, the wine merchants. Stevens was President of the Association that year. 'My Dear Keith,' he began, 'I have received the enclosed from Rennie Maudslay this morning – he was my fag at school and is now assistant keeper of the Privy Purse as you know – taught and trained by me

of course!!' The school in question was Eton.

Two days later Colonel Keown-Boyd wrote formally to Keith Stevens applying for the job. He was fifty-three years old, educated at Charterhouse and Sandhurst, commanded a battalion of the 60th Rifles during the war, retired in 1958 'for personal reasons' after twenty-six years' service and since then had worked for a trading company and an advertising agency as well as running his own small estate and being chairman of his parish council. 'My hobbies', he

told Stevens, 'are fishing and shooting and I am a member of the Army & Navy Club and Whites.'

On 23rd May he was interviewed by a selection committee at Buckingham Gate and on 17th June Keith Stevens phoned to tell him that the job was his. A formal letter followed and on 12th July he was introduced to the Council at twelve noon. It was a classic example of how the Old Boy Network used to organise such matters. It could not happen in the twenty-first century but in the event the appointment was not only made very fast and with minimal fuss, it also worked out extremely well. Keown-Boyd

Left: *The Queen is escorted by Keith Stevens (President) and Mrs Stevens when Her Majesty joined Warrant Holders at the Guildhall in February 1967, to commemorate the 60th anniversary of the Association's Royal Charter of Incorporation, on 25th February 1907.*
Sam Twining

remained as Secretary until 1979, much liked and respected by the Warrant Holders and by the Palace, though unlike his early predecessors and his two successors he only worked a three-day week and seldom left the office. 'If you wanted to see him you had to come to Buckingham Gate,' said one President a touch ruefully. 'He did not come to see you.'

In February 1967, in the closing days of the presidency of Keith Stevens, the Association felt sufficiently removed from war-time constraints to hold a special event at the Guildhall to commemorate the 60th anniversary of its Royal Charter of Incorporation, on 25th February 1967. To the delight of Warrant Holders, Her Majesty The Queen accepted an invitation to join them - the first time ever a Royal Warrant Holders' event had been honoured by the presence of the reigning Monarch.

Also in 1967 Sir Geoffrey Hardy-Roberts was appointed Master of the Queen's Household. Unlike some of his predecessors, Hardy-Roberts came to this job with a proven record as an administrator. As a young wartime brigadier he had been in overall charge of supplies during the D-Day landings. In peacetime he was for twenty ground-breaking years administrator for the Middlesex Hospital Group. At the time of Hardy-Roberts's retirement from the Middlesex the Chairman of Governors was Lord Cobbold, who at the time also happened to be Her Majesty's Lord Chamberlain. Lord Cobbold decided that Hardy-Roberts was just the man to 'reform and revive an organisation still suffering from the utilitarian measures and low-funding of the post wars'. Those words are from Sir Michael Tims who served as Hardy-Roberts's deputy and was an influential figure at Buckingham Palace for many years, and they were delivered at his funeral in Arundel Cathedral in 1997.

As Master, Hardy-Roberts was a crucial figure in the Palace's dealings with the Warrant Holders. In theory the Lord Chamberlain is the single most important courtier when it comes to dealing with the 'Royal Tradesmen' but in practice matters concerning the Warrant have, historically, fallen to various other officers in various departments. It is also a matter of historical fact that some such officers have been content to maintain the status quo, while others have been reformers. Hardy-Roberts was firmly in the latter camp.

In Sir Michael Tims's memorial address he said of his old boss, 'He said at the start, "Let's throw everything up in the air and see how it lands!" – and this he did. He changed whatever needed change and built on much existing excellence. New and ample funding was *needed* and his force of character and strength of argument soon weakened the resolve of tough financial colleagues.'

The President of the Warrant Holders in the year of Hardy-Roberts's arrival at the Palace was (Lord) George Hayter, Chairman of Chubb. Members of the Chubb family have held the Warrant since Charles Chubb was King George IV's locksmith. Although the company has modernised and diversified, relationships with the Royal Family were, at least in George Hayter's experience, close if not entirely intimate.

Lord Hayter remembers a moment in 1947 when My uncle, Emory, had our Royal Warrant before me. He was summoned to the Palace to discuss with Queen Mary the provision of a safe as a wedding present to the present Queen to hold her jewellery. On his return he told me: 'all was well – a large safe to be lined with velvet was chosen'. Unfortunately he inadvertently said in conversation with her, 'I think Elizabeth would like that' instead of referring to her as HRH. He didn't think Queen Mary had noticed.

At that moment the telephone rang and Queen Mary's secretary said she would be obliged if Mr Chubb would attend the following morning. Queen Mary could be formidable. Anyhow I got him off in time and awaited his return with anxiety.

He came back wreathed in smiles. Her Majesty had found some discarded velvet curtains and just wanted to know if they would be suitable.

Five years earlier Peter Coleclough had been invited to join the Council by Sidney Hine and Rupert Carr. Coleclough's company was Howard Rotavator Co. Ltd., who made agricultural equipment. Both Carr and Hine had been Presidents of the Association and in due course, in 1971, nine years after joining the Council, Coleclough assumed office himself, and as President, acted as host for the 1971 reception at the Guildhall attended by Her Majesty The Queen and by the Duke of Edinburgh. Coleclough was also instrumental in moving the annual luncheon to the Savoy, where it remained for a couple of years. And it was Coleclough again, as President, who managed to get women admitted to the annual cocktail party held in the Association's offices. 'A giant step forward!' he comments laconically. And at the time it was.

Apart from this sort of jollification and similar 'PR activities' Peter Coleclough said that 'nothing very remarkable occurred'. Money was short. Office and general expenses amounted to only about £7500 a year. Minutes of Council meetings were taken in hand writing and read out at the next meeting. There was no question of their being distributed as there was no

copying machine other than a Gestetner used by the assistant secretary Mrs Carver only in moments of extreme need.

The twenty-fifth anniversary of the Queen's wedding in 1972, was the year in which Sam Twining of Twining's Tea was President. Not only had his father been President but the Twining Warrant was one of the oldest on record. In Twining's year the annual luncheon, which had moved in the Coleclough presidency from the Connaught Rooms to the Savoy, had to be cancelled because the Duke of Windsor died. The next year it was removed to the Park Lane Hilton, where it has remained ever since.

More significantly, it was decided during the Twining presidency to establish a 'Joint Silver Anniversary Trust' which was to commemorate the twenty-fifth wedding anniversary and also the twenty-

Right:
Sam Twining, on becoming President at the age of 39 in 1972.
Sam Twining

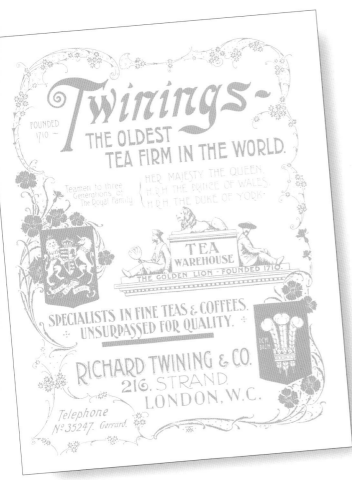

the time it was felt at Buckingham Palace that, at twenty-three years old, The Prince was still too young and, moreover, as a serving naval officer, was too often away from home. He had yet to establish the sort of permanent working household which made all the appropriate demands on Royal Tradesmen.

The matter lay fallow during the next few presidencies, which were those of a tobacconist, T. E. Davies of Ardath, William Douglas of Gray's the Edinburgh ironmongers, and John Connell of the Distillers Company who held the Warrant for Scotch whisky. John Connell remembered a number of difficult cases involving misuse of the Warrant during his time. These were not all straightforward. In the case of his own company, for instance, they owned a distillery in Mexico, which made Gordon's gin. Were they entitled to display the Royal Coat of Arms on bottles of Mexican Gordon's? It was a tricky question.

John Connell's recollection of this period was that Colonel Keown-Boyd had, after more than a decade in office, become a dominating presence. 'Bill did rather run the show,' he said.

In 1976 the then Warrant Holders' President, William Palmer, of Huntley & Palmers, the cake and biscuit manufacturers, made another overture to Lord Maclean. The Prince of Wales, he argued, was now slightly older than his predecessor, the late Duke of Windsor, when he, in 1921, gave his first Royal Warrant. Palmer told Lord Maclean that from the Warrant Holders'

fifth anniversary, five years later, of the Accession. The idea was to help The Queen provide for her pensioners by providing money to build retirement homes for former royal servants at Balmoral, Sandringham and Windsor. Sam Twining wrote to all the grantees and received a response he described as 'terrific'. As a result the houses were built on land donated by The Queen. They were finished in 1974, and Sam Twining and his successor, Ted Davies, went to Windsor Castle to present The Queen with a scrapbook of the buildings and their construction.

It was also in 1972 that Sam Twining wrote to the Lord Chamberlain, Lord Maclean, suggesting that The Prince of Wales might wish to become a Grantor, giving his own Royal Warrants of Appointment. At

point of view there was a 'problem to maintain the impetus of the Royal Warrant under modern conditions'. He and his colleagues believed that 'the introduction of a third-generation Grantor, and particularly one who is young and commands such national and international respect as His Royal Highness The Prince of Wales, would put this problem behind us for a long time to come'.

Palmer was at pains to emphasise that Warrant holding and all that went with it was not at all the old-fashioned and snobbish business which some ill-informed critics supposed. 'I do not believe', he wrote, 'that the diversity of outlook, social background and politics that covers the membership of the Royal Warrant Holders Association is generally realised. It is, in fact, a truly democratic organisation in the widest sense, united in its common service and loyalty to the Crown. Where else would you find a Lord Chamberlain and a Chimney Sweep sitting down together at Top Table?!'

On 12th July 1976 Lord Maclean wrote back, 'In Confidence', to say that he had now had an opportunity to discuss the proposal with The Queen and subsequently with The Prince of Wales. The answer was that The Prince would like to start granting Warrants. The first grants would be made in 1980 to firms who could 'give evidence of a continuous, satisfactory and direct supply of goods or services to The Prince of Wales, or His Royal Highness's Household, over the preceding three-year period which will start on 1st January 1977'.

A Victorian illustration of 7 Buckingham Gate
RWHA Archive

Sir Edward Rayne, CVO, President in 1964 and Hon. Treasurer from 1979-1991.
Over a period of forty years, Sir Edward (Eddie) Rayne represented his company, H & M Rayne,
Shoemakers and Handbag Manufacturers, as their grantee, and acquired legendary status
as the Association's senior advisor and guide.
Lady Rayne

At first glance the appointment of Hugh Faulkner as Secretary of the Association in 1979 looks like a simple case of more of the same: a commander succeeded a colonel who succeeded a brigadier. The changes involved some alterations of rank and a switch from the Army to the Senior Service, but basically it looks like a case of one retired officer after another.

At that time the idea of engaging professional head hunters was never entertained. Instead, members of the Council agreed to seek candidates by discreet advertising and word-of-mouth contact. By this means they arrived at a long short list of eleven candidates, mainly but not exclusively from the Armed Services and these were interviewed by a select subcommittee chaired by Sir Edward Rayne.

Sir Nevil Macready of Mobil, who was the first President of the Faulkner era, later recalled that at the selection meeting one of the other candidates was an admiral. He was an acquaintance of Macready's and was extremely miffed to be turned down – so miffed, indeed, that he rang Macready to complain. 'I was relieved to be able to tell him that he was too grand for us,' said Macready. There was an element of truth in this. As Macready put it, 'You have to get on with some quite senior people and be chums with the Household but at the same time you're only running a small office and there's a lot of dogsbody stuff to deal with. You can't be above licking envelopes.'

The Admiral's disappointment was given added piquancy by the fact that he was much favoured by the Association's Treasurer, Sir Edward 'Eddie' Rayne. Rayne, who for forty years held the Warrant for making the Queen's shoes, had been since 1974 the *éminence grise* of the Royal Warrant Holders and was used to getting his own way. One President of the 1980s later revealed, 'When I became President, I was taken to lunch by Eddie Rayne and he explained how he liked Presidents to carry out their duties.' Another remarked that 'he acted as father figure to each President in turn with the result that nothing much happened without his approval . . .'.

On this occasion, in Faulkner's phrase, 'Eddie had picked his man.' For once, however, Rayne was outgunned. Dick Roberts, the Managing Director of Roberts Radios, was another strong character and also one of the small selection committee. He was strongly opposed to the Admiral. Sadly, both Roberts and Rayne were to die prematurely: Roberts of cancer and Rayne in a fire at his home less than a year after being 'dined out' as Treasurer in 1991. They were both, in their different ways, considerable personalities and devoted to the Warrant and the Association. Their deaths left a big gap.

'The Admiral's big mistake', in Faulkner's recollection, was that he brought his wife along to the interview. 'That finished him,' said Faulkner. Sir Nevil Macready remembered, more positively, that Faulkner made a particularly good impression. He was not pompous but on the other hand he made it clear that he was not someone who was going to be pushed around. 'Hugh was very affable,' he said. 'He got on with everyone. That's how he is. He gets on with everyone.' Faulkner later remembered telling the selectors that he had once been secretary of a hunt, which he thought impressed them. More important, he was able to say, with absolute conviction, 'I love people.'

This clubbable conviviality was to be the key to his seventeen-year term of office. His predecessor, Colonel Keown-Boyd, was, in Faulkner's words 'A lovely man'. He too was much loved by the relatively small group of people who knew him. He worked part-time and was not keen on leaving the office, preferring to entertain his 'chums' to lunch round the boardroom table. When Keown-Boyd was originally interviewed for the job, it was recalled, he had interviewed the selection committee rather than the other way round.

In Keown-Boyd's day the Association organised an annual banquet, lunch and cocktail party but that was about it. It was all very civilised but Faulkner, looking back on his inheritance, described it in the single word 'moribund'. The lease on the offices at 7 Buckingham Gate had little more than ten years to run. The working capital was a mere £65,000. All member companies paid the same subscription – £15 a year. The financial future looked bleak. Worse even than the money worries in the view of the incoming Secretary was the lack of day-to-day contact between the office and the bulk of the membership.

Faulkner resolved to change this. The first thing he told Eddie Rayne as Treasurer was that he wanted to work a full five-day week. The second resolution he made to himself was: 'A day in the office is a day wasted.' Later, at one of the Grosvenor House banquets, the President, Victor Watson of Waddington, made a joke of Faulkner's habitual absence from his desk. 'Who', asked Watson, 'does the work when Hugh's not in the office?' The response from Faulkner's right-hand woman, Annie Wycherley, was swift and succinct. 'The same people who do the work when Hugh *is* in the office,' she said. It is a story Faulkner liked to tell against himself.

He felt strongly that the Secretary should know the members and have at least a passing acquaintance with their business. His natural gregariousness and curiosity made him an ideal person to fulfil this aim. 'I remember very early on', he said, 'I went to see one firm and their managing director said, "How nice to see you! We've been Warrant Holders since 1914 and this is the first time we've seen anyone from the office."' Faulkner was shocked.

Sir Nevil Macready, the first President of the Faulkner years, remembered that the new Secretary was keen on travelling round to meet the troops and especially the members of the local Associations in Edinburgh and Aberdeen. The somewhat old-fashioned all-male atmosphere of the Association was being changed. The annual drinks party for members of the Household at the Association office had, for instance, become an event to which wives were invited. Faulkner, however, told Macready that as he wanted to concentrate on learning the job he would not be bringing his wife along to any functions at least during his first year in office. He made it clear that for this reason it would be inappropriate for Macready to bring Lady Macready. Sir Nevil did not demur. 'It was only shortly before I joined the Council that wives began to be invited to the President's December reception. Before that, Palace officials had been entertained without their wives once a year in the Council Chamber at Buckingham Gate. The change was undoubtedly much appreciated since Palace wives are so seldom included in official functions.'

As the Managing Director of an American-owned company, Mobil Oil Company Ltd, Macready was an unusual President though he compensated for the foreign ownership of his company by being a British aristocrat – a baronet, indeed. Actually, he was the third baronet to have been President since the war – the others being Sir Frederick Wells of Sanitas and Sir Richard Burbidge of Harrods. Macready had joined the Council at the instigation of Jack Charrington, the managing director of Charringtons, who were Mobil's distributors for the south of England. Almost immediately after joining the Council he was posted to Paris. 'Never mind,' said Bill Keown-Boyd. 'You just come over for meetings whenever you can.' In

Left: *Sir Nevil Macready (left) attends The Queen Mother, signing the Visitor's Book when she visited Mobil House for their centenary in 1986. Right is John Lowein, Chairman of Mobil Oil Co. Ltd.*
Nevil Macready

the event he didn't and when his turn came to become President he was in the difficult position of never having attended a single Council meeting.

There were several high spots during his year as President. Partly as a result of the new policy of the Association's officers getting out and about, the Sandringham Warrant Holders were encouraged in their ambition to form their own Association for the first time. There was also a memorable occasion when Sir Nevil invited Princess Anne to be the Association's guest. The reply was that Her Royal Highness would be delighted to accept but unfortunately she had another engagement later that evening so would the Warrant Holders mind terribly if they came to her at St James's Palace rather than her coming to them. 'Mind?' said Macready, shaking his head. The Princess was dressed in full formal evening dress and the surroundings were, of course, splendid. But what made the biggest impression was the interest and enthusiasm Princess Anne displayed. 'She was so knowledgeable,' he said. 'So well briefed.'

The atmosphere at that time was, in Macready's words, 'very clubby'. The Association was focused on the three annual social events. Relations with the Royal Household were cordial. 'Chips Maclean, the Lord Chamberlain, and I got on very well. I took him to the opera. But there's much closer and more regular contact nowadays. Then as now we all took great pride in our Warrants and though we recognised that they could be commercially valuable I think the important thing was that holding the Warrant meant that we had to maintain certain standards.'

Macready's successor as President was another oil man, John Riddell-Webster, though he was as unlike the popular conception of the breed as was Sir Nevil. Riddell-Webster had won an immediate MC with the Seaforth Highlanders in Sicily and was described by the *Daily Telegraph* as 'happiest with a rod in his hand'. After Harrow and Cambridge he joined the Anglo-Iranian Oil Company, which subsequently became BP. At the time of his presidency he held the

Warrant for both The Queen and The Queen Mother in his capacity as chairman of the BP subsidiary, National Benzole, which supplied the Royal Households with motor spirit.

The organisation of the Association is such that it is not always clear where initiatives come from. In the case of Riddell-Webster, however, it is generally acknowledged that he was the originator of the Warrant Holders' appeal to mark The Queen Mother's eightieth birthday. This raised £86,000 which was used to install a hydrotherapy pool in the King Edward VII Hospital for Officers in London.

This gift represented a subtle shift in the history of the Warrant Holders' charitable enterprises. In earlier times royal milestones were commemorated with gifts to the Royal Family itself. The most notable such precedent was the purchase of the 'King's House' on the occasion of George V's Jubilee. By 1980 that sort of gesture was no longer considered appropriate, but for the Warrant Holders it was still too early to become entirely egalitarian. The hydrotherapy pool was a much needed benefit and a worthy cause, but the King Edward VII Hospital was nonetheless a privately funded institution reserved for the exclusive use of officers and their relations. Other ranks were specifically excluded.

Within a few years the gift-giving philosophy had changed even more so that the Association's philanthropy was extended to encompass society as a whole and precisely to encourage those who needed it most.

David Part was President in 1981. He had always believed that the charitable activities of the Association were important and apart from playing his own part in The Queen Mother's eightieth birthday appeal and the building of staff bungalows on the royal estates, he was also instrumental in starting the 'germ' of The Queen Elizabeth Scholarship Fund. Later, too, he was a strong supporter of the creation of the Plowden Medal. Along with others, Part takes a particular pride in 'creating our developing role down the years in our charitable activities which I have

The General Trading Company, one of only seven companies to hold, in 2001, the Warrant of all four Grantors, seen here displayed above their new premises in Symons Street, London SW3.
David Part and GTC

always felt are so important a facet of the Association'.

Part's General Trading Company in Sloane Street was one of the few concerns to boast a coveted 'full house' of four Warrants. The company's Warrants are as 'Suppliers of Fancy Goods'. 'Ah,' said one Lord Chamberlain on meeting Part for the first time, 'Fancy Goods at fancy prices.' Part's reaction to this sally was a particularly rueful smile. However philanthropic the Warrant Holders became and however cordial their relations with the Palace, there was, as always, a certain creative tension in what was a commercial as well as a loyal relationship. Business, after all, is business and trade is trade. Warrant Holders have always had to live by their business and trade; the servants of the Monarch have always been obliged to keep costs as low as possible. The two interests do not always coincide – at least not in the short term.

On the whole, however, Warrant holding was an affable affair and members of the Association kept to the spirit rather than the rules of the game. Victor Watson of Waddingtons Games Ltd, who was President of the Association in 1983, was an embodiment of this in several different ways.

Waddingtons held the Warrant for supplying playing cards to the Monarch but this was a relatively new

appointment. The traditional supplier was Thomas de la Rue. Waddingtons had entered the market in the 1920s and thanks to technological innovations they had made great progress. A price war ensued but a rapprochement of sorts was engineered when the rival managing directors discovered a shared love of bridge and of cricket. Victor Watson of Waddington and Bernard Westall of de la Rue agreed to an annual cricket match between the two firms. This, they felt, would at least ensure that they became friendly rivals rather than deadly enemies.

During the Blitz the de la Rue factory in Bunhill Row was destroyed by German bombs but even as the ruins lay still smouldering Victor Watson went to the City, saying that to see a rival forced out of business by enemy action was definitely not cricket. He therefore offered de la Rue half his firm's wartime capacity and the two companies entered into a joint production arrangement. This lasted until 1967, when de la Rue decided that banknotes were more lucrative than playing cards and sold out to Waddingtons. Thus, after due process, the Royal Warrant passed to Victor Watson. 'Apart from ensuring satisfactory supplies to The Queen,' he says,

I took no interest in the Royal Warrant

Holders Association. Then, in the late 1970s, I suddenly had the idea that it would be interesting to attend the Annual General Meeting. I was impressed by what I saw. The assembled company seemed to be composed entirely of people who were established in life. They were cheerful, friendly and exuded an air of ineffable confidence. The sun was shining. As the meeting began a band marched past playing a lively tune. All seemed right with the world. The business of supplying the Monarch took on a new meaning for me. I realised that we had a priceless asset in the Warrant, not for promoting the product, but for building a feeling of loyal pride in the workforce. I felt that by association with other suppliers to the Royal Household we would gain access to a fine club and become more aware of the privilege we enjoyed.

The following year he turned up again for the

Victor Watson, Chairman of the Way Ahead Committee, at Waddingtons. Picture taken by Mayote Magnus for By Appointment *published in 1990.* Sheila Watson

Annual General Meeting. The sun shone again and the band played outside, and he made a little speech. Soon afterwards he was invited to lunch at Wiltons by the Treasurer, Sir Edward Rayne, and the Secretary, Bill Keown-Boyd. He liked Wiltons but he knew that the object of the lunch was 'to see if I could hold a knife and fork properly, take soup without slurping and refrain from being too argumentative'. He realised that he had passed the test when he was invited to join the Council in 1976. He was originally told he would have to wait nine years before becoming President, but others dropped by the wayside and he succeeded to the post in 1983.

Other Presidents in the 1980s reflected the wide range of Warrant-holding activities although just as 1979 and 1980 produced two oil industry presidents so the 1980s produced no fewer than three Presidents from the worlds of wines and spirits. This was entirely coincidental and, indeed, Comte Alain de Vogüé of Veuve Clicquot, Tim Sandeman of the eponymous wine merchants and David Palengat of Allied Domecq could hardly have been more different. The Comte de Vogüé, who served in 1985, was the first foreign President and greatly enlivened his banquet with a speech in immaculate though heavily accented English in which, during the miners' strike, he somehow managed to inveigle both Peter Rabbit and Arthur Scargill into Mr Macgregor's garden!

He also became the first President to hold a Council meeting outside London. As this was to be at his company's headquarters in Champagne it was an enticing prospect. Unfortunately the event got off to an inauspicious start when the Council's aircraft was diverted to Belgium because of a French air traffic controllers' strike and the delegates had to complete their journey by bus. However, Veuve Clicquot's hospitality saved the day and it remains one of the most enjoyable Council meetings yet held.

Then there was a builders' merchant from Aberdeen, Graeme Wilson, and a sweet manufacturer, John Marks of Trebor mints and Sharp's toffees.

Wilson, like Alain de Vogüé, was an accomplished and individual after-dinner speaker – though in a markedly different style. His greatest accomplishment was probably his crucial role in persuading the Windsor and Eton Association to forsake its complete independence and come into the national Warrant-holding fold.

Marks also made an impact on his banquet. His guest of honour was Sir John Harvey Jones. Marks had read that Harvey Jones's wife once said that when her husband died he would be found to have the letters 'ICI' stamped right through him like a stick of rock. Marks's company had long since abandoned the unprofitable business of manufacturing sticks of rock but he managed to find an old hand who remembered how to do it and was able to present his dinner guest with a customised stick with 'ICI' printed in pink from one end to the other. He also managed to produce a sugar Bishop's crook with a mitre running through it for his other speaker, the Bishop of Reading.

Towards the end of the decade Hugh Faulkner, the Council and successive Presidents turned their thoughts increasingly to the 150th anniversary of the formation of the Association and to The Queen Mother's ninetieth birthday, both of which were in 1990. Many individuals were involved in devising the various projects to mark the two dates and in making sure that they came to fruition. However, the first written proposals were submitted by Hugh Faulkner to Eddie Rayne in July 1986, the Association's long-standing and influential Honorary Treasurer. It is interesting, though unsurprising, that they were sent to Rayne and not to the President! In the event and after considerable debate, these first proposals were almost all adopted.

According to Barry Reed of Austin Reed, its first chairman, The Queen Elizabeth Scholarship Trust was really born on the day Hugh Faulkner despatched this initial memorandum: 28th July 1986. It was not an easy birth because 'there was to be much internal debate before it became a reality', but the seminal thoughts were contained in that confidential paper.

At first Rayne was unimpressed. Faulkner wanted the membership to stump up serious money for a brand-new scholarship scheme to be administered by the Warrant Holders themselves. Rayne didn't believe that people would be willing to part with the sort of money Faulkner envisaged. He also preferred to keep things simple and to stick to the precedents. This meant that whenever a significant royal anniversary occurred, any money raised should be given to an existing charity nominated by the relevant royal Grantor. The Association simply wasn't equipped to become a serious charity in its own right, which was, fundamentally, what the Faulkner proposals implied.

Faulkner and his sup-

Left: *The Queen Mother with Lowrie Sleigh (left) President of the Edinburgh Association at Distillers House, St. James's Square where she had lived as a child. Behind stands Lady Rayne, with Sir Edward (behind Her Majesty).*
Joy Sleigh

Below, both pictures: *Telegram exchange between the President and The Queen before the 150th Anniversary Banquet.*
Barry Austin Reed

INCORPORATED BY ROYAL CHARTER
[1907]
TELEPHONE: 01-828 2268
FACSIMILE: 01-834 5912

7, *Buckingham Gate,*
London.
SW1E 6JY

HER MAJESTY THE QUEEN,
BUCKINGHAM PALACE,
LONDON SW1.

ON MONDAY 25th MAY, 1840, A GATHERING OF TWENTY-FIVE ROYAL TRADESMEN HELD AN ANNIVERSARY DINNER AT THE FREEMASONS TAVERN IN CELEBRATION OF HER MAJESTY QUEEN VICTORIA'S BIRTHDAY.

ON THE OCCASION OF THE 150TH ANNIVERSARY OF THIS EVENT, WHICH MARKED THE FOUNDING OF OUR ASSOCIATION, THE COUNCIL AND ALL MEMBERS OF THE ROYAL WARRANT HOLDERS ASSOCIATION JOIN ME IN TENDERING TO YOUR MAJESTY OUR MOST SINCERE GREETINGS AND GOOD WISHES. THE MEMBERSHIP LOOK FORWARD TO PROVIDING LOYAL AND DEVOTED SERVICE TO YOUR MAJESTY FOR MANY YEARS TO COME.

BARRY AUSTIN REED
PRESIDENT

porters, including Barry Reed who, crucially, was to be the Association's President in the year of its 150th anniversary, pointed to clause 8 of the Association's Royal Charter, which said that one of its purposes was 'to establish and administer Funds, Institutions, Scholarships etc. for the benefit of Trade or the encouragement of apprenticeship or learning.' Reed realised that since its incorporation in 1907, virtually nothing had been done to achieve this end. All that could possibly be said to fit the bill was 'a small charity fund at the disposal of the President'.

Reed felt strongly that the Association was failing in its duty. He believed that this time there should be a genuine attempt to get back to part of the original roots of the Association and do something to nurture the cause of true craftsmanship. To this end The Queen Mother should be invited to approve the setting up of a trust fund from the money raised. The income from this Trust should be used to 'support bursaries and scholarships connected with promoting British craftsmanship'. Like many Presidents, nearly all of whom come from the upper echelons of British trade and industry, Reed was a strong character and he expressed himself with force. 'My memory', he recalled later, 'is that I put this point rather vigorously, muttering that I would not be happy to take office in 1990 unless we pursued such a course.'

Reed carried the day and by the next meeting it was agreed that there should be one concerted appeal to celebrate both the 150th anniversary and The Queen Mother's ninetieth birthday. As a compromise with tradition it was agreed that while one-third would be given to the charity of The Queen Mother's choice, two-thirds of the

money would go towards establishing the new Trust. To Reed's considerable pleasure he was only just beginning his term of office when a message came to him from Clarence House saying that The Queen Mother wished to give 'her' third of the money to the newly established Trust as well. So honour was satisfied and the Trust got *all* the money.

This was considerable. Hugh Faulkner's policy of getting out and about now paid dividends, for he was able to approach many of the members on the basis of personal friendship. Nevertheless the original aim was comparatively modest. The sub-committee was hoping to raise enough money to fund a single scholarship of £5000 a year in perpetuity. It was planned to send out a formal letter of appeal but in the meantime Barry Reed hosted a series of lunches in Austin Reed's London flat at which some forty leading members were entertained. Hugh Faulkner also promoted the appeal wherever he went so that by the time Reed's presidential letter went out in January 1990 much of the spade-work had been done.

The money came in far faster than expected. The big Council members rallied round. Weetabix for Richard George, Stephens Brothers for Barry Reed, Barbours for Margaret Barbour and Twinings for Sam Twining all entered large sums. Their generosity, as Council members, might perhaps have been expected, but among the other founding fathers were Vauxhall, Bass, DER, Benson & Hedges, Whitbread and BOCM Silcock, all of whom gave £10,000 or more. By 1st May, 401 companies had given a total of £600,000 and by the autumn that had risen to more than £700,000.

At the same time the Trust was being established, thanks to considerable efforts from Peter Smith of Securicor, himself a former President, and Farrers, the Association's solicitors, as well as Hugh Faulkner and what Reed referred to as his 'small but superb team of ladies'.

The first Trustees were an interesting cross-section of Warrant Holders. Apart from the Secretary, they

BUCKINGHAM PALACE

Barry Austin Reed, Esq.,
  President,
    The Royal Warrant Holders Association.

Thank you for your kind message sent on the 150th Anniversary of the founding of the Royal Warrant Holders Association at the Freemasons Tavern.

Many congratulations on achieving this notable Anniversary. I was deeply grateful to you for your expression of loyalty, as I am for the devoted service which Warrant Holders have given to me and my Household for many years.

I send you, and all those whom you represent, my warm good wishes.

ELIZABETH R.

were a men's outfitter (Barry Reed – Stephens Brothers), a supplier of 'gold and silver laces, insignia and embroidery' (Bryan Toye – Toye, Kenning) a tea man (Sam Twining – Twinings), a butcher (Colin Cullimore – Dewhurst), a tailor (Michael Skinner – J. Dege) and a restorer of fine arts objects (the Hon. Anna Plowden – Plowden & Smith).

Time was of the essence. The plan was to make the first awards at the Association's annual luncheon in

June 1991. That meant publicising the scheme in the autumn of 1990 so that the applications could all be in by the end of January 1991. The unexpectedly generous funding meant that far from providing one scholarship of £5000, the Trustees were able to disburse £42,000 to six Scholars each of whom would receive in addition a specially minted medal from Garrard, the Crown Jewellers.

The 150th anniversary was also celebrated with a book, a plate and a rose. The anniversary plans were delegated to a small sub-committee, chaired by Rayne and including as well Hugh Faulkner, Barry Reed and Sam Twining. Reed held the Warrants of The Duke of Edinburgh and The Prince of Wales as Managing Director of Stephens Bros, the shirt-making sub-

sidiary of Austin Reed. Twining, a former President, was the senior member of the eponymous tea-making family.

The Committee first met in 1987 and continued to do so at regular intervals thereafter. A number of additional ideas were mooted and rejected for various reasons. These included regional parties in the North and Midlands, a gala ball at Syon House and a grand exhibition of Warrant Holder products intended as part of a national export drive. Barry Reed thought one of the best ideas came from his wife Mike, who suggested that The Queen be approached to see if she would consent to a Buckingham Palace garden party exclusively for members and their staffs. This was done and The Queen graciously agreed.

The commemorative book was a lavish production published by Queen Anne Press written by Tim Heald and copiously illustrated with original photographs by Mayotte Magnus and Jorge Lewinski. The book was principally a celebration of the diversity of the hundreds of widely differing 'Tradesmen' who held the Royal Warrant. Handsome leather-bound volumes were presented to Her Majesty The Queen and the other Grantors by the 1989 President, Richard Woodhouse. Woodhouse held the Warrant on behalf of Sandicliffe Garage as suppliers of motor horse boxes to The Queen.

The reply from Queen Elizabeth The Queen Mother's Comptroller at Clarence House was characteristically gracious, saying that 'Queen Elizabeth thought it a most interesting volume, containing such a multitude of excellent photographs from every represented trade'.

The rose was chosen by a small sub-committee of Council members and wives who visited the Harkness Rose Gardens at Hitchin in July 1988. They chose 'an elegant apricot/buff coloured floribunda' which, like the celebratory book, was named 'By Appointment'. Barry Reed, as President, together with Peter Harkness presented a bouquet of 'By Appointment' roses to The Queen at the Chelsea Flower Show. All

Left: *The 150th Anniversary Rose: 'By Appointment'*
RWHA Archive

the Grantors were given bushes for their gardens and a decade later Barry Reed himself was able to report that his own bed of 'By Appointments' was still flourishing in the garden of his north Yorkshire home. Another Warrant holding company, Mobil, even bought 150 of the roses to line the approach road to their oil refinery.

The last in this commemorative trio was an anniversary plate designed by Royal Doulton. A limited edition of 1000 was produced and they have now become prized collectors' pieces. The plate has the Association's logo with the Royal Coat of Arms in the centre and on the terracotta-coloured rim are gold drawings depicting various crafts and trades associated with the Warrant: a soda siphon, a fish, a loaf of bread, a horseshoe, a cup and saucer, a shot-gun and a fishing rod, a wash-basin – even a sweep's brush poking through the top of a chimney. Almost all Warrant-holding life is there.

In addition to the normal high days of the Warrant Holders' year the anniversary year was celebrated with a number of special events. The first of these was a Thanksgiving Service at St Lawrence Jewry, followed by lunch at the Guildhall hosted by the Lord Mayor of London, who that year was Sir Hugh Bidwell, fortuitously an old friend of Barry Reed.

Right: The 150th Anniversary plate.

During his reply to the Lord Mayor's speech, Reed read the text of the message he had sent to Her Majesty The Queen to mark the anniversary. 'On Monday 25th May 1840,' it ran,

'a gathering of twenty-five Royal Tradesmen held an Anniversary Dinner at the Freemasons Tavern in celebration of Her Majesty Queen Victoria's birthday.

On the occasion of the 150th Anniversary of this event, which marked the foundation of our Association, the Council and all members of the Royal Warrant Holders Association join me in tendering to Your Majesty our most sincere greetings and good wishes. The membership

look forward to providing loyal and devoted service to Your Majesty for many years to come.'

In her reply from Buckingham Palace The Queen said

'Thank you for your kind message sent on the 150th Anniversary of the founding of the Royal Warrant Holders Association at the Freemasons' Tavern.

Many congratulations on achieving this notable Anniversary. I was deeply grateful to you for your expression of loyalty, as I am for the devoted service which Warrant Holders have given to me and my Household for many years. I send you, and all those whom you represent, my warm good wishes.'

The Queen and the other Grantors were able to convey those warm wishes in person a few weeks later on 17th July at the Buckingham Palace Garden Party. At the express wish of The Queen as wide as possible a sample of Warrant Holders and their staff were present, so that each company was encouraged to bring not just the grantee but also a director, a supervisor

'Royal Warrant Holders March' and, in a revival of the ancient custom, the sovereign sent a gift of venison from the royal herd.

The final and least expected celebration that year was made possible by the Japanese firm of Kumagai Gummi. Their London headquarters at 20 St James's Square had been the town residence of The Queen Mother's family – the Bowes-Lyons – in the early years of the century. She had expressed a wish to see the old house once more and the Association was able to arrange this one evening that December. At this glittering reception The Queen Mother was presented with the portrait of her by Mara McGregor, which the Association had commissioned for her ninetieth birthday. She was delighted with this – not least with such personal touches as the inclusion of her favourite corgi, Ranger, and the Castle of Mey in the background. Since the presentation the portrait has hung in a prominent position on the first floor at Clarence House.

The 150th anniversary had been an enjoyable time, marked by several memorable events and a number of tangible souvenirs. But of all the achievements associated with this period none was as important as the creation of The Queen Elizabeth Scholarship Trust.

and a shop-floor worker together with their spouses. In the event the day was sunny and over 3000 Warrant Holders, staff and partners thronged the Palace gardens in the presence of The Queen and The Duke of Edinburgh, The Queen Mother and The Prince and Princess of Wales.

It was many years since a member of The Royal Family had attended one of the Association's formal luncheons or banquets. The consensus at headquarters was that the last occasion had been in the 1930s when The Prince of Wales had been guest of honour at a banquet, but over half a century after the event there was no one left who remembered the occasion at first hand. The Association was delighted, therefore, when The Duke of Edinburgh agreed to propose its health at the Grosvenor House banquet on 1st November. The Duke spoke with characteristic wit and pungency, and also cut a 150th birthday cake; the band of the Life Guards played a specially composed

Right: *The Council in session in the Buckingham Gate Boardroom, 1988.* RWHA Archive

Below: *The anniversary portrait of The Queen Mother, with Ranger, in front of Glamis Castle, by Mara McGregor.* RWHA Archive

In a different part of the Warrant-holding world another new initiative was being proposed. On 8th November 1990 The Prince of Wales launched 'Business in the Environment'. This organisation is part of 'Business in the Community', of which HRH had been President since 1985. It is dedicated to persuading 'business to be responsible corporate citizens. In his capacity as its President, His Royal Highness, well known for his commitment to the environmental cause, advocated three steps for medium and small companies to improve their environmental practices: conducting critical self-examination, taking expert advice, and publicly stating their environmental policy and objectives.

More to the point, he was able and prepared to practise what he preached.

'Anyone who has a choice of possible suppliers,' he said, 'can do this by making it clear that one of the key criteria to be used when choosing a supplier will be their record on environmental matters. As it happens, I am in this position myself – amazing as it may seem – and will be asking all future applicants for my own partic-

ular Royal Warrant to meet various environmental criteria, in addition to other requirements. They will be invited to complete an environmental questionnaire (which will be based on the Business in the Environment Workbook), to demonstrate a clear commitment to improving any aspects of their performance which do not accord with current best practice in their sector, and to publish a statement of environmental policy. Those companies who already hold Warrants will be asked in due course to meet the same criteria when their Warrants come up for periodic review.'

All Grantors have, of course, given Warrants on the basis of their own taste and judgement, but this was the first time that a member of The Royal Family had used the Warrant as an instrument of deliberate policy. From now on The Prince of Wales's Warrant became not only very personal but also a declaration of environmental intent. Anyone applying for the right to display The Prince of Wales's feathers had to do more than provide evidence of supply. They had also to demonstrate a genuine commitment to sound environmental practice. Those who applied for his Warrant were sent a letter setting out this environmental policy, together with a copy of the 1990

Left: *1997 advertisement for Start-rite shoes*
Start-rite Library

'Business in the Environment' speech, a list of the five fundamental criteria they would have to adopt and a detailed breakdown of how exactly these criteria should be met.

Firms were asked to develop a clear environmental policy – appropriate to the size and nature of their activities – which had to be submitted with the application. They were asked, too, to appoint a senior member of staff to promote 'best possible environmental management' and to carry out an initial environmental review which, if appropriate, also set out 'improvement targets in the key environmental performance areas'. In addition, applicants were encouraged to review their environmental targets 'at least annually' and to produce an 'Annual Environmental Report,' which could either be produced specifically for the purpose, or could be taken from the relevant section of their company's annual report. A copy of this had to go to The Prince's Private Secretary. This was 'green' Warrant holding in practice.

One company which took part in trials to test the usefulness of these ideas was Start-rite, the children's shoe manufacturers. In 1991 the company conducted an in-depth review of their packaging materials and gave a short presentation to The Prince. The following year he came to the Start-rite factory and subsequently made a speech in which he cited Start-rite's reforms as not only environment-friendly but also cost-effective. 'We changed to one hundred per cent recycled board for our shoe boxes, one hundred per cent recycled polythene for carrier bags and seventy per cent

recycled tissue paper for wrapping shoes,' commented the Start-rite Chairman, David White. 'Sadly, with time and experience we have lost some of those savings, but we moved further into the factory and have successfully replaced solvent-based adhesives with water-based adhesives for sticking soles to uppers. In short, HRH definitely made us more environmentally aware and greener in our use of materials'.

Barry Reed's successor as President was Bryan Toye of Toye, Kenning & Spencer, suppliers of gold and silver laces and embroidery. Toye, an eminent City personality and liveryman, was the chairman of one of the oldest family businesses and Warrant Holders in the country. The first Toye to arrive in Britain was a Huguenot lacemaker who fled France in 1685, and founded the company which still bears his name and is managed by his descendants.

In 1993 The Prince of Wales demonstrated his interest in the Royal Warrants by accepting the Association's invitation to the annual luncheon – at which The Queen Elizabeth Scholarships were formally presented. This was the year of Sir Richard George's presidency. George was the chairman of Weetabix who held Warrants as manufacturer of breakfast cereals to The Queen, The Queen Mother and The Prince of Wales. Another highlight of his

The Prince of Wales addressing the Warrant Holders and their guests at the 1993 luncheon, flanked by the President, Sir Richard George (right) and Barry Austin Reed.
RWHA Archive

year was a helicopter expedition to the far north where he entertained local Warrant Holders to a luncheon at Ackergill Tower outside Wick and visited The Queen Mother's house, the Castle of Mey. All Presidents like to create precedents but there was one which Richard George regretted. He was forced to miss his own presidential reception on account of illness.

Sir Richard was to have been succeeded by Ian Ross of the Distillers Co., and the next president after him was due to be David Williams-Thomas of Royal Brierley. However neither man was able to assume office. The first took early retirement and the second succumbed to pressure of business. Margaret Barbour was next in line but was unable to advance her year, so the ever-inventive Hugh Faulkner suggested that the Council should turn to Douglas Kinloch Anderson.

Kinloch Anderson, the kilt-maker, was well known as a stalwart of the Edinburgh Association. He had served as its President, and from 1993, had represented it on the Council of the national Association. The election of such a prominent Scot, especially one so intimately associated with the traditional dress of his nation, was a felicitous demonstration of the Association's connections north of the border.

Kinloch Anderson did not disappoint. Appearing whenever possible in highland dress and holding his presidential reception in the Caledonian Club, he also arranged the most Scottish banquet in living memory. Arbroath smokies were followed by haggis, accompanied of course by neeps and tatties. A baron of magnificent Scottish beef appeared, to be followed by cranachan for dessert, washed down by Laphroiag. Pipers played and the kilt was flamboyantly to the fore.

Margaret Barbour, whose company, J. Barbour & Son, manufactures the distinctive dark-green country rainwear which has passed into the sartorial vocabulary of Britain, succeeded him and proved to be an innovative and self-styled 'housekeeper'. She felt that in some regards the Association was too much like a Gentleman's Club and, as the first lady President, believed strongly that the presidency should not be the sole preserve of men who were willing and able to spend large sums of money during their year of office. Honoraria were introduced for both national and regional presidents; local secretaries were granted a degree of financial compensation from headquarters; but in generous contrast, she herself staged the most lavish of president's receptions at Spencer House in Mayfair.

Margaret Barbour also encouraged the Association and its presidents to look beyond the Royal Palaces in their travels, pointing out that many people in Northumberland, Cumberland, Durham and North Yorkshire seldom, if ever, attended Warrant-holder functions in London. By hosting a reception in her native north-east, she attracted to the Gosforth Park Hotel in Newcastle a notably wide variety of relatively unfamiliar Warrant holders, from Procter & Gamble to the antique restorer at Heddon-on-the-Wall.

The menu card for the Caledonian Banquet in 1994, devised by The Scottish President, Douglas Kinloch Anderson of Kinloch Anderson, Tailors & Kiltmakers.
RWHA Archive

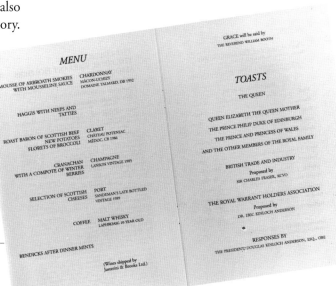

MENU

MOUSSE OF ARBROATH SMOKIES
WITH MOUSSELINE SAUCE
CHARDONNAY
MÂCON-UCHIZY
DOMAINE TALMARD, DB 1992

HAGGIS WITH NEEPS AND
TATTIES

ROAST BARON OF SCOTTISH BEEF
NEW POTATOES
FLORETS OF BROCCOLI
CLARET
CHÂTEAU POTENSAC
MÉDOC, CB 1986

CRANACHAN
WITH A COMPOTE OF WINTER
BERRIES
CHAMPAGNE
LANSON VINTAGE 1985

SELECTION OF SCOTTISH
CHEESES
PORT
SANDEMAN'S LATE BOTTLED
VINTAGE 1989

COFFEE
MALT WHISKY
LAPHROAIG 10 YEAR OLD

BENDICKS AFTER DINNER MINTS

(Wines shipped by
Justerini & Brooks Ltd.)

GRACE will be said by
THE REVEREND WILLIAM BOOTH

TOASTS

THE QUEEN

QUEEN ELIZABETH THE QUEEN MOTHER
THE PRINCE PHILIP DUKE OF EDINBURGH
THE PRINCE AND PRINCESS OF WALES
AND THE OTHER MEMBERS OF THE ROYAL FAMILY

BRITISH TRADE AND INDUSTRY
Proposed by
SIR CHARLES FRASER, KCVO

THE ROYAL WARRANT HOLDERS ASSOCIATION
Proposed by
DR. ERIC KINLOCH ANDERSON

RESPONSES BY
THE PRESIDENT, DOUGLAS KINLOCH ANDERSON, ESQ., OBE

Nº 1 Buckingham Place, London SW1

Hugh Faulkner retired as Secretary in 1996 after an eventful seventeen years. His predecessor, Bill Keown-Boyd, had been an army colonel and so had his successor, Christopher Pickup. At first glance this transition, like the one that had taken place in 1979, looked like another case of *plus ça change, plus c'est la même chose.* Whereas all previous Secretaries had been appointed on the basis of the Old Boy Network, intuition and interview, this one, in keeping with the current climate of political correctness, was conducted by a professional head hunting agency. It was interesting that Chris Pickup, though selected according to state-of-the-art scientific principles, was widely regarded as very much the choice that the Association would have made if left to its own unacceptable old-fashioned devices of an earlier era.

Right:
Col. Christopher Pickup, OBE, who became Secretary to the Association in February 1996.
Anthony Buckley and Constantine Ltd.

The two men were actually more different than one might originally have suspected. Hugh Faulkner, for instance, belonged to a pre-computer generation and was sceptical about their efficacy. Annie Wycherley and Patricia Norsworthy, his trusty support, were equally opposed to new fangled machinery. They were happy with typewriters and telephones, but preferred personal contact to anything else. Faulkner himself had an aversion to offices and did not enjoy driving a desk. It was perhaps symptomatic that when he was in the office he worked at one end of the magnificent boardroom table. It could be said that the boardroom doubled as his office, were it not for the fact that Faulkner never gave the impression of regarding the room as his office in any conventional sense. For him the office was where he was. His filing system existed in his head. Years later, Annie Wycherley was to recall, with amusement, that when Faulkner originally interviewed her for the job they chatted over a glass of sherry and it was only as she was leaving that he remembered to enquire, without much enthusiasm, 'By the way, luvvy, can you type?'

Chris Pickup belonged to a different generation of serviceman. Not only was he brought up in a more technological age, where a degree of computer literacy was a prerequisite, he came from the Army Air Corps. This meant helicopters and helicopters imply a degree of technological sophistication. Pickup was perfectly sociable and gregarious but, unlike Faulkner, he was equally at ease behind his desk punching the keys of his laptop.

One can overemphasise the importance of the Association's Secretary, but in an organisation where the unpaid President serves only a year at a time he is likely to be at a disadvantage when confronted with a Secretary who is a full-time salaried official, particularly when the Secretary has already had several years in the job. However powerful and experienced a President might be in his own business life, he only had a year in the Association's top job. It was inevitable that he should lean heavily on the Secretary and his staff, particularly when the secretary had had time to play himself in.

The Warrant Holders also operated a tradition whereby former Presidents did not retire gracefully but remained as members of Council for as long as they wished. This meant that an incoming President could find himself confronted by more than twenty

years' worth of Presidents sitting around that great oval table exercising, consciously or not, a daunting aura of collective wisdom and experience. This could be inhibiting especially as there is a natural tendency among yesterday's men to opt for caution and conservatism. Sir Edward Rayne, great servant of the Association though he was, exemplified this. Some naturally innovative Presidents felt themselves constrained by the weight of elder statesmen's experience.

Margaret Barbour was still President when Colonel Pickup took over but her presidency had only a few weeks to run. The first President with whom the new Secretary had to build a day-to-day working relationship was therefore Robert Gieve who held the Warrant on behalf of Gieves & Hawkes, the naval and military tailors of 1 Savile Row. Gieve's great-grandmother Elizabeth was Queen Victoria's favourite seamstress and Gieve himself could remember first visiting Buckingham Palace with the company's head cutter as an eleven-year-old in 1949. He held the chalk and pins, and was amazed to witness 'the easy rapport between The Monarch and "the man from Gieves"'. Later he himself made many such visits in his own right 'sometimes with my own chalk and pins'. It was Gieve who was mainly responsible for instigating the 'London reception'. Because London was the headquarters of the national organisation it sometimes seemed to be forgotten that the city was home to a significant number of Warrant Holders who felt as close-knit as their early West End predecessors or as their regional colleagues in Ballater or Sandringham. Robert Gieve's recognition of this fact with what was, in effect, a party for the 'Buckingham Palace branch' proved a great success. 'The Secretary negotiated good terms with the RAC Club on Pall Mall,' he said, 'and it was held in the last week of

Left: *Robert Gieve (left of centre) on his visit to Holyroodhouse in October 1996. Beside Gieve stands Iain Campbell (far left), and Brian Smellie, with the Secretary, Christopher Pickup on Smellie's left.* RWHA Archive

Below: *Buckingham Palace, painted by in 1846 by Joseph Nash (1809-78).* The Royal Collection Trust

September with over a hundred guests in attendance. All enjoyed the opportunity to meet each other, learn about each other's business interests, and talk of their shared responsibilities as fellow Warrant Holders. This London Reception has since become a permanent fixture in the Association's London calendar.'

Another presidential tailor, Michael Skinner of Dege & Skinner, President in 2000, remarked that when you have seen your great and good clients stripped to their underpants you tend to be slightly less overawed than you might otherwise be. Perhaps this had something to do with the fact that almost the first thing Gieve did as President was to respond to a paper, written the previous year by Roger Mitchell (of Holland & Holland, gunmakers) asking pertinent questions about the purpose of the Association. Mitchell was to be President in 1999. Gieve proposed the establishment of what became the 'Way Ahead Committee'. He did not do this because he thought there was anything seriously wrong but because he believed that any organisation should take stock from time to time and the Association had not done this for some years. He also thought it would be helpful for the new Secretary. A complete overhaul and re-examination would be the best possible way for the new Secretary to learn about the strange organisation he had just joined.

The Way Ahead Committee was chaired by Victor Watson of Waddington Games. The other members were David Part of the General Trading Company, Sheila Pickles of Penhaligon, Roger Mitchell and Alan Britten.

Britten, like Sir Nevil Macready a Mobil man, had been a member of the Council since 1988 after being 'Boodled' by Eddie Rayne under the watchful eye of the then President John Marks. 'I held my knife and fork properly and showed my genuine enthusiasm for the venerable institution of Warrant holding,' said Britten.

Britten may have had respect for the Association's venerability but along with other younger members of

Council he pressed for a change to the rule that former Presidents could remain on the Council for life. (Both Britten and Gieve were born in the 1930s so their youth was relative rather than absolute!) Their efforts to introduce a compulsory retirement age met

Right: New Badge developed for the RAC to celebrate the granting to them of a Royal Warrant by King Edward VII on February 27th, 1907. The badge features the wheel, with Mercury below and the crown above, surrounding a portrait of The King.
Royal Automobile Club/Art Archive

with failure, though there was 'vigorous and extensive debate'. Some of the older members took the hint and absented themselves from meetings but another side effect was that 'other very serious proposals were hardly noticed'. According to Britten, 'these involved greater participation by Council members during the run-up to their Presidency, improved communications, and a critical recommendation that the Association should celebrate The Queen's Jubilee in 2002 rather than the millennium.'

The most important aspect of the 'Way Ahead' deliberations was a confrontation with the essential dilemma facing the Association. There was an ambivalence. Was it a club with a mainly social function, or was it a trade association with an obligation to serve the professional and commercial interests of its members? With a tactful instinct for compromise the Committee decided that the prevailing 'admix of both' was satisfactory, but they still 'nudged it towards a trade association'. This was not a dramatic change, but it did represent a switch of emphasis. The changes were of style rather than substance. Victor Watson, with characteristic impishness, suggested that his Committee might be re-named The Way Sideways.

The basic aim of the Association remained much as it was at the time of the 1907 charter, though the wording of it was brought up to date so that the new version read:

> 'To unite in one body all those who hold a Royal Warrant of Appointment: to serve the members of that body by promoting and when necessary protecting their interests to the best of its ability – subject always to the maintenance of the highest standards of craftsmanship and service.'

To achieve this the Way Ahead Committee recommended five 'objectives'. These were: ensuring the continuance of the Warrant as 'a treasured and respected institution'; to serve as a link between its members and the Household; to assist the Lord Chamberlain in safeguarding the good reputation of the Warrant; to represent the Warrant and its holders to the media and others and finally, through The Queen Elizabeth Scholarship Trust, to encourage training in the crafts and skills exemplified by those who held the Warrant.

It was Britten's job as President from 1997 to 1998 to implement the Committee's recommendations. With the help of The Queen's Press Secretary, Geoff Crawford, the flow of information between the Palace and the Association was improved. There was a series of informal office lunches to consult grantees and a first ever get-together at The Prince of Wales's country home at Highgrove.

For some time there had been a feeling among the Household that the formal lunch and banquet could be made a little less starchy. This year the fifty strong high table at the banquet was drastically curtailed and members of the Household were distributed among grantees in the body of the hall.

The low point of this year was the untimely death, through cancer, of the Vice-President, the conservator Anna Plowden, joint founder and manager of the innovative firm of conservators, Plowden & Smith. Although she never achieved her ambition of succeeding to the presidency her memory is now perpetuated by an annual Plowden Medal awarded for particularly distinguished service to the profession of conservator. It carries no financial reward but already in its short life it has acquired considerable prestige.

A not untypical citation was that which accompanied the Award to Dr Jonathan Ashley-Smith, Head of the Conservation Department at the Victoria & Albert Museum since 1977. This applauded his 'tireless and visionary commitment to the conservation of the moveable heritage' and the 'significant impact' his research had made 'on both the public and professional perception of conservation'. Other recipients all measure up to this sort of standard and the medal aptly commemorates Anna Plowden's own 'lifetime of commitment to and achievement within the field of conservation' – albeit a lifetime which was tragically curtailed.

For years the Association had faced the inevitable expiry of the lease of 7 Buckingham Gate and Sam Twining the Treasurer and Hugh Faulkner had been building up a financial reserve to help with whatever new plan had to be produced. The Buckingham Gate

Left: *The Hon Anna Plowden CBE inspecting an 18th century marble cherub and eagle group, prior to undertaking its restoration, c. 1979.*
Plowden & Smith Ltd.

office was a curate's egg. The position, just opposite the diplomatic entrance to Buckingham Palace, was almost perfect. The council chamber, which doubled as the Secretary's office, was magnificent as a council chamber but less appropriate as the Secretary's office. The offices of Annie Wycherley and her team, one of which was not much better than a cubbyhole halfway up the stairs, were little short of a disgrace.

Buckingham Gate was to be redeveloped by the Crown Estate and there was no place for the Association in the new offices. Alternatives considered included a house next to Berry Brothers & Rudd in St James's; several other nearby properties and even a corner of Buckingham Palace. In the end the diligence of the new Secretary, Christopher Pickup, discovered an elegant Edwardian 'Georgian-style' property at Nº1 Buckingham Place just around the corner. It was too big but it was already divided and sub-let to very reputable tenants. The real estate market was disturbingly buoyant so the Association, backed by the new but very experienced Hon Treasurer Sir Richard George, put in a bid significantly in excess of the asking price and won the tender by 'a whisker'.

Britten was wholeheartedly supported by the Council, whom he kept fully informed throughout. However, he discovered, after the event, that one of the past Presidents was actually Trustee of a charity which had put in a competing bid. The individual concerned acted with commendable propriety throughout and took no part in the bidding nor what Britten described as 'the inevitable post-facto wrangling which followed'.

It was a lucky deal. The Twining/Faulkner war chest was sold at just the right time and the Association extricated itself from the unexpired portion of the Buckingham Gate lease on very favourable terms. The freeholder of the new premises was The Queen Elizabeth Scholarship Trust and the Association became the head leaseholder. The Association occupied, for the first time in its life, a secure, freehold home, and the Scholarship Trust now

had a large part of its income underpinned by the bluest of blue-chip tenants. It was all eminently satisfactory. The staff working conditions were vastly improved, the Secretary had his own office and the treasured council table fitted into the new boardroom as to the manner born.

Meanwhile there had been a significant review of the Lord Chamberlain's Tradesmen's Warrants Committee and Warrant holding in general. The old 'Green Book' was revised and reissued in a transformed guise as 'The Lord Chamberlain's Rules'. Key figures in this were Sir Malcolm Ross and Sir Michael Peat.

In 1991 Peat had joined the Royal Household on secondment from his family business. After two years his position at the Palace became permanent. In some ways this looked like a thoroughly conventional appointment. Educated at Eton and Trinity College Oxford, Peat had worked in the family business for just over twenty years. His father, Sir Gerrard, was a Knight Commander of the Royal Victorian Order – The Sovereign's personal order – who from 1969 to 1988 was assistant auditor and then auditor to the Privy Purse. All this seemed to fit the traditional bill. Nothing looked more predictable than for Michael Peat to follow his father to the Palace and to become Treasurer to Her Majesty the Queen and Keeper of the Privy Purse.

In some respects, however, Peat's appointment was unusual. After Oxford he went to the Institut Européen d'Administration des Affaires (INSEAD) at Fontainebleau, where he took a Master's degree in Business Administration. The family business he then joined was Peat Marwick, one of the country's best-known firms of accountants. It is not usual for accountants to hold high office at Buckingham Palace.

Peat's brief was reform. Under the approving eye of the Lord Chamberlain, the Earl of Airlie, his job was to scrutinise the existing management systems within the Royal Household and, where appropriate, bring them into line with current practice in the world outside. Part of his remit was to examine the system of granting and maintaining Royal Warrants.

He concluded that it was an excellent system but that it was in some respects 'a house built on sand'. Part of the problem lay in the image. In Peat's estimation the Royal Warrant Holders Association looked old-fashioned. Words that he used were 'sleepy', and 'dusty'. He sensed that there were Warrant Holders who took their Warrants for granted and that the Palace might occasionally give Warrants too easily.

He also questioned whether, in an increasingly litigious age, the use of the Royal Coat of Arms might be considered an endorsement by the monarchy. If this was legally the case then a member of the public who was dissatisfied with a purchase of something carrying a royal 'seal of approval' might be able to sue the Crown. It seemed unlikely but nevertheless he thought it was something that required legal clarification. Another grey area that required clarification was the 'national interest' issue. One or two larger companies maintained that being stripped of their Warrant would damage their exports. This would be contrary to the national interest. Peat was sympathetic but insisted that it was a false argument. It was an argument not dissimilar to the one advanced by Schweppes in the previous century, but it was still firmly rejected. Warrants were intended to recognise personal service to The Royal Family. Export performance was recognised through The Queen's Awards for Enterprise.

Whether or not he was correct in his assessment – and some Warrant Holders contested the 'sleepy' and

'dusty' verdict – it was clear that nobody had really examined the system's working at least since the time of Geoffrey Hardy-Roberts more than twenty years earlier. The Peat view was that all organisations need to be looked at periodically even if they appear to be functioning well. The mere fact that no such examination had taken place was justification enough for a serious review.

Of course, it was not all bad. The Queen Elizabeth Scholarships were going well and they represented precisely the sort of initiative he felt the Warrant Holders should be taking. He also relished the clubbable aspect of the Association. After all, he had captained the Household in the recent golf match with the Association, and he thought that for Warrant Holders and Household members to get together on social occasions was not only fun but also beneficial. He noted the parties that Prince Charles held at Highgrove for his Warrant Holders and The Queen Mother's hosting of events for 'her' Scholars.

On the other hand there had been some mistakes. A case in point was the House of Windsor débâcle. In the early nineties a Bahamas-registered company announced that it would be trading by mail order under the name 'The House of Windsor'. Their stock-in-trade was the sort of upmarket luxury British goods which are associated with a significant section of Royal Warrant Holders. The company approached the Association and the then Secretary, Hugh Faulkner, went to the Palace who, surprisingly, let him know that they would have no objection. The company even managed to secure the patronage of a member of The Royal Family: Prince Michael of Kent.

Eventually and quite by chance the *mail order* House of Windsor came to the attention of the *real* House of Windsor and the Palace executed a swift but embarrassing volte-face. Their disapproval was made plain and the mail order plans were aborted. 'Of course,' said Sir Michael, 'We should have jumped on it at the beginning.'

After due deliberation some old rules were modified and some new ones introduced. Four areas were considered.

The first innovation was what Sir Michael described as 'a significance test'. In order for someone to qualify for a Warrant the service provided must have real significance. Products, and the services which support them, must be significant for either the member of the family who grants the Warrant or to the company which provides them. Products provided in such a routine, impersonal manner that the provider scarcely knows (or perhaps cares) whether the product is used by the Royal Household or not are likely to fail the 'significance test'.

Quantity is not the only criterion. For the small shopkeepers of Ballater. for instance, the services they provide to Balmoral are hugely significant. In the overall scheme of the Household budget the amounts involved might be infinitesimal but the 'significance' – the sense of pride, of duty and above all of service to The Queen – would be beyond doubt. 'Because the public *think* it means something,' said Sir Michael, 'it *must* mean something. If there is no "significance" for either the giver or the receiver then there should not be a Warrant. For the system to be built on rock it's got to have "significance".'

Then there was the matter of price. Very difficult. A vital part of Sir Michael's brief was to run a tight ship and to save money wherever possible. If the Warrant means as much to companies as it obviously does there must be a temptation for them to offer their services at way below the normal commercial rate – or even completely free of charge.

'I was nervous about discounts,' conceded Sir Michael. 'We like them. Of course we do. But they must be "reasonable". We are nervous about accepting things for free. That might be construed as selling the Warrant. On the other hand we have an obligation to the taxpayer to drive a hard bargain.' In other words he expects to be treated like any other important and valued customer. No more, no less.

Third, there was a lack of clarity about whether the use of a product by the Royal Household was, by itself, a sufficient justification for granting a Warrant. This issue revolved round whether a Warrant should be given even if the applicant had not supplied the goods or services to the Royal Household. For example, if a building contractor used a certain type of paint to redecorate one of the Palaces, should the paint's manufacturer be eligible to apply for a Warrant? The guideline suggested was 'only if the Household itself had specified the particular paint'. This was on the basis that if the paint type had been chosen by the contractor without reference to the Household then there was no relationship between the supplier of the paint and the Household and its 'significance' was minimal.

Finally, Peat suggested that the existing practice of reviewing Warrants every ten years might be out of line with modern business practice. In the modern world ten-year contracts were unusual. So, in a change which did not find sympathy with some of the traditionalists, the period was halved to five years.

'Yes,' he conceded, 'it's tougher, but it *has* to be tougher. It's part of The Queen's role to recognise and reward excellence. In that sense it's like the honours system with a rigorous approach and applying the highest possible standards.'

Meanwhile, after ten years the system, instigated in 1990 in The Prince of Wales's household, had taken root and flourished. In putting his personal imprint firmly on Warrant-granting policy and in making his Warrant Holders a vivid reflection of his own tastes, preferences and principles, The Prince evoked memories of Queen Victoria's patronage of the Honiton lace industry. By encouraging one man bands practising traditional crafts, The Prince recalled the practice of ancestors stretching back well before the Industrial Revolution. The Prince has made sure that all his Warrant Holders have been invited to receptions at Highgrove, his Gloucestershire country home. Here they could expect to be greeted by name and to be subjected to friendly but rigorous questioning, not

least on their implementation of his environmental requirements.

Among his 160-odd Warrant Holders were some whose companies had been started with backing from his own Prince's Trust. The photographer Paul Burns was one of these. So was Fiona Rae, whose enamelled work is often given by The Prince as personal gifts.

The rules governing The Prince of Wales's Warrants are rigorous but not inflexible. Very small companies are not expected to produce the same level of supporting environmental documentation as very big ones. And Business in the Environment offers detailed guidance to applicants. Each request is looked at with the overriding imperative that the business should demonstrate a concern for its impact on the environment.

The Prince is therefore intimately involved with the granting of his Warrant. Decisions are taken with the greatest care. Discussion at every stage in the process and at every level is mandatory. Where appropriate, he is particularly sensitive to the individual circumstances of a company. It is the relatively small size of his Household which makes this flexible and individual approach possible, and allows The Prince to grant and maintain his Warrant in his own distinctive and personal way. Two of the eight new Warrants in 2001 went to Rollo Whately and Gino Franchi who, respectively, mount and frame the water-colours that

he himself paints.

An even more recent example which illustrates this is that of Billings & Edmunds, the Eton College outfitters. Under the overall rules, no one receives a Warrant until he or she can demonstrate five years of continuous supply. By the end of 2000 Billings & Edmunds could do that but Prince William had already left school and Prince Harry had only two years before he also left. The supply provided by Billings & Edmunds would then cease. It would be wrong, all agreed, if the company were to go on displaying the Warrant after the two Princes had abandoned school uniform for ever. This was an obvious case for compromise. Billings & Edmunds were therefore granted a Warrant after the requisite five years, but will relinquish it as soon as Prince Harry leaves Eton. Their service has been 'special' and 'significant', but by its nature short-lived. All this is reflected in The Prince's decision to grant them a two-year Warrant.

It is difficult to put a commercial value on the holding of a Royal Warrant and companies are understandably reluctant to do so. The Warrant is not intended as a boost to trade, but there is no doubt that it is widely regarded as a help, particularly in the export market. Japan, the Gulf States and, perhaps to a lesser extend, the United States of America, are all places where it is thought that the Royal Coat of Arms is a significant incentive to would-be purchasers. There is, of course, a sort of snob appeal connected with it, but it is also generally seen to be a guarantee of superior quality.

An integral part of the Association's 'Way Ahead' was recognition of the increasing importance of The Queen Elizabeth Scholarship Trust. QEST had already got off to an auspicious start, thanks to the financial generosity of so many Warrant-holding companies. In the first year of the awards the Scholars were a tapestry conservator, a farrier, a stonemason, a glassmaker, a shoemaker and a homeopath. Over the next decade this proved to be not untypical. The 2000 Scholarship winners, for example, garnered around £100,000 between the fourteen of them. They were a stone conservator, an artist, a bench joiner, a gold-and silversmith, a farrier, a painter and decorator, a milliner, a weaver and a basket maker.

These simple descriptions, however, give little clue to the particular characteristics of the Scholars and the often exotic nature of the projects for which they use their funds. Roy Youdale, the basket maker, for example, was forty-nine years old – the QEST scholarships are determinedly non-ageist – and already a skilled independent willow basket maker, growing his own willow and instructing others in his craft. To hone his skills, however, he wanted to study privately in Switzerland with one of Europe's leading basket makers. QEST made this possible. The weaver, Louisa Wood, wanted to go to the centre of Chinese hemp production in Yunnan to learn their techniques of spinning and weaving, and thus revive the moribund use of hemp as a fabric in England. The bench joiner had had a special course in ecclesiastical joinery designed for him by Hackney Community College. Rod Kelly, the gold-and silversmith, already skilled enough to be represented at the Goldsmiths Hall Millennium Exhibition, wanted to perfect his skills, particularly in the area of gold inlay, by studying with two master craftsmen. Robert Ogborn, the self-employed painter and decorator wanted to perfect *his* skills by attending a formal course in Brittany's Ecole de Peinture Décorative et de Trompe l'Oeil.

In all these cases a common factor emerges. The Scholars are already expert at their craft but feel unable to extend their expertise without outside help. The Trustees are proud to recognise the fact that in their pursuit of excellence many Scholars suffer 'loss of income' and this factor is built in to the awards. As former QEST Chairman, Christopher Rowe of Findlater Mackie Todd says, 'Craftspeople live from hand to mouth. Every day away from the workbench is a day most of them can't afford. We need to recognise that the provision of travel costs and the cost of study courses is not, by itself, enough.'

And so on. After the first ten years many of the Scholars had achieved all sorts of success – making hats for the West End musical *Fosse*, building the world's first straw bale sauna, opening a shop selling 700 different hand-made honey-based products, making a pair of tables which were the Association's wedding present to the Earl and Countess of Wessex, designing fourteen ceramic pieces for Thomas Goode, which are now in the Victoria & Albert Museum's permanent exhibition. The portrait painter Rupert Atkinson now has commissions to paint all four Grantors and Davina Chapman, the calligrapher, now regularly produces place names for royal banquets.

It is, of course, impossible to say whether such successes would have been achieved without the stimulus and benefit of The Queen Elizabeth Scholarships but nevertheless the roll of honour is impressive. Barry Reed's successor as Chairman of the Trust is Alan Britten. He says, 'if any candidate of any age comes forward who can demonstrate genuine excellence in his or her craft, and who has a clearly

On his return from Florence, where he attended the Charles Cecil Studio, QEST Scholar Rupert Atkinson was commissioned to paint all four Grantors. His portraits of The Duke of Edinburgh (far left) *and The Prince of Wales were completed in 2000.*

identified, well-supported plan for self-development, the Trust stands ready to help. That is our primary message.'

It is a message which finally fulfils the promise embedded in the ringing declaration of 1907 and has attracted the approbation of even the most sceptical onlookers. In the summer of 2000 Holly Finn, editor of the 'How to Spend It' pages of the *Financial Times*, was invited to the Association's Annual Luncheon, which she described in a subsequent full-page article as 'a very staid, very old-boy affair', adding that she felt as if she was one of very few people present who had not 'had personal experience skirmishing in India'.

This good-natured scepticism did not last. 'Like the lunch,' she wrote, 'the Warrants are not as superficially ceremonial as they sometimes appear and are sometimes treated.'

By the time she had finished her review Holly Finn had been genuinely won over. After interviewing some of the successful Scholars she concluded:

> Talk to them, and you are reminded of the passionate knowledge it takes to become truly skilled in a specific trade. Commission them, and you see how much they care about each and every item they make.
>
> The Royals single out Royal Warrant Holders for exceptional ability, and Royal Warrant Holders now single out craftsmen for the same. It's a trickle-down system that, by rewarding demonstrably superior workmanship and service, benefits both craftspeople and you, the consumer.

The Association obviously feels the accolade is well merited but it was all the more so because it came from someone who was not originally disposed to be so generous.

QEST represents a blending of respect for the past with hope for the future which Warrant Holders believe is emblematic. It is what they believe in and what they stand for, and in awarding these scholar-ships they are properly grateful for the very real support not just of The Queen Mother, in whose honour they are named, but also of The Queen herself, the other two Grantors, The Prince of Wales and The Duke of Edinburgh, as well as the other members of The Royal Family who do not themselves award Warrants. QEST is, perhaps above all, the way forward but it is part of a continuing tradition. It would not be possible without the example of the past and the efforts of the present.

Another of the first contributors to QEST funding was Findlater Mackie Todd & Co Ltd., the wine and spirit merchant who first held the Warrant in King George V's reign when independent and now, as a branch of the John Lewis Partnership. John Lewis, in the form of Peter Jones, have since 1996 arranged the displays of Scholars' work at the Association's annual luncheon. 'As soon as I received Barry Reed's letter,' says Christopher Rowe who holds the Warrant on behalf of Findlater, 'I felt that we had launched a project that would make a significant contribution to British Arts and Crafts.' Rowe himself went on to serve as a QEST Trustee for six years with three as Chairman.

In due course Rowe became President of the Association, stepping into the breach caused by the untimely death of Anna Plowden. Like all Presidents, there were high spots unique to his year of office. One was the reception for possibly the most remote body of Warrant Holders, namely the group of Royal Tradesmen clustered around the northern fastness of The Queen Mother's Castle of Mey in Scotland. Sir Richard George had made the first known visit by a national President, and this had whetted appetites in both London and Caithness. When Christopher Pickup started examining the possibility of holding some sort of reception for the Association's Caithness members he soon got a message from The Queen Mother saying that she thought that much the best place for such a party would be the drawing room at the castle. Which is what happened.

The Queen Mother also came to open the new offices at Nº1 Buckingham Place. Her only stipulation about doing this was that it should happen on a day when there was no racing within driving distance of Clarence House. This was achieved. Christopher Rowe recalls that Parkers, who held the Warrant for their writing implements, presented the Association with a special fountain pen with the Royal Arms on top. 'When I proffered this to Her Majesty for signing our visitors book,' he said, 'she declined and produced a biro from her handbag.'

Christopher Rowe has always felt strongly that Warrant Holders are a powerful force as ambassadors on behalf of the concept of Constitutional Monarchy. 'One of my objectives during my Presidential year', he said, 'was certainly to continue along the path of improved relations with the Household. However, almost more importantly, I was very keen to stress the support that Royal Warrant Holders give to the Monarchy.' This is a universal Warrant Holder maxim.

Michael Skinner, the tailor, was President in 2000. Oddly, Skinner's family are old-established Warrant Holders but not through what has now become the family firm. His father held King George VI's Warrant through Wilkinson & Son and his father-in-law, W. R. Vincent of Vincent's of Reading, once made Queen Elizabeth II's motorised horseboxes. Dege had for years made the splendid uniforms for the Honourable Corps of Gentlemen at Arms. The skirted red coats with Garter blue cuffs and facings are modelled on the uniforms of Dragoon Guards officers of the 1840s but Dege were making royal robes even before that. They started with William IV, continued with Victoria and George V, and were responsible for Queen Mary's Coronation robes.

One of Michael Skinner's presidential coups was securing the attendance of The Princess Royal as guest of honour at the 'Millennium Banquet'. The Princess proposed the health of the Association and charmed everyone by speaking with her customary informality, obvious knowledge of her subject matter and barely a note in sight. Despite the white tie and tails, this great banquet was now much reduced by contrast with Victorian times. There were only three speeches – from The Princess, Michael Skinner and Sir Brian Jenkins, a former Lord Mayor of London. Sir Brian, though himself an accountant by trade, was a former Master of Michael Skinner's own Livery Company, the Merchant Taylors.

The Band of the Royal Signals played incidental music, but there were no longer any singers and the most obvious nod to the traditions of the last century was the serving of a savoury – Welsh rarebit – to stand alongside the Sandeman's port. On a more substantive level Michael Skinner played a considerable role in raising £300,000 for QEST from the Association membership, to mark the hundredth birthday of The Queen Mother.

Skinner's year closed in March 2001 with a Clarence House reception at which he presented Her Majesty with a commemorative book written by Juliet Bankes, the calligrapher, and bound by Bex Marriott, both of whom –

Left: *Christopher Rowe, of Findlater Mackie Todd & Co Ltd., as Chairman of the Queen Elizabeth Scholarship Trust, greets The Queen Mother outside Nº1 Buckingham Place on the occasion of her visit to open the Association's new headquarters.* RWHA Archive

Below: *The bust of The Queen Mother, by Vivi Mallock, which Her Majesty unveiled during her visit to Buckingham Place on 20th November 1998. The plinth and column for the bust were designed and made by QEST Scholar Jonathan Harris.*

appropriately – were QEST Scholars. The Queen Mother, well into her 102nd year, invited all her recent QEST Scholars to join her party and spent the best part of two hours wandering among them, chatting happily as she inspected the examples of their work on display in her drawing room. It was a tribute to The Queen Mother's indefatigible enthusiasm that while all present were charmed and delighted, none seemed unduly surprised.

Michael Skinner was succeeded by Adam Brett-Smith, of the wine merchants Corney & Barrow, who were not only long standing Warrant Holders but had also provided a previous President in the form of Keith Stevens, who held the position in 1966 and had been one of the key players in the appointment of Bill Keown-Boyd as Secretary.

Right: Alan Britten, Chairman of the Queen Elizabeth Scholarship Trust, is presented to The Princess Royal by the President, Michael Skinner, at the 2000 Banquet in the Grosvenor House Hotel. Adam Brett-Smith, Vice President, stands behind.
RWHA Archive

Below: *Warrant Holders and their guests at the Millennium Banquet in the Grosvenor House Hotel.*
RWHA Archive

Brett-Smith confessed to a certain anxiety when confronted by the long line of ex-Presidents at Council meetings but seemed happily unfazed by it. Nearer in age to The Prince of Wales than to any of the other Grantors, and the holder of his Warrant, he seemed particularly sympathetic to The Prince's innovative approach to the Warrant. He himself was conducting serious researches into organic wines. 'Holding the Warrant', he said, 'governs the whole way in which you do business. If you hold the Warrant there are certain things you simply would not do. The Warrant imposes the most rigorous standards.'

Like all Warrant Holders, he is enough of a traditionalist to be careful about preserving such standards but he is also concerned to get the message across to a wide audience. He regards one of the greatest challenges of his presidency as 'How to better communicate to the public what's involved'.

In its recommendations the Way Ahead Committee had expressed a wish to 'project a public image which both supports and reflects the character of its member firms, namely: excellence, quality, reliability and discretion'. In addition, 'Every opportunity should be taken to stress the charitable support given to craft and skill training'. The role of President is pivotal in projecting this image and to do so effectively Brett-Smith, like his predecessors, has to be mindful of the two essential elements in the Warrant-holding equation – the Palace on the one hand and the

Royal Tradesmen on the other.

Within the organisation the most important figure is, in a sense, the Secretary. Christopher Pickup and the Council would be aghast if it were ever suggested that, like that earlier Secretary, he really 'ran the show', but his is a full-time salaried job and he provides continuity and permanence even though policy is a matter for the Council.

In 1995 when he answered an advertisement in *The Times,* he 'knew not a thing' about the Warrant or how it worked. By 2001, however, he seemed to the manner born. Many of his duties are similar to those of Secretaries for the previous hundred years or so. The Warrant still has to be 'policed' and 'people **DO** transgress' but the number of cases is minimal com-

pared with the early twentieth century. He deals with perhaps half a dozen a year. This is a murky world of improbable Scotch whisky bottles on the shelves of Turkish supermarkets, of trading standards officers in provincial towns, of sharp letters from the Colonel's office or the Lord Chamberlain's or even from Farrers, the Royal solicitors. 'We spend a lot of time advising on packaging,' he says, 'But most Warrant Holders want to do the right thing and abide by the Lord Chamberlain's rules. And if people do step out of line the sharp letter usually suffices.'

Membership is very slowly declining, mainly because the Lord Chamberlain's rules are being applied more stringently. Members pay to join the Association. Hugh Faulkner and the then Treasurer Sam Twining 'beefed up' the subscriptions in 1995. Not before time, some felt. Some fifty member companies have an annual turnover of more than £500 million a year. They pay an annual subscription of more than £2000 but the smallest, the seventy or so with a turnover below £100,000, pay around £60. And there is a tiny minority of about a dozen who are dealt with under special arrangements.

For the Secretariat, in addition to providing guidance to all who hold, or would like to hold a Warrant, there is the lavish Grosvenor House banquet to organise, as well as the Park Lane Hilton luncheon and the London reception. Anyone who has ever tried to organise an official occasion will know how time-consuming and difficult it is to produce such apparently mundane necessities as seating-plans, menus, and accurately printed invitation cards. Here, in the case of the banquet, we are talking about a white tie occasion with a thousand guests. In addition, Colonel Pickup and his staff have to organise presidential visits to the four regional Associations, and the sporting events involving golf, tennis and fishing. In a sense, these are the sort of largely social tasks one associates with any convivial club however grand.

Over and above all this, however, the staff at Buckingham Place also have to administer the selection process for the Plowden Medal and the burgeoning Queen Elizabeth Scholarship scheme. The Secretary is required to screen some 300 applications a year, prepare briefs for the Trustees to short-list and interview candidates, and arrange the final presentations of their awards.

It is clear that for the Colonel it is this charitable arm of the Warrant Holders Association which bulks largest. The Plowden medal is now established as the 'Blue Riband' of its field. QEST – the first time the Association REALLY started looking outwards – is growing all the time.

Over the century, the generosity of the Royal Warrant Holders Association has taken on a markedly different form. In the 1930s, the King's House was a gift from the Association to the Monarch, albeit a gift intended to display to the world the sophistication of modern living and the skill of English craftsmen. Since then the scale of gifts has been reduced: an encyclopaedia (specially requested by Princess Elizabeth) for the 1947 Royal Wedding; a pair of cufflinks for Prince Charles's twenty-first birthday. The Silver wedding in 1972 and the Silver Jubilee in 1977 were jointly commemorated by the gift of some retirement homes for former royal servants on land made available by The Queen, and The Queen Mother's eightieth birthday by a hydrotherapy pool for the King Edward Hospital for Officers. Since The Queen Elizabeth Scholarship Trust was established as the Association's major charity, gifts have tended to be pieces of fine craftsmanship, produced by Scholars of the Trust. By the time of The Queen's Golden Jubilee however, the emphasis had shifted entirely. The Warrant holders were no longer making a gift to the monarchy. Instead they were sharing in the Monarch's own gift to the nation. The Association is paying for the sculpture scheme by the Scot Sandy Stoddart, which will decorate the entrance pavilion of the rebuilt Queen's Gallery at Buckingham Palace.

The concept is heroic,' says the Colonel, 'an allegorical depiction of the whole of The Queen's reign.'

Listening to the Secretary's enthusiasm, one can almost envisage a day when the charitable and philanthropic tail of the organisation comes to wag the trading, industrial, Warrant-holding dog.

Around the corner at Buckingham Palace another Colonel, Sir Malcolm Ross, formerly of the Scots Guards and, since 1991, Comptroller of the Lord Chamberlain's Office, muses on Warrant holding from a different perspective. 'We ARE the authority,' he says. He works closely and cordially with the Royal Warrant Holders Association but, at the end of the day, it is he and his master, the Lord Chamberlain, who advise the Grantors. He was a little sceptical when he first came to the Palace, knowing no more about the Warrant than Colonel Pickup when he first joined the Association. But Sir Malcolm has long since ceased thinking of the Association simply as a smart dining club. He understands the value of the Warrant and of its holders. 'Communication is much more frequent and regular,' he says. 'There has been a lot of change and one is always thinking about ways forward.'

He is particularly bothered about the relatively impersonal service rendered by some Warrant Holders, by comparison with the very personal relationship which other grantees have with their Grantor. He has wondered if perhaps a new distinction might usefully be made between those Warrant Holders who serve or supply The Queen herself and those who deal at a remove with the Royal Household and its officers. Could this distinction be formalised by the creation of some form of differential Warrant, so that some companies might be 'By Appointment to the Royal Household' rather than to an individual member of the Royal Family?

If such an idea were to be pursued, however, it would be done with the utmost tact and consideration. 'Christopher and I would talk,' said Sir Malcolm. 'And if we agreed, it would be discussed with all the representatives of the different Households at the Royal Household Tradesmen's Warrants Committee. And if we all agreed then we would present our conclusions to the Council of the Royal Warrant Holders Association.'

It would, in other words, all be very civilised. It has been ever thus, with a few regrettable exceptions, for hundreds of years. There will, inevitably, be change, but it will be change within the context of tradition and politeness, loyalty and professionalism.

What else would one expect from what Captain Tom Simpson Jay, Silk Mercer to Her Majesty Queen Victoria and first President of the Royal Warrant Holders Association, so aptly and so memorably described as 'A Peerage for Trade'?

Sandy Stoddart's Detail from working drawings for the sculpture scheme for the rebuilt Queen's Gallery at Buckingham Palace

The Local Associations

The Lower Ward, Windsor Castle. After Joseph Nash (1809-1878).
The Royal Collection Trust

Windsor Castle is the only building in the United Kingdom which has been in continuous use as a royal residence since the time of William the Conqueror. Holyroodhouse has an ancient but much interrupted royal history and Balmoral, Sandringham and even Buckingham Palace are Victorian parvenus. This seniority is reflected in the pride and independence of the Warrant Holders clustered in and around the ancient boroughs of Windsor and Eton. Not only do they claim that their Association pre-dates the National Association, they actually continued as a separate and autonomous organisation for well over a hundred years.

The Windsor and Eton Association claims to have been founded in 1823 though legend – unsubstantiated – has it that the Royal Tradesmen of Windsor first dined formally together in 1810. Being a small community, the tradesmen inevitably played a prominent part in local life and were often members of the Corporation or even Mayor. This tradition persists today.

The earliest recorded communal Royal Tradesmen's celebrations are those mentioned in the *Windsor and Eton Express* whose owner, Charles Knight of Castle Street was to acquire a Royal Warrant of his own as a printer. His newspaper, still going strong, was founded on 1st August 1812 and a fortnight later it carried a report of Windsor being 'brilliantly illuminated' in honour of The Prince Regent's birthday. That night, apparently, 'the Mayor and Corporation testified to their loyalty to the Prince Regent in bumpers at the Town Hall'. Clearly this was not a Warrant Holders' occasion per se but, although we do not know for certain, the odds are that a majority of those charging their bumpers in honour of The Prince would have been Royal Tradesmen.

The custom of local burghers, especially tradesmen, illuminating their houses with flares, lamps and torches on special occasions was one which continued throughout the century and beyond. Only a week after The Prince's birthday they were at it again in

honour of the 'glorious victory at Salamanca'. The *Express* reported that these illuminations 'though chiefly confined to the houses of the tradesmen were as brilliant and tasteful as the enthusiasm of the moment could adopt'.

The following year the paper recorded similar illuminations to celebrate the birthday of The Princess Charlotte of Wales. A week later it was The Queen's birthday which meant 'demonstrations of joy', more illuminations and a Ball in the Town Hall 'attended by a numerous and elegant party'.

In 1820 the *Express* identified some of the most prominent Royal Tradesmen in Windsor. The occasion was the funeral of George III and those concerned were Mr Tebbott 'Builder to his late and the present Majesty' and Mr Jenner, 'His Late Majesty's joiner'. This is not Mr Tebbott's first appearance. A few years earlier to mark The Prince Regent's birthday he had built a brilliantly illuminated arch across Sheet Street from his own premises to the house opposite. This included a coronet, plumes of feathers and festoons of lights. For The King's funeral Mr Tebbott built a platform 1065 feet long, fifteen feet high and nineteen feet wide with 70,000 feet of boarding and 49,000 feet of quartering. 'This most extensive work' commented the *Express* with admiration, 'was finished through the indefatigable energy of Mr Tebbott and those employed between the interval of Monday and

Right: *Robert Tebbott, from the portrait in the Guildhall, Windsor.* David Lunn and the Royal Borough of Windsor and Maidenhead/Betty Lambourne

The King's 1826 birthday – his sixty-fourth – was marked by yet more royal generosity. The Castle was the subject of extensive renovation, mainly because the King had moved to Windsor from his earlier haven at the Brighton Pavilion. More than 700 workmen were employed on the project. At one o'clock they all assembled on the new eastern terrace and 'at the signal of their directors of the work, hailed the occasion with repeated cheers'. They then trooped off to pubs all over town where they were provided with dinners at His Majesty's expense. And in the evening, of course, 'The Town was brilliantly illuminated'.

At the 1827 birthday dinner the Lord Steward was commanded by The King to provide a buck to the Mayor and each of the fourteen Stewards. This provision of royal venison on these occasions became a regular custom until it was finally discontinued in 1947.

It was not all sycophancy and jollification. In 1829, less than a year before his death, The King 'signified his displeasure at the exorbitant profits derived through combination by some of the Tradespeople'. His Majesty let it be known that if his Tradesmen did not supply goods at 'the fair price current in London', he would take his custom elsewhere. Within a few days of this policy being pronounced the price of meat alone fell by two pence per pound.

Something seems to have been seriously amiss for in 1844 a letter under the sobriquet 'Civic' asked, 'Did you observe yesterday, Mr Editor, the absence of the usual brilliant illuminations at the houses of the Queen's Tradesmen? Butchers, Bakers, Grocers, Inn keepers, all conspired to show their teeth instead of their loyalty.' It sounds as if a wind of change was blowing through the Royal Household and economies were being introduced. Does one detect a new broom in the person of Prince Albert?

Five years later, despite the continuance of the venison-fuelled Tradesmen's dinners, the *Express* reported that the Royal Tradesmen of Windsor and Eton 'are complaining bitterly'. The 'Office of Woods

Friday evening.' Both Mr Tebbott and Mr Jenner were clearly significant figures in nineteenth-century Windsor and Eton. Mr Jenner was Mayor in 1827 and Mr Tebbott not only succeeded him the following year, but came back for a second term in 1842. In their capacity as Mayor, each man took the chair at the increasing number of these celebratory dinners.

Shortly after George III's funeral, his successor's birthday was celebrated with the ringing of castle and parish bells, the firing of cannon and public dinners at the White Hart and Swan Inn where, in the evening, the houses of the 'Warranted' Tradesmen of the Royal Family were 'brilliantly illuminated with variegated lamps'. This appears to be the first use of the term 'Warranted Tradesman'.

Later in the year the new King George IV with 'that considerate kindness by which he is so peculiarly characterised' invited all his Tradesmen to a ball at Cumberland Lodge where his health was drunk with 'thunders of applause'. Afterwards a Mr Bannister 'took occasion to express with great feeling and propriety, the sentiments which HM's tradesmen and the inhabitants of Windsor generally felt at this gracious mark of HM's patronage and approbation'. Those present then went back to dancing and 'the company did not separate till the sun was gilding the surrounding scenery with his morning hues'.

and Forests' had been reformed and taken over by a new 'Board'. Contracts were thrown open to tender and the locals – some of whom had been working for the Castle for half a century or more – found themselves being undercut by 'London and other Tradesmen'. Windsor tradesmen who lost their royal employment included carpenters, joiners, plumbers, glaziers and painters.

These tradesmen obviously took this very much amiss. They saw no reason for suddenly being deprived of a royal patronage which they had come to take for granted. The official response was that business is business and sentiment can only be allowed to play a minimal part in the arrangements between Royalty and trade. At the end of 1850 all Castle contracts were ordered to expire at the end of a three-month period because London people were so consistent in coming in with lower tenders than the locals. Similar tensions were still apparent more than 150 years later.

By the end of Queen Victoria's reign, however, there seemed to have been an outbreak of peace, for on The Queen's eightieth birthday a small delegation of Royal Warrant Holders was allowed to present The Queen with a basket of roses. They were introduced, in the corridor after luncheon, by the Master of the Household. The Queen said 'what lovely flowers. It is most kind of you!' and then the Warrant Holders' President read a short address humbly tendering congratulations on this auspicious occasion and promising to pray daily that she might 'continue to enjoy the blessing of health and happiness with the

Right: *The Coronation Banquet for George IV, held in Westminster Hall on 19th July, 1821. "The bringing of the first course". Lithograph by David and Robert Havell.* Guildhall Library/Bridgeman Art Library

undiminished loyalty and affection of your people'.

The Queen, characteristically terse, replied, 'Excellent. I am most obliged to you.' After which the delegation 'retired much gratified with the exceptional honour that had been granted by Her Majesty'.

By now the Windsor and Eton Tradesmen had formally banded together as an Association with a set of rules and regulations, and an annual subscription of twenty-five shillings to include the cost of an annual banquet. The first meeting recorded in the minute book was at Messrs Caley & Son, The Royal Family's corner shop in the High Street, first started at the beginning of the century by Mrs Caley, The Queen's milliner. The original

Caley Warrant was granted by George IV in 1820.

Quite why it was felt necessary to give themselves a formal structure after the best part of a century of successful socialising, illuminating and networking, it is difficult to say. The minutes are succinct, not to say cryptic, on the matter, saying simply that Mr J. Bedborough and Mr Cobden proposed and seconded a motion saying, 'It is desirable that an Association of Royal Warrant Holders of Windsor and Eton be formed.' The motion was duly carried on 11th May 1898 but no mention is made of the arguments for or against.

Almost immediately the Windsor and Eton Association seems to have begun an apparently scratchy correspondence with 'the London Association' (as they always referred to the national body), but otherwise the affairs of the Windsor and Eton Warrant Holders proceeded much as before. Wreaths were ordered for the anniversary of Queen Victoria's death and for the funeral of Edward VII with strict stipulations about cost (no more than a guinea for the former and two for the latter). The annual banquets were discontinued during the war but resumed afterwards and in 1925 there was a daring attempt to get ladies admitted. Despite the fact that one of the Committee was a Mrs Manley and that Caley's, had been founded by Mrs Caley, this proposal was turned down.

In 1928 members of the Royal Household were invited to the banquet for what appears to be the first time. The guests of honour were Colonel the Hon. Sir George Crichton, the Comptroller of the Lord Chamberlain's Office, and Owen Morshead, the King's librarian. A year later the Association's Secretary had a meeting with Lord Stamfordham to see whether His Majesty would accept a loyal address. In 1933 the Association invested in a badge and chain of office

Left: *Caley Bros. handbill dating from between 1853 and 1861.* John Lewis Partnership archive collection

for the President for which each member contributed ten shillings. Two years later a special meeting was held to discuss what should be done about the appeal for the 'King's House Fund' and it was agreed that the Association would not make a corporate donation but would send out a letter to all members asking them to give generously but directly to the London Association. In 1944 an Association flag was made to be flown by the President when appropriate.

Immediately after World War Two there seem to have been no meetings but in 1947 they were revived. The annual banquet also appeared to have fallen by the way and the Committee agreed to revive it. Unfortunately the Association was told that the deer stocks in Windsor Great Park had dwindled to such an extent that the Monarch would no longer be able to provide the customary venison.

Coupled with the fact that rationing was still in force, the Committee decided that they could not put together a menu worthy of the occasion.

Even in drab and austere times Warrant Holders could be eccentrically inventive. One unique dispensation of the 1950s was the approval of perhaps the most particular Coat of Arms ever to grace Warrant Holding premises. This was the privilege of Mr Hussey of Wellmans, the ironmonger on the corner of Peascod Street. Being an ironmonger, Mr Hussey naturally wanted to display his iromongering expertise and so asked if the Coat of Arms above his shop could reflect his trade. The Lord Chamberlain was pleased to acquiesce and the Peascod Street Arms go into the records as the only version of the Royal Arms ever to be displayed by its grantee in wrought iron.

In 1948, however, a banquet was held at the Castle Hotel. It was the first since 1938. For several years the ventriloquist Peter Brough (together with his famous puppet, Archie Andrews) provided the main entertainment.

Throughout these years there seems to have been a regular correspondence with the 'London Association' about some form of affiliation. Finally it was agreed in 1955 that the Windsor and Eton Warrant Holders should send a representative to the London Council meetings while at the same time preserving their jealously maintained independence.

In 1962 The Duke of Edinburgh attended an Association lunch at the White Hart – the first time a member of the Royal Family had joined the Tradesmen since the nineteenth century. That same year the President voiced a recurring fear of the smaller Warrant Holders, namely that they would be squeezed out by larger companies who would be able to offer the Household preferential rates and discounts, which they could not. Evidently he was assured by London that if details of this practice could be proved they would take the matter up with the Master of the Household.

From time to time the Association also gave pre-

sents to members of the Royal Family – not just the loyal addresses and baskets of flowers associated with earlier years but an encyclopaedia for the Royal Wedding of 1947 (specifically requested by Princess Elizabeth) and a pair of cuff links for Prince Charles's twenty-first. They even chipped in towards the cost of a polo pony which was presented to him by the 'London Association'. The Tradesmen also made donations to charity and, in 1973, planted a cherry tree in the parish churchyard. Twenty-five trees for a small estate for retired Crown employees followed in the year of the Silver Jubilee, two for Royal Lodge to mark The Queen Mother's eightieth birthday and a further two for Highgrove to mark The Prince of Wales's wedding.

In 1974, fifty years after the idea was first mooted, women were admitted to the annual banquet, which had now been downgraded to just 'dinner'. In 1981 the Lord Chamberlain was guest of honour for the first time.

The most significant development in recent years came in 1987 when the Windsor and Eton Association finally affiliated with what was still referred to locally as the 'London Association' but which was in reality the national Royal Warrant Holders Association. The person who can take most credit for the move was Graeme Wilson, that year's national President. Wilson was an Aberdeen Warrant Holder whose family company, William Wilson & Co., supplied building materials to Balmoral. 'He was

really a breath of fresh air,' recall approving Windsor Warrant Holders. 'It helped, of course, that he wasn't English. Until he came along London used to treat us as second-class citizens. But Graeme changed all that.'

On 27th October Wilson wrote to Uma Patel, proprietor of the Castle Pharmacy in Peascod Street. Patel was that year's Windsor President. As someone born in Kenya of Indian ancestry, Patel was able to look at the issue without the baggage of past prejudice.

Wilson made two points in his letter. The first was that the common link between all Warrant Holders was that they 'all supply one family'. He argued from this that it seemed 'appropriate for those Warrant Holders who wish to have some form of Association, that the Association should also be one family'. His second was that as President of the national Association he represented the Edinburgh, Aberdeen and Sandringham branches but not Windsor. He felt this was an anomaly.

Uma Patel, passing the letter on to his members, took issue with the second point because he said that,

Left: *Wellman Bros., with the wrought iron version of the Royal Arms facing Peascod Street, Windsor.*
Jacqueline Hussey

Below: *A quartet of Presidents: Graeme Wilson (seated) with (left to right) Kinloch Anderson (Edinburgh), Donovan Fry (Sandringham) and Gordon Baxter (Aberdeen). Uma Patel, the President of Windsor and Eton is absent, since Windsor had not, at that time, joined the National Association.*
RWHA Archive

as individuals, most, if not all, the Windsor and Eton Warrant Holders belonged individually to the national Association and therefore were represented by the national President. What seems to have exercised the Windsor and Eton Warrant Holders most was the idea that they should be referred to merely as a 'branch' of the national organisation. They were insistent that they were an 'Association' with the history to prove it. Wilson was keen to reassure them that there was no question of a 'takeover' and indeed that 'strenuous efforts must be taken to record your history to ensure it has its rightful place in the Royal Warrant Holders Association story'. (I'm pleased to think that I am now making just the 'strenuous effort' that Graeme Wilson had in mind.)

Right: Douglas Hill, Secretary of the Windsor and Eton Association, standing beneath the Coat of Arms of his Grantor, Queen Elizabeth The Queen Mother, outside his shop in Eton High Street.
Derek Bishop

In the event the semantics were ironed out so that Windsor and Eton remained an 'Association' under the overall umbrella of the national Association and not merely a 'branch'. A vote was taken and passed so that, at last, Windsor and Eton became, truly, part of the Warrant-holding 'family'. Years later when Uma Patel and others who were present at the time reflected on the affair they agreed unanimously that it needed a man like Wilson to bang heads together and make the necessary change. He was so patently Scottish, proud and independent while being committed to the cause of unity, that only the most insular and reactionary could possibly believe that he was conniving in a plot which would in any way downgrade or compromise the status of the Windsor and Eton Association.

Nevertheless the Windsor and Eton Royal Warrant Holders do impress one still as being fiercely independent and, as on some occasions in their history, they are worried about the machinations of those they perceive as 'Big Brother'. Recent changes in Royal Household procedures made several of them believe that their Warrants were under unfair threat – just like those of their predecessors in 1849. One of their number, the jeweller Harold Cox & Sons, had recently lost the Warrant. For years they had been responsible for maintaining the Windsor Castle clocks but now new brooms had decreed that it would be more efficient if the Windsor clocks were maintained by the same people who looked after the Buckingham Palace ones. Other Warrant Holders feared they might lose their cherished Warrants for similarly 'unfair' reasons.

At the time of writing, however, the membership remained buoyant with a very similar emphasis on small local companies which has characterised the place since the reign of George IV and before. Douglas Hill, the Secretary, is typical. His Eton High Street chemist's shop doubles up as an off-licence specialising in the elegant Sauvignons blancs and Chardonnays of his native New Zealand. He used to run the Token House, a Windsor gift shop, where he also had the Warrant. Now he does the Royal Family's prescriptions, a highly personal service for which, of course, those members of the Royal Family above pensionable age pay no charge. He also supplies prescriptions for the boys of Eton College and so, for a time, had royal custom there too. In order to retain his Warrant he must demonstrate 'regular supply'. This may seem like an acceptable criterion, but as he says, the fewer royal prescriptions he has to write the happier he is because the healthier they are. 'You don't want to keep them full of medication,' he said, smiling wryly. And yet, perversely, keeping 'them full of medication' is precisely what would guarantee the continuation of his Warrant.

Fred Newman of the Abbey Rose Gardens at Nashdom had a similar problem. He recently supplied 250 'Double Delight' roses for the sunken bed at the Castle. This is right under the royal apartments and the roses are admired and enjoyed by The Queen whenever she is in residence.

'How long will they last?' I asked him.

'Twenty five to thirty years', he replied.

If he were less excellent at his craft the roses might have to be replaced within a year or so but because he is a master of what he does he will have no need to supply more Double Delight for a quarter of a century or so. Which means he won't be able to demonstrate 'continuous supply'.

His situation is made worse because under the old system his dealings were all with the Privy Purse. This meant that his supply made him eligible for the Warrant. After the new reforms, however, he found himself transferred from the Privy Purse to the Crown Estate. Tradesmen supplying to the Crown Estate are not eligible for the Royal Warrant. Nothing about the way in which Fred Newman supplied his roses had changed but the Household system *had*. As a result Newman's Warrant was threatened. Yet he had done nothing wrong and had continued as he always had done. It was the Royal Household that had moved the goalposts.

But one must not exaggerate their discontent, genuine though this is. 'No-one runs down The Royal Family in front of us,' said Fred Newman, summing up the attitude of the entire Windsor and Eton Association.

Uma Patel produced an unusual example of the unique prestige conferred by holding a Warrant. 'When I originally arrived here', he said, 'I was the first brown man on the High Street. And when some people came into the chemist's they didn't even talk to me. They talked to the girls, my assistants, instead. Then I was awarded the Warrant and suddenly the same customers spoke to me.'

Most of the members of Windsor and Eton deal exclusively with the Castle. There are exceptions such as Hypnos beds and Sanderson wallpapers but the most unexpected is Thomas Day whose Warrant is for the supply of automobiles. Day has a company nearby at Fleet, which provides vehicles in bulk for large businesses. Originally his Warrant had nothing at all to do with Eton or Windsor. It all began during his national service in Malaya with the Seaforth Highlanders and although he now supplies working vehicles for the Royal Family on a nation-wide basis his first contract was with Balmoral, where his former Seaforth Commanding Officer had become the Factor. That is why, although he is a proud Windsor and Eton Warrant Holder, most of Day's story belongs in the Balmoral section of this book. You could not describe him as a typical Windsor and Eton Warrant Holder, but then there is no such thing.

After all, they include Warrant Holders who have acquired their Warrants as recently as Day and as long ago as Caley's. They include several gardeners apart from Fred Newman. Indeed, Derek Bishop, owner of William Wood & Son, was able to produce one old advertisement describing his company as 'The Royal Horticulturists'. (They not only supplied British Monarchs from Edward VII onwards, they also served such foreign Royals as the Empress Eugenie, the Grand Duke Michael of Russia

Left: The Queen Mother receiving roses from Fred Newman at the Windsor Rose Show, 1989.
Fred Newman

Below: Handbill for William Wood & Son, 'The Royal Horticulturalists'.
Derek Bishop

and H H the Jam Sahib of Nawanagar.) Mr Bishop was also able to produce an endorsement for the company's special 'Le Fruitier' manure from the head gardener at Windsor long ago, as well as a picture of the founder's grandson showing off his personally created rock garden to the Duke and Duchess of York (later King George VI and Queen Elizabeth) at the Chelsea Flower Show in 1936.

Then there is Ray Parry of Alden & Blackwell the Eton booksellers; John Gamble of Kleenway of Bracknell who sweeps the Castle chimneys; Kathy Pow, the royal manicurist from Chalfont St Peter, Jeremy Piercy of Protim in Hayes, the damp-proofing

and timber treatment company and Roy Graf of Olan Conservation who holds the Warrant for drawing restoration. These Warrant Holders are far too individual and diverse to be described as 'typical', yet they all belong to a tradition which began with the King's builder, Mr Tebbott and his joiner, Mr Jenner, back in the early 1800s. In fact, that tradition must go back in some shape or form to the middle of the eleventh century when William the Conqueror first came to Windsor. It makes the Windsor and Eton Association a unique institution which still, in its heart of hearts, thinks itself superior to the younger upstart headquartered down river at Nº1 Buckingham Place.

The Duke and Duchess of York visit the Chelsea Flower Show in May 1936. Mr Wood (centre) shows
them his rock garden representing an alpine meadow, which was awarded the Silver Cup.
Derek Bishop

Old Balmoral Castle from the back, looking towards the Dee, by William Giles (1801-1870).
Royal Collection Trust

Balmoral was bought by Prince Albert for his wife, Queen Victoria, in 1852. The estate is in mountainous country on the banks of the River Dee some fifty miles from the granite city of Aberdeen. The original castle was considered too small so a new one was built to a design which owed more than a little to the Prince Consort himself – a fact which goes some way to explaining its slightly schloss-like appearance.

It is an isolated spot and throughout its history most of its needs have been serviced by tradesmen in the immediate vicinity, in particular the village of Ballater, and from Aberdeen.

In May 1898 George Thomson, then the Secretary of the Warrant Holders who served Queen Victoria at Balmoral, drew up a document which he introduced with a 'Prefatory Note'. This explained: 'For the information of Younger Members, as well as to record in type the initiation of the Association of Her Majesty's Tradesmen in Aberdeen, and mark some of the outstanding features of its later years, the following notes have, by desire been strung together by the Secretary.'

He strung them together to invaluable effect, for his twenty-five years provides a unique record of the origins of the Aberdeen Association of Royal Warrant Holders that would otherwise be shrouded in the same sort of mystery which, to outsiders at least, surrounds the famous royal home whose life lies at its heart.

George Thomson's notes were written 'Fifty years since Her Majesty first came to Aberdeenshire, and during that long period the Merchants of the City have been the recipients of Royal patronage from all departments of The Queen's Household – little indeed, has gone past the local trader that could by any possibility be obtained in the neighbourhood'.

From the very earliest days it seems that those local tradesmen would dine together to celebrate The Queen's birthday on 24th May. They were not totally exclusive for they also welcomed 'in honour of the occasion, friends and brother tradesmen who have not the good fortune to belong to the charmed circle'. This 'Citizens' Dinner' was held at the Royal Hotel under the 'direction of that most gentlemanly of hosts, Mr David Robertson'. By the time George Thomson came to write his notes both David Robertson and the Royal Hotel had passed away but, he recalled, 'there are those among us still who have lively recollections of the pleasure of these meetings and the many eminent and worthy Aberdonians who gathered round the board in those bygone days to pledge with Highland honours Her Gracious Majesty's health.'

In 1871 the Aberdeen tradesmen decided to formalise their organisation with a set of rules laying down conditions of membership and 'setting forth the objects'. Very broadly these consisted of holding an annual birthday banquet and 'the conservation of its special privileges, and the Royal Arms and Badge of Membership'. These last, in particular, were 'guarded with jealous care'.

The most recognisable name among the early Presidents is that of James Chivas of the eponymous whisky company and for the first twenty-odd years the Secretary was William Jamieson. George Thomson, the writer of the notes, took over in the early nineties and largely thanks to him there was a full-scale reorganisation in 1893. Changes in the 'Management Committee' led to one of the most significant achievements in the Association's history.

This concerned the statue of Queen Victoria on the Town and County Bank corner of St Nicholas

Street. 'It had often been remarked with regret', wrote George Thomson, 'that the rigour of our northern climate was eating into and wasting the beautiful Marble Statue by Brodie, representing Her Majesty in Her earlier years . . The happy thought suggested itself to some of the members that it would be doing a service to the town and an honour to the memory of the sculptor, as well as paying a graceful tribute of respect to Her Majesty, if the statue could be removed indoors to save it from exposure to the weather, and replaced in more lasting material on the same site'.

Not only was this done, thanks to the new and obviously energetic Management Committee, but a new statue of Her Majesty 'in maturer years' was commissioned and duly unveiled on 9th November 1893 (The Prince of Wales's birthday). It was cast in bronze and stands as a prominent and popular landmark in the centre of the city to   this day.

In 1895 the Aberdeen Association 'joined Membership with a similar Institution in London'. This, of course, was the newly incorporated national body, though it is plain that the Aberdonians of the day regarded themselves as at least the equals of their Sassenach counterparts. In the same year a presidential Gold Medal was presented by George Shirras of Shirras, Laing and an Official Seal by David Taylor of Taylor & Henderson.

George Shirras was President during The Queen's Diamond Jubilee celebrations in 1897. His company described themselves as 'Wholesale and Retail Ironmongers and Blacksmiths, Bell Hangers, Brass, Copper and Tinsmiths, Stove and Kitchen Range Manufacturers, Lamp Makers and Oil Merchants, Electric Light and Heating Engineers, Illuminators and Decorators'. The company, dating from 1839, was awarded its Victorian Warrant in 1889 as 'Purveyors of Brazier to Her Majesty'. On the occasion of one royal visit to Aberdeen Shirras, Laing decorated the city and rivalled even the traditional displays at Windsor by putting out 10,000 flags and 7500 lamps and illuminations.

At a 'more than usually brilliant' banquet in 1897 Shirras proposed a loyal toast in proud and resonant words: 'To those of us who have the honour to provide for the needs of Her Majesty's household whilst she is at Her Highland home, she has been pleased to show condescending kindness and consideration which we keenly appreciate and gratefully acknowledge,' he said. This was greeted with cheers and he continued, 'The Queen possesses no more devoted servants or loyal subjects than the Royal Tradesmen of Aberdeen, and our congratulations and humble duty we venture to lay at her feet.' This was met with further cheers but even greater cheering broke out as he concluded by saying, 'That Her Majesty may continue long to rule over us, and may in God's good time exchange an earthly for a heavenly crown is our earnest hope and prayer.'

It was stirring stuff.

A few years later the organisation appointed the first of three generations of McBain to be its Secretary. For ninety-one years the McBains, grandfather, father and son, took it in turns to administer the Association's affairs but, sadly, much of their reign is lost to history. The oldest minute book still extant dates only from the 1950s. The McBains were not Warrant Holders themselves but worked for a family firm of accountants – A. & J. McBain. The present

Left: The statue of Queen Victoria in Aberdeen, by Alexander Brodie in Sicilian marble, inaugurated by The Prince of Wales in 1866. Due to weathering, the statue was relocated in 1888.
Diane Morgan

Below: 1897 Advertisement for Shirras, Laing & Company, "By Special Appointment to The Queen".
Diane Morgan

Right: *St. Nicholas Street, Aberdeen, at the turn of the century and Centenary of the Aberdeen University Library. The 1893 statue of Queen Victoria is clearly visible on the right of the picture.*
Diane Morgan

Below: *The bronze statue of Queen Victoria "at a more mature age", which replaced the original on the corner of St. Nicholas Street and Union Street, Aberdeen and was unveiled on 9th November, 1893.*
Diane Morgan

Secretary, George Alpine, isn't an actual Warrant Holder either, being an Aberdeen lawyer.

While careful to pay tribute to the dedicated service of the McBains, without whom the Association would not be in such excellent shape, Mr Alpine seems, as befits a lawyer, somewhat more concerned about such matters as records and constitutions. He says, for example, that the present unwritten constitution is so unclear that he and the millennium year President, Colin Sutherland of the building contractors Hall & Tawse, are not even clear about who exactly the Aberdeen members are.

In 2000 there was no subscription although there were plans to institute an annual fee of £25, payment of which would unquestionably confer membership. Hitherto there was a school of thought which believed that membership of the national Association automatically involved membership. Others disagreed. And what of Brian Shepherd who regularly went from Aberdeen to Balmoral to cut Prince Philip's hair? He had The Duke's Warrant and yet he did not belong to the national Association. Was he, de facto, a member of the Aberdeen Association? And there were some Warrant Holders such as 'Scottish Hydro' who supplied Balmoral but belonged to the Edinburgh and not the Aberdeen Association. It could be quite confusing, though the position should become clearer with a written constitution and the charging of an annual subscription. The situation was oddly reminiscent of that in London almost a century earlier when only half the Warrant Holders of the time were members of the Association.

Balmoral tends to be the focus for the Aberdeen Association but fifteen or so members hold The Queen Mother's Warrant and supply her needs at the Castle of Mey, where the Factor is Martin Leslie who for some years fulfilled the same role at Balmoral. The Factor is roughly the equivalent of the English land agent. He is the boss and

but when Sir Richard George of Weetabix was President of the national Association he visited Balmoral by helicopter and then took Martin Leslie on up to Caithness, where he hosted a memorable lunch for the local Warrant Holders. A few years later the new Secretary, Christopher Pickup, visited the area with Christopher Rowe of Findlater, Mackie, Todd who was then President. This time Her Majesty The Queen Mother was in residence, and entertained them and the local Warrant Holders at the Castle.

although, naturally, he is responsible to the owner, he exercises considerable authority on his own account.

Martin Leslie started to look after The Queen Mother's Castle of Mey Estate at the beginning of 1975. When he was translated to Balmoral in June 1979 he was able to continue managing the Castle and when he retired from Balmoral he was 'even more fortunate' in being able to go on looking after the estate from his home on the Isle of Skye. In 1996 Her Majesty handed the Castle of Mey Estates over to a Trust and now leases the Castle from the Trust. This means that the Royal Warrants regarding the Castle will remain the same for her lifetime. Because Martin Leslie is The Queen Mother's Factor, and also Factor to the Trust, he says, 'I sometimes have to negotiate with myself.'

The handful of Warrant Holders serving the Castle of Mey are far away from their colleagues – two are over the water on Orkney – but despite occasional suggestions of forming their own local Association it has always been felt that there are too few to justify it. Visits from London have been few and far between

When an estate is as far away from headquarters as Balmoral and the Castle of Mey are from Buckingham Palace and Clarence House then the man on the spot obviously has a greater level of autonomy than someone who operates nearer home.

An example of this is the Warrant first issued to Tom Day during the 'factorship' of Colonel McHardy who came to Balmoral in 1965 and, though long retired, still lives on the banks of the Dee just a few miles from his former bailliwick. When he arrived the Colonel found that three vans needed replacing. He tried locally but the responses did not satisfy him, so he telephoned 'Happy' Day who had served under him as a Corporal in the Seaforth Highlanders in Malaya. Day was now running a garage down south near Camberley and said he could deliver the vans, in whatever colours the Colonel wanted, on the following Tuesday. He and two friends drove the vehicles all the way to Scotland, and a professional relationship was born. From this small beginning Day, who as we have seen is a member of the Windsor and Eton Association, has become the major provider of cars for the royal fleet.

'The Royal Warrant means a hell of a lot,' says the Colonel, 'and I was very, very particular when I was at Balmoral. I never changed any of the suppliers if they held the Royal Warrant unless there was a very strong reason to do so.'

Of course, the correct procedures had to be followed, just as they have to be followed today by the present Factor, Peter Ord, who moved to Deeside after a successful spell as Factor at The Queen Mother's ancestral home, Glamis Castle. Sometimes, however, sound common sense and a loyalty which is best described as a true family feeling can override or at least reinterpret the rules.

For example, Robert Pringle runs the garage in Ballater and holds three Warrants. He says that when the Royal Family are in residence he deals with all of them on a regular almost daily basis. It is nearly as if he were part of the household staff himself and he is one of the rare Warrant Holders who is always asked to the 'Ghillies' Ball' – the Deeside equivalent of the staff party. Some years ago his father, who held the Warrants before him, died sadly young. As the rules insist, Robert Pringle accordingly removed his Coats of Arms. Almost immediately 'a certain person' (all Warrant Holders are discreet but the Ballater tradesmen especially so) phoned and asked him why he had taken down the Arms. When he explained, he was told to put them straight back up. Within days rather than the usual months Pringle Junior was form-

Below: *Robert Pringle greets The Queen Mother as he prepares to leave on the 'Motability Land Rover' challenge, with an AA Patrolman and two Policemen, to raise money for disabled drivers.*
Robert Pringle

ally granted the Warrants previously held by his father. It is a reminder that whatever regulations may be in force it is the Royal Grantor who always has the last word and also that sometimes conspicuous loyalty and service are repaid in kind whatever the fine print may say.

Peter Ord employs about fifty people on the 50,000-acre estate. He and his heads of department have a particularly close relationship with the tradesmen and shopkeepers in Ballater. The outward manifestation of this bond comes in the form of the cluster of Royal Coats of Arms on the shopfronts of Sheridan the butchers, Chalmers (formerly Leith's) the bakers, Davidson's the chemist (who bought the business from Ian Murray, now an enthusiastic and respected local ghillie), Pringle the motor engineer, Cassie the television shop, and George Strachan, the general merchant.

'Strachan's', said Colonel McHardy, 'was the sort of place you could go in and say that you needed ninety-six quails' eggs that afternoon, and he'd provide them. It's as if London's St James's Street had been airlifted to the Highlands and set down in the middle of Deeside.' Ballater may be only a village but it boasts enough Royal Warrants to make most cities envious. Those who live there can shop for all the necessities of life at premises which are 'By Appointment'.

Some of the Aberdeen Warrant Holders, such as Harry Jamieson who repairs The Prince of Wales's fishing rods (he'd never willingly buy a new rod, least of all a carbon fibre one), live in isolated spots away from their fellows. Another local but isolated one man band is Andrew Lawson Johnston, the self-taught engraver (he began with a second-hand dentist's drill), who holds Warrants for supplying exquisite pieces of decorative glassware.

But the majority of those who are not in or around Ballater are natives of Aberdeen. Some of these have a very close Balmoral-based relationship with the Grantors. Archibald's, the cabinet makers and upholsterers, started in the centre of Aberdeen and first came to royal attention when they were commissioned to work on Birkhall, the other big house on the Balmoral Estate when Queen Elizabeth The Queen Mother took it over in the 1950s. 'My father was up there constantly,' says Alan Archibald, now retired from the company and a cousin of the present grantee, Michael. 'After Birkhall he was called in to do new loose covers at Balmoral.' These were followed by carpets and curtains too. 'It certainly wasn't a great spending spree,' he says. 'It's *NOT* a luxurious place. Her Majesty liked things the way they were. I remember father coming back once and saying that she didn't want felt under the carpets – she wanted them laid hard to the floor as they had been in Queen Victoria's day.' Colonel McHardy recalls this incident. He remembers The Queen looking at the carpets and saying they seemed 'spongy'. In any event the underlay came out.

'In those days we did a lot of work with the Castle,' says Archibald. 'Now it's on a minor scale. The buying pattern seems to have changed. We're ready to do anything but we seem to get asked less often than in the past . . .' This, of course, is a reflection of a growing tendency towards centralised purchasing and a general rationalisation of the way in which overall Household affairs are conducted. It affects some members of all the local Associations and a number of smaller companies throughout Britain.

The highlight of the Aberdeen Association's year used to be the luncheon which followed the Annual General Meeting. This was held in Trinity Hall, home of the 'Seven Incorporated Trades of Aberdeen'. The trades include such ancient crafts as the wrights and coopers, the weavers and, more unusually, the 'hammermen' and their headquarters is now in a 1960s building conveniently opposite Archibald's showrooms. The Seven Incorporated Trades of Aberdeen are unique in that members still have to be proficient in their trade and must provide evidence to prove it. To be a hammerman – a joiner or carpenter in modern parlance – you must submit a piece of furniture as an entry requirement.

In recent years the lunches have changed to dinners and these have been enlivened by after-dinner entertainments, an idea keenly promoted by the energetic former national President, Graeme Wilson of William Wilson & Sons, suppliers of plumbing, electrical and building materials to The Queen. Wilson's Warrant is another which dates back to the days of Colonel McHardy. Indeed, he says that he knew little or nothing about the Warrant until one day when the Colonel was in his premises making a small purchase – it could have been something as mundane as nails

Below left: The main entrance to Trinity Hall, repaired and enhanced in 1999. Taken from the Seven Incorporated Trades' Millennium Brochure.
Deacon Convenor, Trinity Hall

Below: Flags displaying the Seven Incorporated Trades outside Trinity Hall. Hammermen are those using hammers in their trade (armourers, gold and silversmiths, blacksmiths etc.); Wrights are those using common tools (wheelwrights, joiners, cartwrights etc.); and Fleshers are butchers and slaughtermen.
Deacon Convenor, Trinity Hall

or screws – when he asked in an offhand way if Wilson had ever thought of applying for a Royal Warrant. He hadn't but he did and the award followed. Had it been the other way round it might not have been so easy. The Factor and his senior staff are very aware that some companies are far too 'pushy' when it comes to the Warrant. Undue eagerness in this respect is quickly recognised. It doesn't pay to look too assertive.

In the 1960s Wilson asked if The Queen might come to a cocktail party but was refused. Instead, Her Majesty suggested that the Warrant Holders might like to come to her instead. And they did. Perhaps the most regular party giver has been Gordon Baxter, the larger-than-life proprietor of the famous foodstuff producers. A keen fisherman, he and his wife Ena have long offered generous hospitality to angling Warrant Holders at their home on the banks of the River Spey.

In 1992 when Mark Fleming, who holds the Warrant for timber products, was President he was impressed by the social activities organised by other local Associations. He accordingly persuaded his successor, Michael Archibald, to organise a barbecue on the lawns at Balmoral. Michael Sheridan, the Ballater butcher, provided the chops and sausages. Mr Sheridan was the first President of the Association to come from Ballater – a distinction in which he takes considerable pride. Another 'first' was recorded on 5th November 1997 when Ian Murray, then the Ballater chemist, managed to get Warrant Holders on board the Royal Yacht *Britannia* just before she was decommissioned after her last voyage to Scotland. The party's success was enhanced when it transpired that The Princess Royal was on board preparing for an evening engagement in the city. The assembled company were delighted when The Princess emerged from her room in full evening dress and spent half an hour happily chatting to them.

Another event which, though only started in 1999, has become an instant tradition is the

Association's participation at the world-famous Braemar Gathering. That first year Calor Gas provided a tent on a site negotiated with the Braemar Royal Highland Society by the Hon. Secretary George Alpine. In the first year it was sandwiches and coffee and soft drinks but in the second year President Colin Sutherland laid on some much appreciated whisky. The Braemar event has not only attracted Warrant-holding visitors from all over the United Kingdom but also seduced such usually isolated Warrant Holders as the fishing-rod manufacturer, Harry Jamieson. Like other Scottish Warrant Holders Jamieson works on his own even though he cares for such celebrities as Billy Connolly and Greg Norman as well as his Grantor, The Prince of Wales. As a one man band he finds it difficult to take a day off but he makes an exception for the Braemar Gathering which

is not only unique but also virtually on his doorstep. So the first Saturday of September is now a fixed date in the Association's calendar and there is the added bonus that at the Braemar Gathering you can be sure that Royalty are always present.

In 2000 Colin Sutherland handed over an impressive Royal Warrant Holders' cabinet made by his firm, Hall & Tawse. This cleverly incorporates many of the panelling and design features which can be found in the Castle itself, and was presented at a reception in the Carriage Hall at Balmoral in May 2000. It is now on display whenever the Castle is open to the public and provides a detailed explanation of Royal Warrants on Deeside as well as the story of the Queen Elizabeth Scholarship Trust.

The Factor, Peter Ord, was able to report: 'Unbeknown to all those who accepted an invitation to attend, I had been able to obtain Queen Elizabeth The Queen Mother's agreement to be present, and it came as a great surprise to everyone when she suddenly turned up fifteen minutes into the reception. As you can imagine, this made the whole party go with a swing, and Queen Elizabeth spent about forty minutes chatting to everyone before heading back to Birkhall for dinner.'

Left: *Passing the Royal Pavilion at the Braemar Games, 2000.* Jim Henderson, AMPA, ARPS

Below: *Queen Elizabeth The Queen Mother, accompanied by Peter Ord, inspects the Warrant Holders' cabinet in the Carriage Hall, Balmoral, in May 2000. The Aberdeen Association President, Colin Sutherland stands behind Her Majesty, with George Alpine on the right.* George Alpine/ Aberdeen Association

Like so much of what happens in and around Balmoral, this was very much a family occasion and it is a tribute to the warmth of the relationship between the monarchy and its Deeside and Aberdonian grantees that in their modest way they too feel that they are a genuine and valued part of a real extended family. As one of the senior Balmoral staff put it, 'With the average company I'm afraid the person on the counter often couldn't care less, but with a Warrant Holder it's different. You have a real name and a real person to go to and you can be sure that you'll be well served.'

Print of the Royal Yacht Britannia, presented to members of the Aberdeen Association commemorating their reception held on board while the yacht was docked in Aberdeen Harbour, 5th November 1997.
Aberdeen Association

The Aberdeen Association of Royal Warrant Holders

This print commemorates the reception held on board Her Majesty's Yacht Britannia in Aberdeen harbour on Wednesday 5th November 1997 attended by members of the Aberdeen Association of Royal Warrant Holders.

PRESIDENT

HON. SECRETARY

The Palace of Holyroodhouse in 1850, by James Duffield Harding (1797-1863).
The Royal Collection Trust

For the first century of its existence the Edinburgh Association described its members not as 'Warrant Holders' but as 'Tradesmen'. This no-messing-around appellation did not always find favour with Warrant-holding Scots and on several well-documented occasions companies refused to take up membership because they considered themselves too grand to be dismissed as mere 'trade'. After a hundred years as Tradesmen, however, at the instigation of a fishmonger President and a 'purveyor of cleaning materials' who was his number two, the Edinburghers fell into line with their colleagues and, with singularly little fuss and no visible dissent, became 'Warrant Holders' like everyone else.

It seemed a small matter but in private, a few years later, there were Edinburgh Royal Tradesmen who regretted the change. It had given them a distinctive character and it was an expression of an aspect of the Scottish character in which they took pride: calling a spade a spade.

Only one Warrant-holding company survives from the eight who convened the first meeting of the Edinburgh Association, which was held on 8th May 1894 in Dowell's Rooms in the city centre. The notice for the meeting took the form of a signed advertisement in the *Scotsman* and the sole surviving signatory is James Gray & Son, the ironmongers. Gray's still occupy their original site in the city's elegant George Street in the heart of the Georgian 'new town' parallel to Princes Street. Although the company is a large traditional ironmongers their Warrant is for the supply of cleaning materials to Holyroodhouse.

For the first hundred years of their existence Gray's was an eponymous family business but by the time the Edinburgh

Association was founded the Grays had been vanquished and their place taken by the Douglases. The Douglases have played a prominent part in the history of the Association, first in the person of Councillor Robert A. Douglas, the founding Secretary and Treasurer from 1894 until his death in 1912, and subsequently in the redoubtable Mr R. E. Douglas, whom the minute books show as becoming 'Major Douglas' on his election to Vice-President in 1930. Major Douglas he remained, throughout his formidable twenty-two year presidency. His son Bill, who died tragically young, was also Edinburgh President and graduated from that office to become the national President in 1974.

There were 'about twenty Edinburgh Tradesmen holding appointments to The Queen and other members of the Royal Family' at the inaugural meeting. Early on in the history of the Edinburgh Association one of the members remarked tartly that he wanted Edinburgh to do better than other such organisations, which were, in his opinion, 'little more than a luncheon club'.

By no means all those eligible actually joined the infant Association. Whytock & Reid, the furnishing company, who later provided two Presidents in the

Right: The Duchess of York releases carrier pigeons at Murrayfield during the Jubilee Juvenile Organisations Display on 11th May, 1935. She is accompanied by (left to right), The Duke of York, the Lord Provost, the Rt., Hon. Louis S. Gumley, and Major R.E. Douglas, President of the Edinburgh Association from 1931-1953.
Brian Smellie

The English (left), and Scottish Royal Coats of Arms

1980s and '90s, had held the Warrant since 1838 – only a year after the accession of Queen Victoria – but they were not among the founding fathers. Nor was the department store, Jenners, another famous Edinburgh name whose grantee, Robert Douglas Miller, was President from 1989 to 1991. But Jenners, perhaps surprisingly, were not granted the Warrant until 1923.

Like Windsor, Edinburgh met for meals, which were an important part of such organisations' lives whatever dissenting voices wished otherwise. The first luncheon was held at the now defunct Dowell's Rooms and over the years a number of different venues were tried – some of them rather more successful than others. There seem to have been regular 'business meetings' in addition to the Annual General Meeting and as early as 1897 an outing was arranged. This was to Melrose and the cost was twenty shillings a head. Unfortunately the jaunt had to be cancelled. Perhaps it was too expensive.

From time to time the Association became involved in policing the Warrant, much as London did on a national scale. There was, for instance, a case involving the National Assurance Company (Standard Life) who misused the Royal Coat of Arms in an advertisement in the *Scotsman* in 1950. Another recurring irritant was the use of the English as opposed to Scottish Royal Coat of Arms. In the sixties the Lord Lyon King at Arms was prompted to order: 'Firms ought to   be using the United Kingdom-Scottish version with the lion rampant in the first and fourth quarters and the unicorn on the dexter side. Unfortunately there are a number who insist on putting up or flying the English version. This is recognised by the fact that the lions in the first and fourth quarters are couchant.'

Erring members were duly admonished.

Over the years, however, the Edinburgh Tradesmen settled into a comfortable and quiet routine much like that which they affected to despise at Windsor. The list of Presidents reflects the dynastic family quality of the membership. The Reids and the Douglases were not the only families to have provided two generations of Presidents. Others include the Kinloch Andersons, kilt makers, and the Inches, jewellers. The former are still very much part of the contemporary Edinburgh scene, although the latter are now no longer associated with their old company, Hamilton & Inches, where Julia Ogilvie is the grantee.

In 1935 the Edinburgh Association marked King George V's Jubilee by presenting him with a 126 piece setting of silver cutlery for the Palace of Holyroodhouse. Unfortunately the Association's reach exceeded its grasp and despite the Secretary's suggestion that members should contribute a minimum ten guineas each to pay for the gift, the money raised fell well short of the required sum. Although the fact is not recorded in the official records, the embarrassing shortfall was made good by the generosity of Langs Biscuits.

The annual lunch or dinner was always the high

Right: *Le Comte Alain de Vogüé visiting Martin & Frost, interior furnishers, in Edinburgh during his year as national President in 1985. de Vogüé stands centre right of the picture, flanked by Robert Martin, the grantee (centre left) and Lowrie Sleigh, the Edinburgh President (right). The national Secretary, Commander Faulkner, stands on the left of the picture.*
Joy Sleigh

Below: *The Rossleigh Showroom, in Annandale Street, Edinburgh, decked out for the 1953 Coronation.*
William Sleigh

spot of the year. The minute books of the earlier years reveal comparatively little about them except for the changing venues, though occasionally one catches a whiff of controversy hidden between the lines.

On one occasion, for instance, the habitual invitation to the Lord Provost was declined. As a result the Association decided not to drink the usual toast to the city and the Secretary was instructed to send a formal letter to the Lord Provost regretting his absence. Major Douglas of Gray's, who served as President from 1934 to 1956, was said to covet the post of Lord Provost but only got as far as Deputy. He was alleged to be too short for the top job! On another occasion the musical programme was cancelled due to financial constraints. This caused one member to suggest that 'the press might be asked to send a reporter who could play the piano'. One can't help feeling that there was more to this remark than meets the eye.

Attendance at the Association's regular luncheons and dinners sometimes ebbed but there was always a hard core of regulars. This included stalwarts such as David Barnes of Dobbies, President from 1991 to 1993 and the late Lowrie Sleigh LVO, President from 1984 to 1986 and an office holder since 1968. Lowrie Sleigh's father, Sir William, succeeded Major Douglas as Treasurer in 1930 and was a Vice-President until his death in 1945. The Sleighs used to have a motor company called Rossleigh but when this was taken over Lowrie established his own private car hire business. So keen was Lowrie that he had, once, to be reprimanded for displaying too many Royal Warrants. His son has succeeded him as Managing Director and, like his father and grandfather before him, is an Edinburgh Warrant Holder. Other regular lunchers and diners have included the Kinloch Andersons, the Reids, the Douglas Millers, the Campbells, Bohdan Nastiuk, who distributes high-class food, especially cheese from his business at Ninemileburn in partnership with his wife Natalia, Jim Mackie of Wilson's the piano and harpsichord tuners and restorers, and Brian Smellie of Gray's .

Apart from formal meals such as the memorable seventy-fifth anniversary dinner in 1969,

attended by over a hundred guests, there were additional high spots such as a cocktail party in 1970 which was attended by The Queen, The Prince of Wales and The Princess Royal. Both these occurred during Bill Douglas's presidency.

In 1992, after a referendum on the matter, it was agreed by a vote of 14 to 7 to open the annual dinner to ladies, a move which proved a great success. Another innovation was the admission of national firms with business in the Edinburgh area. These companies included Justerini & Brooks, Calor Gas, Allied Domecq and Corney & Barrow.

Change accelerated in 1993 when Iain Campbell became President. The twenty-three members who attended the AGM the following year agreed that for the first time an annual fee should be introduced to offset expenses. This was set at £25. One of the high spots of Campbell's term of office was a centenary reception in the city's beautiful Signet Library. This was attended, appropriately enough, by His Royal Highness The Duke of Edinburgh.

'I was very keen,' admits Campbell, 'and our business was much smaller then so I could devote time to the organisation. But really it was a whole group of us who chivvied things along.' Another progressive was Brian Smellie who bought James Gray & Sons from the Douglases and succeeded Campbell as President. The two formed a strong reforming team when, after being President, Campbell volunteered to take on the secretaryship from the lawyer, Robin Blair, who had served with distinction for a quarter of a century.

Campbell, Smellie and their like-minded associates introduced a number of changes. One of them was the name. Another was the introduction of a proper sit-down lunch at the New Club following the Annual General Meeting. When the national President came up from London they rang round members to arrange informal visits to local factories and offices not only in the Edinburgh area but further afield as well.

Appropriately enough in the country where the game began, golf began to feature on the Royal Warrant calendar and an annual Hugh Faulkner Putter competition was inaugurated at Bruntsfield in honour of the recently retired national Secretary who had moved to a country house near Crichton, half an hour's drive to the south of the links. After an inaugural Edinburgh versus South game at Muirfield in 1999, Morris Miller of John Dewar & Sons presented the 'Dewar Quaich', which is to be the prize in future years.

Even the outings, so abortively inaugurated with the cancelled trip to Melrose in 1897, were reinstated. In 1999 President Andrew Dewar-Durie and his wife hosted a party at the Laphroaig distillery on Islay (the only single malt to be honoured with a Royal Warrant) complete with the Laphroaig pipe band. The following year Allied Domecq laid on an even more spectacular visit to Jerez. Leiutenant-Colonel David Anderson, the Holyroodhouse superintendent, was an honoured guest on several of these occasions and was soon regarded by many members as 'one of us'. It was useful for both sides to know whom they were dealing with if problems arose involving the Royal Family and the Warrant Holders.

Another coup was finding an energetic Secretary to succeed Iain Campbell whose burgeoning fish business was becoming too time-consuming to allow him to spend enough time on the Association's affairs.

Left: *Hugh Faulkner (right), presents the Faulkner Putter to the 2000 winner, Iain Campbell, at Bruntsfield.* Willie Munro

This was Willie Munro, a former building society boss, who turned out to be as energetic and enthusiastic as any Warrant Holder.

In 2000 the AGM was held outside Edinburgh for the first time, the venue being President Andrew Dewar-Durie's favourite Western Club in Glasgow. This break with tradition reflected the fact that only sixteen of the fifty-two members were actually based in Edinburgh itself. After one or two experiments such as the Merchants' Hall when Douglas Kinloch Anderson was the Master there the dinner seems to have settled at the chic Caledonian Hotel ('That was a venue which sent out a message,' says one prominent member) and the 2000 dinner drew an attendance of 130 members and guests.

Edinburgh is now a capital city with a Royal Palace at its hub which is next to the national parliament. At times in the past Holyroodhouse, very much the focus for the city's Warrant Holders, seemed to attract relatively few visits from the Grantors but now members of the Royal Family are using the Palace with increasing frequency. Another of the Royal Family's favourite homes, the Royal Yacht *Britannia*, is now moored at Leith but she, of course, has become a museum and conference centre, her royal days sadly gone. However, after the annual dinner of 1998, David Reid of Whytock & Reid, who had assisted in the yacht's refurbishment when she arrived in Leith, was able to arrange a tour of the ship for the visiting President.

Whatever the future holds, the Edinburgh Association seems to be increasingly active. Iain Campbell, one of those who have contributed to its high profile, describes the perfect display of a Royal Warrant as being 'tastefully visible' and this seems to be the condition to which Edinburgh now aspires.

It should not be thought, however, that the Association takes itself too seriously. A sense of fun is important to the new regime and a recurring claim is that its proceedings have been 'loosened up'. They seem to exhibit an endearing collective sense of self-deprecation. David Reid tells one story which is a good example of this. When his father, the legendary Campbell Reid, was President the guest of honour was Lord Home of the Hirsel. Another distinguished presence was the Chief Constable of West Lothian. Unfortunately, however, Campbell and his committee had not realised that many of the waiters on duty at the Archers' Hall that night were moonlighting members of the Chief Constable's own force. Off-duty policemen are not allowed to take on paid employment, so when they realised that their boss was dining with the Warrant Holders they simply failed to show. Service that evening was the slowest experienced by the Edinburgh Royal Tradesmen in over a hundred years!

Sandringham House painted by the Prince of Wales in 1991.
The Prince of Wales

The Sandringham Association was founded in 1979. This makes it very much the junior partner among the local Associations, but in a relatively short period this stripling branch has, in terms of numbers, overtaken its more venerable siblings so that by the turn of the century membership stood at no less than 160 members.

The Sandringham 'Warrantdom' (a word yet to appear in the Oxford Dictionary but minted by the founding Secretary, John Storrs, on page 163 of the immaculate original minute book) was modelled on the form already established by Aberdeen, Edinburgh and Windsor, although its proximity to the Royal Family's East Anglian country home obviously gave it certain unique features.

The original conception was that of Sir Julian Loyd, the Sandringham Land Agent from 1964 to 1991. At the 1978 Grosvenor House banquet he was sitting at the top table and suddenly realised that he recognised none of the people with whom he dealt on a day-to-day basis in Norfolk. When he consulted his programme he found that only three of the Sandringham Warrant Holders were represented. Moreover these three were all represented by the grantees from Head Office. Sir Julian did not know any of them, because he was used to dealing with their local people.

The more he thought about it the more he saw that those who serviced Sandringham tended to be small shopkeepers, specialist craftsmen or local representatives, all of them people of relatively modest means who could not afford the price of travel and accommodation, much less the hire of white tie and tails, which were a necessary part of the great Grosvenor House banquet.

After consultations with the then President, Sir Nevil Macready, an informal pub lunch was arranged at the Black Horse in Castle Rising. The participants were the Association Secretary, Colonel Bill Keown-Boyd, former President Sam Twining and Julian Loyd himself. The three of them agreed that there was a good case for forming a Sandringham Association, and representations were then made to the new national President, John Riddell-Webster, who in turn approached the Lord Chamberlain, Lord ('Chips') Maclean, and the Keeper of the Privy Purse, Sir Rennie Maudslay. It was unanimously agreed that a Sandringham Association should be formed forthwith.

Colonel Keown-Boyd had retired by now but the new Secretary, Commander Hugh Faulkner, came down to King's Lynn to look round the Berol ballpoint pen factory, where he met John Storrs and suggested to him that he might like to be the Association's first Hon Secretary.

The following month Hugh Faulkner wrote to Julian Loyd proposing Bill Lusher as the founding President. Lusher's family firm of building contractors had carried out the extensive alterations to Sandringham House in 1973 and were now regularly involved in the annual maintenance of the Sandringham fabric. The Hon. Secretary was confirmed as John Storrs of Berol, and the Chaplain was the Rt Revd. Aubrey Aitken, Bishop of Lynn. On 20th June Storrs and Lusher met at the Black Horse, Castle Rising, to discuss details. They had never met before and recognised each other from their self-descriptions

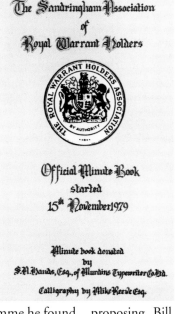

Right: *Title page of the 'immaculate' original minute book of the Sandringham Association.*
Frank Morris/ SARWH

Bottom right: *John Storrs (right), with Pippa Dutton at the Emmanuel Dinner, 1997.*
RWHA Archive

– 'small rotund and bearded' for Storrs, 'tall, debonair and wearing yellow socks' for Lusher. From that moment the Sandringham Association has never looked back. It has become a tradition that Bill Lusher wears yellow socks at every Council meeting.

After an informal buffet reception on 14th November 1979 it was agreed that the first formal event should be held the following year. On 21st March President Lusher was formally installed at a reception for 150 guests including the Lord Chamberlain and the Keeper of the Privy Purse in the Sandringham ballroom – the first time the room had ever been used for a private function. The Queen sent a personal message wishing the Association 'a lively and successful future'. For more than twenty years her wish has been coming true.

In the beginning Lusher and Storrs identified sixty-nine potential members. These were the names on a list given to them by Julian Loyd at a meeting at the estate office in York Cottage. All were approached and forty joined. The qualifications were straightforward. Members had already to hold the Royal Warrant but they could either be local companies or the local branches of national companies. The defining factor was that they had to serve 'The Sandringham Estate, Sandringham House, the Home Farm or the Stud'. The aim of the branch – unlike that of the Association as a whole – was entirely social, although as John Storrs himself remarks 'a tremendous amount of business is conducted' on the occasions when members get together.

The original membership qualifications have now been broadened so that any East Anglian Warrant Holder may belong irrespective of whether or not they supply Sandringham. The family atmosphere survives, however. William Lusher's successor, Colonel D. K. M. Gilbert DSO, of the timber treatment specialists, Protim Services is quoted in the Association's minutes as saying that he wanted to maintain the 'informal, warm and friendly atmosphere' originally created by the founders. The words 'informal', 'friendly' and 'family' occur again and again in the Association's minute books. In 1984 the Hon. Secretary even wrote an 'encouraging letter' to lax attenders who, in the words of the Committee, should not be 'cast out of the fold'.

This friendly family approach did not preclude an element of mutual self-help. As early as 1982, for instance, William Lusher congratulated May & Baker on winning the Queen's Award for Industry, adding that award-winning members such as this would, in future, be able to 'offer advice and help to those who were striving to achieve a similar honour'. A decade later the minutes reveal that members had got into the habit of visiting each other's offices. As so often in the affairs of the Sandringham Association, these visits seem to have been a judicious mixture of business and pleasure, though the Secretary commented wryly that 'it is always relaxing to enjoy other people's problems'.

The Sandringham year has come to be built round three principal events: the annual President's reception in April; the magnificent Sandringham Flower Show in July and the Annual General Meeting and luncheon in October.

The President's weekends are a close reflection of the Sandringham family style. On the Saturday evening there is a buffet reception at which members are able to indulge in a traditional Norfolk-style 'mardle'. The evening always concluded with another Norfolk tradition – the serving of marshmallows and hot chocolate, a combination which is believed by

on
Friday 21 March 1980
at
Sandringham House

by gracious permission of
Her Majesty The Queen

Left: *Bill Lusher, left, founder President of the Sandringham Association, is greeted by the national President, John Riddell Webster, at the inaugural ceremony on 21st March 1980.*
Bill Lusher

Below: *Dinner programme for the inauguration of the Sandringham Royal Warrant Holders Association.*
John Storrs/SARWH Archive

the natives to have formidable aphrodisiac properties.

The Presidents of all the other local Associations are invited – a Sandringham innovation which has now been copied by everyone else. Locations have varied. In the initial year the venue was the Sandringham ballroom and this has been repeated on four subsequent occasions. In 1994 the Association was the first organisation to use the new Sandringham Visitors' Centre. For the tenth anniversary the Association met in the officers mess at RAF Marham where The Queen's Private Secretary, Sir William Heseltine, was guest of honour.

Four times the Association has been invited to Holkham Hall, the ancestral home of the Earls of Leicester. On the fourth of these visits, in 1997, the Earl and Countess had engagements elsewhere but returned unexpectedly early. Because of this Jonathan Bowman, that year's President, receiving guests with his wife Janet at the top of the impressive staircase, found himself in the acutely embarrassing position of welcoming the Leicesters into their own house.

On the following Sunday there is a religious service in the parish church where so many members of the Royal Family have worshipped over the years. The President traditionally reads a lesson and holders of the office always confess to a considerable sense of trepidation when they do so. For years Bishop Aitken of Lynn officiated and joined members for a glass of sherry in the rectory afterwards.

In 1998 the Sandringham President was a Lincolnshire man, Geoffrey Bottom of Witham Oil & Paint, and the event was held in Lincoln with the 'Lincolnshire Poacher' stirringly rendered in the Judges' Lodgings, matins in the cathedral and lunch in the Masonic Rooms. This prompted a certain unease among traditionally minded Norfolk members and in millennium year President Mark Lusher, son of Bill the founding President, responded to the Lincolnshire challenge by laying on the Norwich Assembly Rooms and morning service in Norwich

Cathedral. In 2001 however, members ventured abroad again, this time to Nottingham where the President, Alec McKee lured them to his John Deere headquarters, with promises of rides on his magnificent fleet of agricultural and horticultural machinery.

For many years the autumn AGM was held at Jesus College Cambridge, with an exceptional deviation during the national presidency of Alan Britten of Mobil, a Sandringham member, who staged a lavish dinner at his old college, Emmanuel, prior to the AGM at Jesus. Latterly, however, the meeting has moved to the Guildhall of the Holy Trinity in King's Lynn.

But the best-loved of all events in the Sandringham calendar is the 120-year-old annual Flower Show. Since 1982 the Association has had its own spectacular marquee at which the products of members, described by John Storrs as 'luscious, delectable and winsome wares', are on sale in aid of charity. This was originally the idea of Colonel Gilbert and the Association regularly plays host to about 250 guests. Since 1995 the marquee has been provided by the good offices of Jim Wilson and the generosity of Calor Gas, and guarded by the imposing figure of Jim Dowdell, formerly of Securicor.

Here the show's patron, Queen Elizabeth The Queen Mother, accompanied by her grandson, The Prince of Wales, invariably stops to inspect the general merchandise and raffle prizes provided by members of the Association.

There is always a cricket match on Flower Show day. By tradition the match, played on the picture-postcard ground beyond the church, is between a Warrant Holders' team and the Sandringham village side. There is even a cup – the Aubrey Aitken Memorial Trophy – presented by Donovan Fry as a memorial to the bishop in 1986.

Before that, Sandringham Cricket Club had hosted the final of a local knock-out cup on Flower Show day. After that lapsed there was a regular fixture against West Norfolk but in 1986 Jeff Hazel of Sandringham CC called in to the Warrant Holders' marquee and formally challenged John Storrs to a match the following year. From the first, the Warrant Holders' XI has been enthusiastically led by Mark Lusher, son of founding President Bill. He has played every year except when he was prevented from doing so by his duties as President or President Elect. It was sad that one of his absences coincided with a famous Warrant-holding victory in the millennium match, and ironic too, for over the years he has been consistently the best cricketer on the team. Mark Lusher confesses that he has sometimes been unpleased by the uncricketing sentiments of some members. Even

Left: The President, Adam Brett-Smith, with Alec McKee and members of the Sandringham Association at John Deere, in April 2001.
SARWH Archive

Below: Annie Wycherley receiving her farewell presentation from Jonathan Bowmans (left), President of SARWH, at the 1997 Sandringham Flower Show. Left is Jill Hurdman and behind Wycherley are Fred Newman (Windsor) and David Reid (Edinburgh).
RWHA Archive

Above: *Mark Lusher (right) shakes hands with Mike Hazel (brother of the match instigator) before the 1988 Cricket Match. Park House is in the background.*
Mark Lusher

Right: *Nick Copeman, then Vice President of SARWH handing a second basket of strawberries to The Prince of Wales in 1994.*
Nick Copeman

John Storrs reported in year ten that the Warrant Holders' team had lost nineteen times. In fact, after the 2000 game the record was 'won 4, lost 8 and rained off 2'.

Despite a healthy rivalry between the two sides the match is always played in a thoroughly friendly spirit even when, in succeeding years, both teams imported 'ringers' from the Norfolk County side. The friendly atmosphere becomes even more convivial as a result of the barrel of beer presented every year by Donovan Fry. This is delivered before the start of play and set up in the pavilion among the trees within sight of Park House in order to allow it plenty of time to settle. Any beer left unconsumed is finished off by the teams the following weekend.

But the best moment of the day comes when Her Majesty visits the marquee and is presented with strawberries provided by John McCarthy of D. & F. McCarthy Ltd. This is the centre piece of an incomparably friendly and informal family occasion. Every year the President offers the strawberries and every year The Queen Mother graciously accepts them. In millennium year, two weeks before her hundredth birthday, Her Majesty arrived in her golf buggy, smiling as radiantly as ever, and found President Mark Lusher (absenting himself from the cricket team!) standing on the royal blue carpet with his wife Sarah and their two children, Kim and Emma.

As usual, he offered strawberries, but this time it was strawberries with a difference. John McCarthy had counted out exactly a hundred and arranged them in three separate baskets so that they spelled out the numbers 'one zero zero'.

Those exquisitely maintained Sandringham Minute Books of Secretary John Storrs will be lucky if they have anything more memorable to report for many years.

John McCarthy displays his 100 strawberries, prepared for The Queen Mother on 26th July 2000.
SARWH Archive

I   The Royal Household Tradesmen's Warrants Committee

II   Foreign Warrants

III   Council of the Royal Warrant Holders Association 2001/02, including Local

             Association Representatives

IV   Association Presidents since 1896

V   Secretaries since 1896

VI   Hon Treasurers since 1895

VII   Queen Elizabeth Scholarship Trust Trustees since 1990

VIII   Queen Elizabeth Scholars since 1990

IX   Full list of Warrant Holders:

                     A: 1900

                     B: 1946

                     C: 2001

X   Officers of Local Associations

XI   Companies holding all four Grantors' Warrants in the yeat 2001

THE ROYAL HOUSEHOLD TRADESMEN'S WARRANTS COMMITTEE

The Administration of Royal Warrants of Appointment is the responsibility of The Lord Chamberlain, who exercises control through the Royal Household Tradesmen's Warrants Committee. This Committee meets formally each year, normally in November, and 'out of Committee' as required, under the Chairmanship of the Lord Chamberlain. The principal departments of The Queen's Household are represented, as are the Households of the other Grantors.

The Committee considers applications for all new Warrants and reviews those that are due to expire at the end of the following year, and makes recommendations to the Grantors accordingly. The final decision is always that of the Grantor.

New applicants, who must have been trading with the Household concerned for not less than five years, submit a formal application through The Royal Warrant Holders Association. Grantees, whose companies are due for review are notified by the Lord Chamberlain's Office 6 months in advance of the Annual General Meeting and invited to submit their trading figures for the last three years.

The results of the Committee's deliberations are never made public but grantees are informed of the Grantor's decisions by the Lord Chamberlain's Office. New Warrants granted, run from the following January for a period of five years. If a Warrant is, for any reason, cancelled, 12 months notice (i.e. to the following December) is normally given.

The Royal Warrant Holders Association maintains a complete list of all current Warrant Holders on its website (www.royalwarrant.org).

The following normally attend, or are represented, when the Royal Household Tradesmen's Warrants Committee meets;

The Lord Chamberlain – Chairman

The Keeper of the Privy Purse

The Master of the Royal Household

The Comptroller of The Lord Chamberlain's office

The Director of the Royal Collection

The Crown Equerry

The Communications Secretary

The Private Secretary to The Duke of Edinburgh

The Private Secretary to Queen Elizabeth The Queen Mother

The Private Secretary to The Prince of Wales

The Assistant Secretary, The Lord Chamberlain's Office – Secretary

FOREIGN WARRANTS

Edward Bujak, MA, PhD

Visiting Research Fellow, University of East Anglia

The practice of granting Royal Warrants of Appointment to tradesmen is not unique to the British Royal Family. During the nineteenth century Royal Warrants were often used by European monarchies to encourage and develop the industrial and manufacturing base of their Kingdoms. In Denmark, during the nineteenth century, more and more shopkeepers, wholesalers and small industrial companies obtained Royal Warrants as the Royal Household was reduced in size and services were contracted out. Latterly with both King Frederick VII (1848-1863) and King Christian IX (1863-1906) of Denmark being "keen supporters of trade and industry" the designation "Purveyor to the King", which came into use at the beginning of the nineteenth century, was used to mark out well-established individuals and firms that were "economically sound and of good reputation".[1]

In the Netherlands, the award of the title *Purveyor to His Majesty the King* was also "actively used" by William I (1815-1840), the "Merchant King" to stimulate the industrial sector of his Kingdom's economy[2]. Unlike the Danes, the Dutch economy had to endure the depredations of Napoleon's roving columns as well as the Continental blockade. Following the war's end and the re-opening of Continental markets, cheap and affordable British goods began to pour into the Low Countries.

To encourage the growth of firms large enough to be able to compete with this flood of cheap imports the Dutch monarchy divided their Royal Warrant into two catagories. The first enabled the King to mark out for special recognition those firms that had made a significant contribution to the economic well being of the Kingdom as a whole. Upon these firms William bestowed the privilege of using the predicate "Royal" in their company names. Besides being a token of his gratitude for their efforts in restoring the country's fortunes, the pursuit of this particular privilege also encouraged competition between companies. This had the added benefit of further assisting the revival of the Dutch economy as the predicate "also counted as a guarantee of sorts…for the product itself and the services rendered."[3] The Dutch monarchy also attached the use of the Royal Crown to the award of the predicate "Royal". This was also intended to distinguish those firms pulling the economy up by its bootstraps, from their "little brothers", the tradesmen and purveyors to the Royal Court. Those in this second category of Warrant Holders were allowed to display the Royal Coat of Arms and to refer to themselves as "Purveyors to the Royal Household" or "Purveyors to the Royal Court."[4]

As a result of the territorial settlement agreed at Vienna in 1815, William, the "Merchant King", in addition to being King of the Netherlands also became King of the Belgians, but whilst he issued Warrants in Belgium these were few and far between. Efforts to unify Holland and Belgium eventually broke down in 1831, whereupon Prince Leopold of Saxe-Coburg-Gotha was proclaimed King Leopold I of Belgium. Having lived

---

[1]Elizabeth Hennessy, "Marks of Distinction" in *By Royal Appointment*, p. 23 RWHA/B2/456. Notes from the Danish Royal Court 12/7/2001, pp. 1-3 [2]Hennessy, "Distinction", p. 24 and Royal Enterprises in the Netherlands, (Groningen, 1990), pp. 11-12 [3]*Royal Enterprises*, p. 13 [4]*Royal Enterprises*, pp. 13 and 29 and *Summary of Purveyors to the Court in the Netherlands*, RWHA/History File, p. 74. Since 1904, the practise in Denmark has been to distinguish between "Purveyors to HM The King" or as at present The Queen, and "Purveyors to the Royal Danish Court". Purveyors to The Queen can therefore use the Royal Arms, whereas those displaying the Royal Household can only display the Royal Crown. Notes from the Danish Royal Court 12/7/2001, pp. 1-3

in England following his marriage to Princess Charlotte, Leopold was, as Elizabeth Hennessy states,

> familiar with the British system of Royal Appointments, which he then set out to use to stimulate the economy of Belgium. Like Britain's Prince Albert, Leopold was greatly interested in trade and industry and rewarded those artisans, traders and companies who provided the Royal Household with goods and services with the title of Royal Warrant Holder.[5]

The codification of Royal Warrants in the Low Countries during the early nineteenth century, was paralleled by a similar development in Sweden. In the early nineteenth century, King Charles XIV overhauled the Swedish system of awarding Royal Warrants. During the eighteenth century there had been a very loosely regulated system whereby tradesmen adopted the appellation "His Royal Majesty's..." followed by their particular trade. Latterly, the phrasing was altered. As result, tradesmen became for example, butchers, bakers or candlestick makers to "the Royal Court." Under King Charles XIV however, the award of a Royal Warrant was put on a much more formal footing.

King Charles XIV was born Jean-Baptiste Bernadotte. After a meteoric military career serving under the Emperor Napoleon, which included being made a Marshal of France in 1804, he was elected Crown Prince of Sweden by Sweden's States General in 1810 and adopted by the childless King Charles XIII. After changing his name to Charles-Jean he ascended the throne as King Charles XIV in 1818.[6] He and the Emperor Napoleon's younger brother, Louis Napoleon, both introduced new practices into the countries they were called upon to rule. It was only after Napoleon placed Louis Napoleon on the throne of Holland in 1806 that the term *Marchand du Roi* came into use in the Low Countries.[7]

The use by Louis Napoleon of the sobriquet *Merchant of the King* coupled to Bernadotte/Charles XIV's reforms suggests that both monarchs were familiar with some pre-existing Napoleonic model. After Napoleon crowned himself Emperor of the French in Notre Dame cathedral on 2nd December 1804, tradesmen and purveyors would have been required to supply the new Imperial Court with the necessary goods and services, just as their forebears had supplied the old Bourbon Royal Court. The new Imperial Court would also have based its procedures on those of the pre-1789 Royal Court, hence the use of the sobriquet *Marchand du Roi*. But while Louis Napoleon, as King of Holland could confer the title of *Merchant of the King*, those individuals supplying and furnishing the Imperial Court would have been styled *Marchand du l'Emperor*. Imperial Warrants were later an integral part of the Imperial Court re-established by Napoleon's nephew in the mid-nineteenth century.

When, on 1st December 1852, Louis Napoleon Bonaparte, the youngest son of Louis Napoleon, the former King of Holland, was proclaimed Emperor Napoleon III, these Imperial Warrants began to be issued to tradesmen and purveyors both at home and abroad. Some went to British tradesmen. Thus in 1858, Henry Poole and Co. of London were appointed tailors to His Imperial Majesty and by 1867, the Bristol chocolate manufacturers J S Fry and Sons had obtained the patronage of both the Emperor and the Empress Eugenie.[8] Four years later, these Imperial Warrants became defunct as the Emperor abdicated following the disastrous

---

[5]Hennessy, "Distinction", p. 20, see also *The Belgian Royal Warrant Holders*, (Antwerp, 1995), p. 11
[6]Correspondence from Maria Gunnarsson, 2/10/2000, pp. 1 and 4, RWHA/History File, Robert Torday, "Call to Arms" in *By Royal Appointment*, p. 38 and David G Chandler, *Dictionary of the Napoleonic Wars* (London, 1979), pp. 52-4
[7]Hennessy, "Distinction", p. 24. The reign of Louis Napoleon lasted from 1806 to 1815
[8]*Royal Warrant Holders Who's Who*, (London, 1920), RWHA/E3/107 and correspondence with Angus Cundy, Henry Poole and Co., 9/3/2001

Franco-Prussian War of 1870-1. In victory, the King of Prussia became the first Emperor of Germany at which point a new set of Imperial Warrants began to be issued to the tradesmen of Europe.

Before the Great War Liptons, the "largest tea and provision dealers in the world", held Warrants appointing them as tea merchants to His Imperial Majesty The German Emperor. Such Imperial German Warrants superseded those of the German Kingdoms and Principalities that were brought together by Prussia to form the new German Empire but unification did not bring about the abolition of these previously independent states. Prince Louis of Hesse, and the Prince of Teck in 1870/1, Prince Christian of Schleswig-Holstein in 1880 and Frederich Grossherrzog of Baden in 1891[9] all continued to issue their own Warrants, despite being subsumed into the new German Empire. These Royal Warrants together with the Imperial Warrants issued by the Kaiser, were finally rendered null and void by the abolition of the Kaiserreich and establishment of the Weimar Republic after the First World War.

The fall of the Hohenzollern dynasty in Germany, of the Habsburgs in Austria and the Romanovs in Russia, dealt a deathblow to Royal Warrants in those three former monarchies. At a stroke the Warrants of the Emperor Karl I (suc: 1916) and all Warrants issued by his predecessors were swept away. The latter included the Warrants issued by the late Emperor Franz Joseph, as Emperor of Austria and King of Hungary and those granted by the Archduke Franz Ferdinand prior to his assassination in Sarajevo in 1914. One such Warrant was issued in Vienna on 30th May 1897 to Mr William John Guy Esq. of 160A Piccadilly London,

> Gentleman,
>
> I beg to inform you that in compliance with your request His Imperial and Royal Highness Archduke Francis Ferdinand of Austria Oste has graciously appointed you as hairdresser to His own person and allowed that you may bear this title accordingly.
>
> The Grand Steward of the Court[10]

Despite the collapse of the Habsburg Empire, Warrants continued to be issued in the Balkans by the Royal Houses of the various "successor" states carved out of the Austro-Hungarian Empire and before that, the Ottoman Empire. For instance, in the 1930s, tradesmen supplying the Bulgarian Royal Family were rewarded with a Royal Warrant of Appointment.

The Russian Imperial Warrants which vanished at the same time, had been bestowed upon, among others in the late nineteenth century, Henry Poole and Co. and James Buchanan, a bow maker and "importer of Flemish and German bow strings" of Regent Circus in London.[11] Evidence from the early twentieth century, suggests the Russians were looking to formalise the whole business of awarding Warrants. In 1911, the Lord Chamberlain's Office dealt with an enquiry from the Russian Ambassador who was interested in the "practice in this country with regard to the issuing of Warrants of Appointment."[12] Whether this correspondence

---

[9]Correspondence with Angus Cundy, Henry Poole and Co., 9/3/2001
[10]Warrant, RWHA/E1/10
[11]Trade card, RWHA/A1/77
[12]Letter dated 4th February 1911, RA/PP/Household Papers/Volume 21

presaged the introduction of any British-style reforms in St Petersburg is unknown as the Bolsheviks obliterated all traces of the Tsarist regime.

Beyond Europe, in South America the Emperors of Brazil issued Imperial Warrants up to the time that Brazil became a Republic in 1889.[13] In Asia and Africa Warrants were issued under the supervision of the Emperor of Japan and the Emperor Haile Selassie of Ethiopia (between 1930 and 1974).

Generally speaking, the twentieth century has witnessed a dramatic reduction in the number of monarchies, particularly in Europe. After 1945, the Balkan monarchies disappeared, as did the King of the Hellenes and the King of Italy. When Italy became a Republic in 1946, the Warrants issued by the various Italian Princes and Dukes who had been brought together by Cavour and Garibaldi to form a united Italy in 1860 became just as defunct as those formerly issued by the ruling House of Savoy. In the Iberian Peninsula, whilst Spain retained its Royal Family after neighbouring Portugal declared itself a Republic in 1910, the former has since ceased to issue Warrants.[14]

In Northern Europe, however, Warrants are still issued by the Royal Houses of Belgium, the Netherlands, Denmark and Sweden. Elsewhere, the picture post-1945 encompasses the disappearance of Shahs, Maharajahs and Emirs, the survival of an Emperor and the emergence of fabulously wealthy Sultans. With Indian Independence in 1947, the Warrants issued by the Maharajahs of the Indian Sub-Continent passed into history to join those that had once been issued by the Egyptian Khedive or the Emirs of Afghanistan. Tradesmen supplying the Shahs of Iran retained their Warrants up to the Revolution of 1978.

Tradesmen can still today obtain Warrants of Appointment from equally exotic rulers. In the Middle East, Dege & Skinner enjoy the distinction of being tailors to the Sultan of Oman while in the Far East, Meyer & Mortimer Ltd are the Sultan of Brunei's military outfitters. Further East, Henry Poole and Co., having been the Emperor of Japan's tailors in the 1920s, continue to enjoy the patronage of the Imperial Household.[15] Thus, despite the loss of numerous Royal and Imperial Houses during the nineteenth and twentieth centuries, on the eve of Her Majesty The Queen's Golden Jubilee, Warrants of both a Royal and Imperial character are still given, and highly valued in many parts of the world.

---

[13]Trade card, RWHA/A1/77 and correspondence with Angus Cundy, Henry Poole and Co. 9/3/2001 and with the Brazilian Embassy 9/3/2001

[14]Correspondence with the Spanish Embassy, 14/6/2000 and the Italian Embassy, 9/3/2001

[15]Correspondence with Angus Cundy, Henry Poole and Co. 9/3/2001, Michael Skinner, Dege and Skinner, 9/3/2001, Meyer and Mortimer Ltd, 9/3/2001. As regard to the Emir of Afghanistan, his shirts were made by one George Watson Esq., my thanks to Keith Sargeant, Thresher and Glenny Ltd.

THE COUNCIL
ROYAL WARRANT HOLDERS ASSOCIATION
APRIL 2001

Past Presidents		Past or Present Grantee for
The Lord Hayter, KCVO, CBE	(1967)	Chubb & Sons
Peter Coleclough	(1971)	Howard Rotavator Co. Ltd.
Sam H.G. Twining, LVO, OBE	(1972)	R. Twining & Co. Ltd.
John Connell	(1975)	The Distillers Company
William Palmer, CBE, DL	(1976)	Huntley & Palmer Ltd.
R.E. Stevens	(1977)	Garrards & Co. Ltd.
Sir Nevil Macready, Bt. CBE	(1979)	Mobil Oil Company Ltd.
David Part, OBE, TD, DL	(1981)	The General Trading Company (Mayfair) Ltd.
Peter Smith, OBE	(1982)	Securicor Ltd.
Victor Watson, CBE, DL	(1983)	John Waddington PLC
Sir Michael Colman, Bt	(1984)	Reckitt & Colman Products
Count Alain de Vogüé	(1985)	Veuve Clicquot-Ponsardin
Graeme Wilson MBE	(1987)	William Wilson & Co. Ltd.
John Marks	(1988)	The Trebor Group
Richard Woodhouse	(1989)	Sandicliffe Motor Group Ltd.
Barry St. G. Austin Reed, CBE, MC, DL	(1990)	Austin Reed Group PLC
Bryan Toye	(1991)	Toye, Kenning & Spencer Ltd.
Sir Richard George, CVO	(1993)	Weetabix Ltd.

Douglas Kinloch Anderson, OBE	(1994)	Kinloch Anderson Ltd.
Margaret Barbour, CBE, DL	(1995)	J. Barbour & Sons Ltd.
Robert Gieve	(1996)	Gieves & Hawkes Ltd.
Alan Britten	(1997)	Mobil Oil Company Limited
Christopher Rowe	(1998)	Findlater Mackie Todd & Co.Ltd.
Roger Mitchell	(1999)	Holland & Holland Ltd.
Michael Skinner	(2000)	Dege & Skinner

President

Adam Brett-Smith		Corney & Barrow Ltd.

Vice-President

The Viscount Marchwood		Moët Hennessey UK Ltd.

Members

Andrew Prendergast		Mayfair Cleaning Co.Ltd.
John Horrell		Dodson & Horrell Ltd.
Ann Rossiter OBE		H. Bronnley & Co. Ltd.
Iain Campbell		Campbell & Neill

Representatives of Local Associations

Brian Smellie	Edinburgh	James Gray & Son Ironmongers & Electricians Ltd.
Nicholas Copeman	Sandringham	BBC Fire Protection Ltd.
Fred Newman	Windsor	Abbey Rose Gardens
Mark Fleming	Aberdeen	John Fleming & Co. Ltd.

PRESIDENTS OF THE ROYAL WARRANT HOLDERS ASSOCIATION
1896 – 2001

1896	T Simpson Jay	Jay's Ltd, Silk Mercers
1897	Algernon Graves, FSA	Henry Graves & Co Ltd Printsellers and Publishers
1898	Ernest Callard	Callard, Stewart & Watt Ltd. Bakers
1899	JM Campbell	Debenham & Freebody, Furriers & Silk Mercers
1900	Daniel Mayer	S & P Erard, Harp & Pianoforte Makers
1901	W Carrington, JP	Carrington & Co, Jewellers & Silversmiths
1902	W Carrington, JP	*ibid*
1903	Thomas Tipton,	Scotts Ltd, Hatters
1904	W Montgomery Wilson	HD Rawlings Ltd, Mineral Water Manufacturers
1905	James G Unite	Mr John Unite Ltd, Tentmakers
1906	George Booth Heming, CBE, JP	Messrs Joseph Heming & Co Ltd, Jewellers & Silversmiths
1907	Francis Edgar Charles	Messrs Charles & Co, Fishmongers
1908	George Heath	Henry Heath Ltd. Hat Makers
1909	Henry C Pearson	Messrs R & S Garrard & Co, Goldsmiths and Crown Jewellers
1910	John Welford, JP	Welford & Sons Ltd, Dairymen
1911	William Bellamy	Bellamy Brothers, Poulterers
1912	William Adlington	S & P Erard, Harp & Pianoforte Manufacturers
1913	Joseph H Whitehorn, MVO	Collingwood & Co Ltd, Jewellers & Silversmiths
1914	HAA Thorn	Charles Lancaster & Co Ltd, Gunmakers
1914	TB Callard	Callard, Stewart & Watt Ltd, Bakers
1915	TB Callard	*ibid*
1916	William C Wise	Paul E Chappuis & Co, Daylight Reflector Manufacturers

1917	William C Wise	*ibid*
1918	Verney Drew, FRSA	James Drew, Glover & Hosier
1919	Lt Col. WM Power, FRSA	WM Power, Picture Frame Makers
1920	James WG Ross	Boilerine Ltd, Manufacturing Chemists
1921	James WG Ross	*ibid*
1922	Charles F Glenny, MVO	Thresher & Glenny, Hosiers
1923	Lionel V Straker	Samuel Straker & Sons Ltd, Account Book Makers
1924	Captain James D Haggart, CBE, JP	P & J Haggart, Tartan Manufacturers
1925	Robert W Wharam	Thomas Crapper & Co, Sanitary Engineers
1926	James Webster, JP	John Knight Ltd, Soap Manufacturers
1927	Captain William F Cooper	Frank Cooper Ltd, Marmalade Makers
1928	The Lord Blythwood, KCVO	General Accident Fire & Life Assurance Corporation, Insurance Providers
1929	Robert Pears	A & F Pears Ltd, Soap Manufacturers
1930	R William Byass	Gonzales Byass & Co Ltd, Sherry Producers
1931	Lt. Gen Sir Travers Clarke, KCB, KCMG, CBE	Express Dairy Co Ltd, Dairy Suppliers
1932	Charles E Newbegin	Garrard & Co Ltd, Jewellers
1933	The Viscount Leverhulme, DL, MA	Lever Bros. Ltd, Soap & Detergent Makers
1934	Sir Duncan Watson, JP, MIEE	Duncan Watson Ltd, Electrical Engineers
1935	The Duke of Atholl, KT, GCVO, CB, DSO	Bovril Ltd.
1936	Lt Col The Lord Herbert Scott, CMG, DSO, DL	Rolls Royce Ltd, Motor Car Manufacturer
1937	FA Simonds	Messrs. H & G Simonds Ltd, Brewers
1938	Howard Hughes	Alfred Hughes & Sons Ltd, Cake and Biscuit Manufacturers
1939-43	Brigadier General A Courage, DSO, MC	White Horse Distillers Ltd, Scotch Whisky Distillers

1944	Howard Hughes	Alfred Hughes & Sons Ltd, Cake and Biscuit Manufacturers
1945	FA Simonds	Messrs. H & G Simonds Ltd, Brewers
1946	The Marquess of Carisbrooke	Electrolux Ltd
1947	The Lord Forteviot, MBE	John Dewar & Sons Ltd, Scotch Whisky Distillers
1948	Oliver Watney	Messrs. Watney, Combe, Reid & Co Ltd, Brewers
1949	Herbert Sulman	Garrard & Co Ltd, Jewellers
1950	Sir Frederick Wells, Bt.	Sanitas & Co Ltd, Suppliers of Sanitas
1951	H Tansley Witt, FCA	Cooper McDougall & Robertson Ltd, Sheep Dip Manufacturers
1952	Sir John Bodinnar, JP	Messrs C & T Harris (Calne) Ltd, Manufacturers of Bacon & Sausages
1953	Reginald HR Palmer, MC, DL	Huntley & Palmers Ltd, Biscuit and Cake Manufacturers
1954	The Hon R Hanning Philipps, MBE	Schweppes Ltd, Manufacturers of Soft Drinks
1955	William B Chivers	Messrs Chivers & Sons Ltd, Purveyors of Jam
1956	Steven H Twining, MBE	R Twining & Co Ltd, Tea & Coffee Merchants
1957	Sir Harry Hague	Messrs A Wander Ltd, Ovaltine Manufacturers
1958	Rupert E Carr	Messrs Peek, Frean & Co Ltd, Biscuit Manufacturers
1959	Sir Richard Burbidge, Bt., CBE	Harrods Ltd, Outfitters & Suppliers of Provisions & Fancy Goods
1960	HM Braid, OBE	John Walker & Sons Ltd, Scotch Whisky Distillers
1961	JW Isaac	Garrard & Co Ltd, Jewellers
1962	SV Hine	Messrs. Day, Son & Hewitt Ltd, Suppliers of Animal Medicine
1963	ED Simonds	Messrs H & G Simonds Ltd, Brewers

1964	Sir Edward Rayne, CVO	Messrs H & M Rayne Ltd, Shoemakers & Handbag Manufacturers
1965	J Williamson	Army & Navy Stores Ltd, Suppliers of Household & Fancy Goods
1966	Keith Stevens	Messrs Corney & Barrow Ltd, Wine Merchants
1967	The Lord Hayter, KCVO, CBE	Chubb & Sons, Patent Lock & Safe Makers
1968	The Viscount Trenchard, MC	T Wall & Sons, Suppliers of Sausages
1969	WDC Hedges	Benson & Hedges Ltd, Tobacconists
1970	JFP Tate	Tate & Lyle Ltd, Sugar Refiners
1971	Peter Coleclough	Howard Rotavator Co. Ltd, Agricultural Equipment Manufacturers
1972	Sam HG Twining	R Twining & Co Ltd, Tea & Coffee Merchants
1973	TE Davies	Ardath Tobacco Co, Tobacconists
1974	William Douglas, DFC	James Gray & Sons Ltd, Ironmongers & Electricians
1975	John Connell	The Distillers Company, Scotch Whisky Manufacturers
1976	William Palmer	Huntley & Palmer Ltd, Biscuit & Cake Manufacturers
1977	R E Stevens	Garrard & Co Ltd, Jewellers
1978	Richard Roberts	Roberts Radios, Manufacturers & Suppliers of Radios
1979	Sir Nevil Macready, Bt.	Mobil Oil Co Ltd (UK), Suppliers of Petroleum Fuels & Lubricants
1980	J Riddell Webster, MC	National Benzole Co, Manufacturers of Motor Benzole
1981	David Part, OBE, DL	The General Trading Company Ltd, Suppliers of Fancy Goods
1982	Peter Smith, OBE	Securicor Ltd, Express Parcel Carriers
1983	Victor Watson, CBE, DL	Waddington's, Playing Card Co Ltd.

1984	Sir Michael Colman, Bt.	Reckitt & Colman Products, Manufacturers of Antiseptics, Air Fresheners, Polishes & Cleaners
1985	Le Comte Alain de Vogüé	Veuve Clicquot-Ponsardin, Purveyors of Champagne
1986	Timothy Sandeman	George G Sandeman Sons & Co Ltd, Wine Merchants
1987	Graeme Wilson	William Wilson & Co Ltd, Suppliers of Plumbing, Electrical & Building Materials
1988	John Marks	The Trebor Group, Manufacturers of Mints
1989	Richard Woodhouse	Sandicliffe Garage Ltd, Supplier of Motor Horse Boxes
1990	Barry Austin Reed, CBE, MC, DL	Austin Reed & Stephens Brothers Ltd, Outfitters
1991	Bryan Toye	Toye, Kenning & Spencer Ltd, Suppliers of Gold & Silver Laces, Insignia & Embroidery
1992	David Palengat	Pedro Domecq SA, Suppliers of Domecq Sherry
1993	Richard George	Weetabix Ltd, Manufacturers of Breakfast Cereals
1994	Douglas Kinloch Anderson, OBE	Kinloch Anderson Ltd, Tailors & Kiltmakers
1995	Margaret Barbour, CBE, DL	J Barbour & Sons Ltd, Manufacturers of Waterproof & Protective Clothing
1996	Robert Gieve	Gieves & Hawkes, Livery & Military Tailors
1997	Alan Britten	Mobil Oil Co. Ltd (UK), Suppliers of Petroleum Fuels & Lubricants
1998	Christopher Rowe	Findlater, Mackie Todd & Co Ltd, Wine & Spirit Merchants
1999	Roger Mitchell	Holland & Holland Ltd, Rifle Makers
2000	Michael Skinner	Dege & Skinner, Tailors
2001	Adam Brett-Smith	Corney & Barrow Ltd, Wine Merchants

THE SECRETARIES OF THE ROYAL WARRANT HOLDERS ASSOCIATION
1896 - Present

1896 - 1897	W Haynes Gibbs and Walter Gibbs
1897 - 1898	W Haynes Gibbs
1898 - 1899	FW Mortimer
1899 - 1900	Harry Frazer
1900 - 1904	Algernon Graves, FSA (Past President)
1904 - 1911	SK Holman
1911 - 1925	James W Coleman
1925 - 1937	Major H Brookhouse
1937 - 1946	Robert Pears (Past President)
1946 - 1952	RHW Hope, OBE, MC
1952 - 1966	Brigadier CE Morrison, DSO, MC
1966 - 1979	Lieutenant-Colonel W Keown-Boyd, CVO, OBE
1979 - 1996	Commander Hugh Faulkner, CVO, RN
1996 - present	Colonel Christopher Pickup, OBE

HONORARY TREASURERS
1896 - Present

1896 – 1900	FW Mortimer
1900 – 1906	Harry Frazer
1906 - 1924	W Carrington Smith
1924 - 1927	Henry Pearson
1927 - 1953	Charles F Glenny, MVO
1953 - 1958	Sir John Bodinner, JP
1958 - 1974	Rupert E Carr
1974 - 1991	Sir Edward Rayne, CVO
1991 - 1998	Sam HG Twining, LVO, OBE
1998 - present	Sir Richard George, CVO

THE QUEEN ELIZABETH SCHOLARSHIP TRUST
TRUSTEES 1990 – Present

Barry Austin Reed, CBE, MC, DL, Chairman 1990 - 1995
Austin Reed Group PLC, Outfitters

Colin Cullimore, CBE, 1990 - 1991
J H Dewhurst Ltd
Butchers

Commander Hugh Faulkner, CVO, RN, 1990 - 1995
Secretary, Royal Warrant Holders Association

Bryan Toye, 1990 - 1995
Toye Kenning & Spencer Ltd
Regalia Manufacturers

Michael Skinner, 1990 - 1993, 1995 - 1998
Dege & Skinner
Tailors

Sam Twining, LVO, OBE, 1990 - 1993, 1995 - 1998
R Twining & Co Ltd
Tea & Coffee Merchants

The Hon Anna Plowden, CBE, 1990 - 1997
Plowden & Smith Ltd
Fine Art Restorers

David Palengat, 1992
Pedro Domecq S.A.
Suppliers of Domecq Sherry

Peter Phillips, 1992
CPC (United Kingdom) Ltd
Manufacturers of Corn Oil, Cornflour and Mayonnaise

John Horrell, 1993 - 1999
Dodson & Horrell Ltd
Horse Feed Manufacturers

Richard Skinner, 1993 - 1999
A E Skinner & Co
Jewellers & Silversmiths

Christopher Rowe, 1992 - 1998, Chairman 1995 - 1998
Findlater Mackie Todd & Co Ltd
Wine & Spirit Merchants

Tom Johnson, 1995 - 1997
Bestobell Service Co Ltd
Maintenance Engineers

Alan Britten, 1998 - Present, Chairman 1999 - Present
Mobil Oil Company Ltd
Suppliers of Petroleum Fuels & Lubricants

Adam Brett-Smith, 1998 - Present
Corney & Barrow Ltd
Wine Merchants

Lee Taylor, 1999
Arthur Sanderson & Sons Ltd
Suppliers of Wallpapers, Paints & Fabrics

Andrew Prendergast, 1999 - Present
The Mayfair Cleaning Company
Window Cleaners

Michael Gregory, 2000 - Present
Arnold Wiggins & Sons Ltd
Picture Frame Makers

Sarah Elton, 2000 - Present
Frank Smythson Ltd
Stationers

Ann Rossiter, OBE, 2001 - Present
H Bronnley & Co Ltd
Toilet Soap Makers

Iain Campbell, 2001 - Present
Campbell & Neill
Suppliers of Fresh & Smoked Fish

Since 1996, all Association Presidents have served as ex-officio Trustees during their year of office.

QUEEN ELIZABETH SCHOLARS

NAME	AGE	PURPOSE	AMOUNT (£)
1991			
Deborah Beasley	29	Tapestry conservation	9,000
Rupert Christie	18	Farriery	5,000
Steven Gravestock	21	Stonemasonry	6,000
Timothy Harris	28	Glassmaking	7,500
Claire O'Flaherty	24	Shoemaking	2,500
Marliese Symons	23	Homeopathy	12,000
1992			
Davina Chapman	44	Calligraphy	3,000
Sandie Ennis	29	Rugmaking	8,500
Martin Enoch	33	Glassmaking	7,500
Sonja Nuttall	27	Tailoring	3,000
Judith Plint	33	Opera singing	3,000
Frances Plowden	26	Artist blacksmith	4,500
David Sax	22	Winemaking	8,000
Graham Williams	29	Antique furniture restoration	10,000
1993			
Spike Bucklow	37	Painting conservation	10,000
Mary Butcher	49	Basketmaking	5,500
Jonathan Darracott	27	Watchmaking and repair	10,000
Denise Durham	26	Chairmaking	4,000
Sarah Goodwin	26	Gold embroidery	1,800
Philippa Hunt	28	Paper conservation	10,000
Bisi Osindero	31	Millinery	5,000
1994			
Ruth Boddington	28	Calligraphy	7,199
Graham Collis	41	Blacksmith training	5,500
Richard Faulkner	23	Horological course	10,000
Janet Wicks	38	Quilting courses	4,800
Catherine Woodforde	30	Gilding courses	6,400

1995

Ros Conway	43	Pâte-de-Vere glass making	6,000
Angela Craft	42	Bookbinding	10,000
Nicola Dunn	29	Antique metal conservation	4,000
Jonathan Fraser	21	Garden design	7,000
James Hamill	37	Bee keeping	5,000
Rodney Harris	29	Brick modelling	10,500
Veronica Main	46	Straw-work	5,000
Stephen Mills	22	Upholstery	3,750
Lisa Shekede	34	Domestic wall painting conservation	10,000

1996

Rupert Atkinson	21	Portrait Painting	11,000
Lee Collins	29	Farriery	6,000
Richard Drayton	26	Wooden boat building	8,900
Rachel Foster	22	Confectionery	2,200
Rebecca Hellen	24	Easel painting conservation	12,000
Bex Marriott	36	Bookbinding	11,700
Peter Norrington	53	Western saddle making	4,200
Tim Wade	40	Woodcarving	3,000

1997

Sean Athow	29	Farriery	7,500
Deborah Carré	30	Shoemaking	10,000
Alan Graystock	22	Scagliola	2,550
Sue Hudswell	43	Apprenticeship in 'closing'	11,550
Anthea Laing	52	Upholstery	4,000
Heather Sproat	27	Haute Couture	9,500
Peter Ting	37	Ceramics	7,700

1998

Claudia Clare	36	Ceramics	5,000
Jonathan Harris	22	Woodcarving	2,500
Barbara Jones	41	Lime plastering & cob building	6,000
Stephen Lewis	27	Stained glass conservation	3,800
James Mackey	40	Musical instrument repair	9,750
James Shoulder	22	Geometrical staircase building	7,000
Lucinda Turner	26	Puppet carving	5,800

1999

Juliet Bankes	49	Wood engraving	3,000
Matthew Caines	34	Classical figure carving	4,500
Charlotte de Syllas	53	Glass jewellery	10,000
Martin Haswell	40	Digital photography	4,500
Deirdre Hawken	54	Millinery	9,000
Sally Hayes	42	Woodturning	2,500
Sarah Hocombe	35	Fresco painting	5,200
Chris Melloy	28	Piano tuning	7,200
John Poole	51	Gilding	4,000
Dunstan Rickhuss	31	Paint effects	5,500
John Rogers	21	Farriery	5,500
Edward Scharer	24	Conservation & restoration	12,000
Roy Youdale	49	Basket making	2,000

2000

Richard Ball	35	Stone carving	9,800
Sarah Berry	26	Architectural woodcarving	1,300
Gabriela Denny	28	Fine art	11,000
Daniel Dorman	24	Boatbuilding	4,500
Steven Garrett	22	Ecclesiastical Joinery	11,000
Rod Kelly	43	Silversmithing	9,300
Christopher McBeth	29	Farriery	5,000
Robert Ogborn	37	Paint effects	9,200
Michael Rhys Jones	17	Farriery	7,000
Sharon Smith	40	Interior design	8,000
Lai Symes	28	Millinery	10,000
Laura West	49	Bookbinding	8,750
Louisa Wood	30	Hemp weaving	3,000

1900

LIST OF TRADESMEN WHO HOLD WARRANTS OF APPOINTMENT FROM THE LORD STEWARD, WITH AUTHORITY TO USE THE ROYAL ARMS

ABERDEEN LIME COMPANY
Fuel
L. ACHARD
Seeds, Plants and Flowers
ADAMS AND SON
Braziery and Ironmongery
AGENCY DUCHY OF BRONTÉ WINES
Wine
PIERRE AILLOUD
Grocery, Tea and Coffee
AITCHISON AND SONS
Confectionery
HENRY ALLNUTT
Farrier
JOHN ANDERSON
Fish
ANGLO-AMERICAN SUPPLY STORES
Grocery, Tea and Coffee
AUSTRALIAN WINES
Wine
BAILEY & CO.
Wine
JOHN BAILY & SON
Poultry
V. BALBONI
Bread & Biscuits
GEORGE BALLANTINE & SON
Wine
BARCLAY AND FRY LTD.
Decorated Tin Boxes
BARCLAY AND SON
Wax
FREDERICK BARRETT
Turnery
BARRINGER, WALLIS AND MANNERS
Decorated Tin Boxes
BARWELL SONS
Wine
JAMES BASDEN (GARDEN BROOMS)
Turnery
BEAL, FRENCH AND CO.
Wine Corks

BECKNELL, TURNER AND SONS LTD.
Tallow and Soap
JOHN BEDBOROUGH AND JOHN WEBB & SONS
Meat
JOHN BEGG
Spirits
BELLAMY BROS.
Poultry
V. BENOIST
Comestibles
A. BERLANDINS
Wine
BEWLAY AND CO. LTD.
Tobacco and Snuff
JOHN BIGNELL
Stationery
P. BIGNON
Wine
JOHN BLAIKIE AND SONS
Braziery and Ironmongery
BLAKE, SANDFORD AND BLAKE
Mineral Waters
F.J. BOGEY
Confectionery
PATRICK BOLAND
Bread & Biscuits
BOLLAND AND SONS
Confectionery
JOSEPH BOLLINGER
Wine
BONO AND BAUDINO
Wine
AUGUSTE BRAUD
Fruit
J. BROMWHICH
Seeds, Plants and Flowers
W. BROOKS AND SON
Vegetables
BROUGHTON AND PLAS POWER COAL CO.
Fuel
CHARLES BROWN AND R.H. MATTHEWS & SONS
Tallow and Soap

BROWN AND SON
Braziery and Ironmongery
BRYMBO COLLIERY CO.
Fuel
JAMES BUCHANAN AND CO.
Spirits
T.W. AND J. BUCKENHAM
Linen
BUDGEN AND CO. LTD.
Oilery
WILLIAM BULL
Seeds, Plants and Flowers
GEORGE BUNYARD
Seeds, Plants and Flowers
P.B. BURGOYNE
Wine
CHARLES HENRY BURT
Linen
CADBURY BROTHERS LTD.
Cocoa and Chocolate
CADBURY, PRATT & CO.
Butter etc.
ALEXANDER CAIRNS
Oilery
CARLO CALDERAI
Comestibles
MARC AND VICTORIE CALENDRET
Seeds, Plants and Flowers
A.J. CALEY AND SONS LTD.
Mineral Waters
CALLARD STEWART & WATT LTD.
Bread & Biscuits
V.A. CAMERON
Bread & Biscuits
JOHN & GEORGE CAMPBELL
Grocery, Tea and Coffee
A. CAMPBELL, HOPE AND KING LTD.
Ale and Beer
JOHN CANNING AND NEVILLE REID & CO.
Ale and Beer
JAMES D. CARD
Braziery and Ironmongery
ROBERT CARMICHAEL AND WOOD BROS.
Meat
JAMES CARTER AND CO.
Seeds, Plants and Flowers

H. CASTLE AND SON
Manufacturers of Garden Seats
CATCHPOLE AND WILLIAMS LTD.
Gold and Silver Smiths
CAWS & SON AND THOMAS KNIGHTON
Meat
W.G. CHAMBERS & CO.
Milk
F.E. CHARLES, W. & J. GILSON
Fish
CHARPENTIER AND CO.
Stationery
CHILD AND CO.
Cider
CHIVAS BROTHERS
Oilery
W.G. CLARKE & SONS
Dog Biscuits
COBETT AND SONS
Grocery, Tea and Coffee
G.J. COCKERELL AND CO.
Fuel
COLLIER AND CO.
Wine
J. AND J. COLMAN LTD.
Mustard
G. CORSINI
Grocery, Tea and Coffee
JAMES COULSON AND CO.
Linen
WILLIAM COULSON AND SONS
Linen
CROSSE AND BLACKWELL
Oilery
VINCENT CRUMP
Confectionery
CUNLIFFE, DOBSON & CO.
Wine
DAIRY SUPPLY CO.
Dairy Utensil Mfrs.
RICHARD PERCEVAL DANIEL AND CO.
China and Glass
A.B. DANIELL AND SON
China and Glass
T. DARRACOTT
Bread & Biscuits

T. DARRACOTT
Confectionery
DAUKES AND CO.
Ale and Beer
J.M. DAVIDSON
Cured Fish
DEAR & MORGAN
Grocery, Tea and Coffee
DE CASTRO AND SON
Grocery, Tea and Coffee
JOSEPHINE DELRUE
Seeds, Plants and Flowers
DEVEREUX AND SON
Hatters
JOHN DEWAR & SONS LTD.
Spirits
DICKSONS LTD.
Seeds, Plants and Flowers
DICKSON, BROWN AND TAIT
Seeds, Plants and Flowers
ALEXANDER DICKSONS & SONS
Seeds, Plants and Flowers
HUGH DICKSON
Seeds, Plants and Flowers
DICKSON AND ROBINSON
Seeds, Plants and Flowers
DIXON GIBBS AND SON
Grocery, Tea and Coffee
DOBBIE AND CO.
Seeds, Plants and Flowers
CHARLES SHIRREFF DODS
Seeds, Plants and Flowers
JOHN DONALD AND CO.
China and Glass
DONEY AND NEVEUX
Confectionery
CLAUDE DONNET
Poultry
JOHN DUNCAN AND SON
Tobacco and Snuff
GRAY, DUNN & CO.
Bread & Biscuits
ZOE DUPREZ
Fruit
ELECTRICAL POWER STORAGE CO. LTD.
Lamps and Lamp Oil

DAVID EVANS
Meat
EXPRESS DAIRY CO.
Milk
FARROW AND JACKSON
Cellar Implements
C. FEUZ
Bread & Biscuits
FISHER SON AND SIBRAY
Seeds, Plants and Flowers
L.D.S. FLAYOL
Meat
FOLKETT BROWN
Grocery, Tea and Coffee
JOHN FORD AND CO.
China and Glass
FORTNUM & MASON LTD.
Oilery
F. FRITTELLI
Lamps and Lamp Oil
J.S. FRY AND SONS LTD.
Cocoa and Chocolate
R. AND S., GARRARD AND CO.
Gold and Silver Smiths
ROBERT GARROW
Fish
GERARD ET CIE
Seeds, Plants and Flowers
JAMES GIBSON
Wine
R & J. GIBSON
Grocery, Tea and Coffee
GILBERTSON & PAGE
Pheasants' Food
GODES-BERGER NATURAL MINERAL WATER CO.
Mineral Waters
THOMAS GOODE AND CO.
China and Glass
A. GORDON AND CO.
Ale and Beer
G. GOULET
Wine
WALTER GRAHAM & CO.
Linseed & Cotton Cake
STEPHEN GRANT AND SONS
Gun Makers

JAMES GREEN AND NEPHEW
China and Glass
THOMAS GREEN & SON LTD.
Horticultural Machine Makers
GREEN AND SON
Cutlery
GEORGE GREENHILL AND CO.
Wax
L. GUILLAUME
Meat
GUNTER & CO.
Confectionery
HALL & SONS
Meat
EDWARD HAMER, JOHN JONES & SONS
Meat
F. & J. HAMMOND
Poultry
MARY M. HARRIS
Turnery
WILLIAM HARRIS
Harness Maker
HARRISON BROTHERS AND HOWSON
Cutlery
JOHN HARVEY & SONS LTD.
Wine
HATCH, MANSFIELD AND CO.
Wine
HAWARD & SON
Oilery
HAWKES AND CO.
Sword Cutlers
HAZELDINE BROTHERS
Van Builders
D. HEDGES
Meat
HEDGES & BUTLER
Wine
HEINRICH HENCKELL
Seeds, Plants and Flowers
JOHN HEYWOOD
Bread & Biscuits
J. HILL & SON
Flour
THOMAS HILL AND SON
Gun Makers

R. HODD AND SON
Gold and Silver Smiths
HODGES AND SON
Braziery and Ironmongery
ROBERT HOGG AND SON
Drugs
HOGG AND ROBERTSON
Seeds, Plants and Flowers
HOLDERNESS & SON
Bread & Biscuits
THOMAS HOLMES, J. MACRAE AND CO.
Fuel
HOWARD & CO.,
Grocery, Tea and Coffee
HUDSON SCOTT AND SONS
Decorated Tin Boxes
MARY, ANNIE & HARRIET HUMPHREYS
Bread & Biscuits
HUNTLEY & PALMERS
Bread & Biscuits
J.J.B. HYDE
Comestibles
IDRIS AND CO.
Mineral Waters
IMPERIAL LAGER BREWERY CO.
Ale and Beer
R. JACKSON AND CO.,
Grocery, Tea and Coffee
JEWSBURY AND BROWN
Mineral Waters
JOHANNIS LTD. AND THE APOLLINARIS CO. LTD.
Mineral Waters
JOHNSON AND RAVEY
Braziery and Ironmongery
H.A. JONES
Confectionery
HENRY JONES
Bread & Biscuits
WILLIAM AND HENRY JOPP
Wine
JUDD AND MALIN
Potatoes
KEARTLAND MOLE
Fruit
KEITH & RALSTON
Bread & Biscuits

CHARLES KELLER
Seeds, Plants and Flowers
WILLIAM KELLY
Fishing Tackle Maker
KELLY'S DIRECTORIES LTD.
Post Office Directory
W.A. KEMP
Fish
W.G. KENT
Refrigerators
KINAHAN AND CO.
Wine & Spirits
KIRKLAND BROS.
Bread & Biscuits
JOHN CHARLES LAKE
Spirits
LAMBERT BRIEN AND CO., AND JAMES JOHN BUTLER
Wax
LANGTON AND CO. LTD.,
Ale and Beer
JULES LAULANNÉ
Meat
LOUIS LAULHÉ
Bread & Biscuits
LAYTON BROTHERS
Fruit
R.E. LEBRASSEUR
Grocery, Tea and Coffee
ANNE LEDERIDGE & SON
Meat
FRANCIS LEMANN & CO.
Bread & Biscuits
LIPTON LTD.
Grocery, Tea and Coffee
LITTLE AND BALLANTYNE
Seeds, Plants and Flowers
LOCKET AND JUDKINS
Fuel
W.H. LOVE & CO.
Fish
LUMSDEN & GIBSON
Grocery, Tea and Coffee
JOHN LUNDEE
Grocery, Tea and Coffee

W. MABEY & SONS
Turtle
MACFARLANE, LANG & CO.
Bread & Biscuits
MACKENZIE & MACKENZIE & LAWSON & SON
Bread & Biscuits
J.W. MACKIE & SONS
Bread & Biscuits
JAMES MACKINTOSH
Meat
MACONOCHIE BROS.
Cured Fish
MAPLES BROS.
Wine
MAPPIN AND WEBB
Gold and Silver Smiths
J.E. MASON
Bread & Biscuits
JAMES MATHEWSON AND SON
Linen
M. MATTIA
Poultry
B. AND W. MCKILLIAM
Confectionery
ANDREW MELROSE & CO.
Grocery, Tea and Coffee
MEREDITH & DREW
Bread & Biscuits
THOMAS METHVEUR AND SONS
Seeds, Plants and Flowers
W.B. MEW
Ale and Beer
MILLER AND SONS
Wax
MILLER AND SONS
Lamps and Lamp Oil
JEAN BAPTISTE MIREMONT
Confectionery
MITCHELL & MUIL LTD.
Bread & Biscuits
MITCHELL AND SON
Confectionery
MOËT AND CHANDON
Wine
STANISLAUS MOORE
Fruit

MOREL BROTHERS
Grocery, Tea and Coffee
MORTLOCKS LTD.
China and Glass
B. MOURRÉ
Grocery, Tea and Coffee
W. MUIRHEAD & SON
Poultry
CHARLES MUMBY AND CO.
Mineral Waters
G.H. MUMM AND CO.
Wine
JOSEPH NÈGRE
Confectionery
WILLIAM NICHOLLS AND CO.
Turnery
T. NIXON AND SON
China and Glass
NIXON & THEW
Grocery, Tea and Coffee
ODAMS CHEMICAL MANURE CO.
Chemical Manure & Nitro Phosphates
F. AND C. OSLER
China and Glass
RICHARD OXLEY AND SON
Stationery
EMILIO PADOA
Wine
WILLIAM PAICE
Seeds, Plants and Flowers
PALMER AND CO.
Wax
JOHN PARRY
Grocery, Tea and Coffee
WILLIAM PAUL AND SON
Seeds, Plants and Flowers
RANDOLPH PAYNE AND SONS
Wine
F.K. PEERLESS
Tallow and Soap
GEORGE PEGLER & CO.
Fruit
J. PEPLER AND CO.
Grocery, Tea and Coffee
J. PEPLER AND CO.
Oilery

LOUIS PETER
Wine
H. PETERS & SON
Fuel
S. PETRZYWALSKI LTD.
Bread & Biscuits
PHILLIPS
China and Glass
WILLIAM PHILLIPS
Meat
J. & G. PIERCE
Hot Water Engineers
ELIZA RADFORD
Bread & Biscuits
H.D. RAWLINGS LTD.
Mineral Waters
BENJAMIN REID AND CO.
Seeds, Plants and Flowers
REMINGTON STANDARD
Type Writing Machine Maker
RICCI BROTHERS
Vegetables
RIDGWAYS LTD.
Grocery, Tea and Coffee
T.R. AND J. ROACH
Seeds, Plants and Flowers
HENRY ROBERTS
Stationery
ROBERTS & SON
Grocery, Tea and Coffee
ROBERTSON, LEDLIE, FERGUSON AND CO.
Leinen
NATHANIEL ROBERTSON
Fuel
R.L. ROBERTSON
Bread & Biscuits
MARY ROBINSON
Fruit
W.H. ROGERS AND SON
Seeds, Plants and Flowers
A. ROMARY
Bread & Biscuits
LAURENT ROUARD
Confectionery
ROWNTREE AND CO. LTD.
Cocoa and Chocolate

ROYAL LAUNDRY
Hot Water Engineers
ROYAL LAUNDRY
Starch
ROYAL LAUNDRY
Tallow and Soap
ROYAL LAUNDRY
Van Builders
RUABON COAL CO.
Fuel
JANE AND GEORGE RUBIE
Oilery
ANTOINE RUMPELMAYER
Confectionery
RUTHERFORD, DICKSON & KAY
Wine
H.F.C. SANDER
Seeds, Plants and Flowers
F.W. SCHICK
Bread & Biscuits
EMILIE SCHWEITZER
Bread & Biscuits
SCHWEPPES LTD.
Mineral Waters
ALEXANDER SHANKS AND SON
Lawn Mowing Machine Makers
SHARP AND SCOTT
Grocery, Tea and Coffee
SHIRRAS LAING AND CO.
Braziery and Ironmongery
SILVA AND COSENS
Wine
JAS. SLATER AND CO.
Cooking Apparatus
SLATERS LTD.
Meat
SMITHS AND CO. LTD.
Lamps and Lamp Oil
H.G. SMYTH
Horticultural Machine Makers
H.S. SODEN
Milk
CAMILLE SOLIGNAC
Seeds, Plants and Flowers
LEWIS SOLOMON AND ISRAEL SOLOMON
Fruit

SPIKING & CO.
Bread & Biscuits
SPONGY IRON FILTER CO.
Filters
SARAH SPRULES
Lavendar Essence
SQUIRE PRIEST
Grocery, Tea and Coffee
F. STAHLSCHMIDT AND CO.
Custom House & Shipping Agents
STANDARD MANUFACTURING CO.,
Horticultural Machine Makers
SUTTON AND SONS
Seeds, Plants and Flowers
TAUNUS WATER CO.
Mineral Waters
TAYLOR, ANDERSON AND TAYLOR
Fuel
S. TERRY
Meat
JESSE THOMAS
Grocery, Tea and Coffee
HENRY THOMPSON
Cutlery
HENRY THOMSON AND CO.
Spirits
J.G. THOMSON AND CO.
Spirits
THOMSON, HILL, THOMSON & CO.
Wine
THOMSON, MARSHALL AND CO.
Ale and Beer
JOSEPH THORLEY
Cattle Food
WALTER THORNHILL AND CO.
Cutlery
A. AND R. THWAITES AND CO.
Mineral Waters
WILLIAM TITT
Fruit
WILLIAM TOOGOOD
Seeds, Plants and Flowers
FRANCIS TUCKER & CO. LTD.
Lamps and Lamp Oil
TULL & SON
Bread & Biscuits

CHARLES TURNER
Seeds, Plants and Flowers
THOMAS TURNER
Cattle Food
R. TWINING & CO.,
Grocery, Tea and Coffee
UNDERWOOD AND FARRANT
Cutlery
JEAN BAPTISTE UTHURBIDE
Grocery, Tea and Coffee
ANTOINE VALENTIN
Lamps and Lamp Oil
JOSÉ VEGAS
Wine
JAMES VEITCH AND SONS
Seeds, Plants and Flowers
ROBERT VEITCH AND SONS
Seeds, Plants and Flowers
F. VERANI
Fish
JOSEPH AND JOHN VICKERS AND CO. LTD.
Spirits
JOHN VIDLER
Flour
F.S. VINE
Bread & Biscuits
EGIDIO VITALI
Wine
F. VOGARD
Confectionery
WACHER AND CO.,
Wine
HIRAM WALKER AND SONS LTD.
Spirits
T. WALL & SONS
Pork
WARRINGTON AND CO.
Engravers
GEORGE WASLEY
Fish
WATERLOO MILLS CAKE & WAREHOUSING CO. LTD.
Forage
HENRY WATERMAN
Poultry

EDWARD WEBB & SONS
Seeds, Plants and Flowers
WELCH WHISKEY DISTILLERY COMPANY
Spirits
WELLMAN BROTHERS AND CO.
Braziery and Ironmongery
WHITE & SON
Pork
ROBERT WHITE
Butter etc.
CHARLES WHITFIELD
Butter etc.
JAMES R. WHITMAN
China and Glass
ROBERT WIGGINTON
Fuel
WILKINSON AND SON
Tailors
B.S. WILLIAMS AND SON
Seeds, Plants and Flowers
WILLIAMSON AND SONS
Tallow and soap
WILLIS AND SON, AND GRUBB & WHEELER
Wheelwrights
WILLMORE AND SCOTT
Stationery
WILLS AND SEGAR
Seeds, Plants and Flowers
J.W. WIMSETT AND SON
Seeds, Plants and Flowers
DAVID EDWIN WINDER, ABSOLOM ANDERSON,
Agent for Whitstable Oyster Fishery
WOOD & CO.
Forage
R. WOOD
Meat
ROBERT WOOD
Drugs
THOMAS WOOD
Confectionery
WOOLDRIDGE AND GRISBROOK
Drugs
WOOLLEY AND COWLEY
Custom House & Shipping Agents

ROBERT WOTHERSPOON AND CO.
Starch

YOUNG AND SON
Scale Makers

G.A. COURROUX, Secretary
Board of Green Cloth, Buckingham Palace
January 1, 1900

1900

LIST OF TRADESMEN WHO HOLD WARRANTS OF APPOINTMENT FROM THE LORD
CHAMBERLAIN, WITH AUTHORITY TO USE THE ROYAL ARMS

LONDON

ARTHUR ACKERMANN
Printers, Publishers and Printsellers
ADAMS AND SON
Ironmongers and Stove Makers
A.J. ARROWSMITH AND CO.
Parquet Manufacturers
FREDERICK ARTHUR
Decorators and Painters
BANTING AND SONS
Cabinet Makers, Upholsterers & Carpet Manufacturers
ALBERT BARKER
Goldsmiths, Silversmiths and Jewellers
ALEXANDER BASSANO
Photographers
ANDREW BEATTIE AND CO.
Dyers and Cleaners
CARL F.W. BECHSTEIN
Harp and Pianoforte Makers
JOHN BEDDARD
Chemists
BELLMAN, IVEY & CARTER
Marble Manufacturers
SIR JOHN BENNETT
Chronometer, Clock & Watch Makers
J.W. BENSON
Goldsmiths, Silversmiths and Jewellers
RICHARD BENTLEY AND SONS
Printers, Publishers and Printsellers
F.P. BHUMGARA
Goldsmiths, Silversmiths and Jewellers
G. AND C. BISHOP
Herald Painters
BLYTH AND SONS
Bedding Manufacturers
THOMAS BONTOR & CO.
Cabinet Makers, Upholsterers & Carpet Manufacturers
JEAN BOUSSOD. MANZI, JOYANT & CO.
Art Printsellers and Publishers
JOHN BROADWOOD & SONS
Harp and Pianoforte Makers

W. BROOKS & SON
Carvers and Gilders
MRS. C.J. BROWN
Chimney Sweeper
JOHN BUMPUS
Booksellers and Stationers
BUTTERWORTH & CO.
Printers, Publishers and Printsellers
HORACE BUTTERY
Picture Cleaners & Restorers
CAPPER SON & CO.
Linen Drapers
CATER & SONS
Hatters
PAUL E. CHAPPUIS AND CO.
Daylight Reflector Manufacturers
CHUBB & SONS
Lock and Safe Makers
WILLIAM CLARKSON
Perruquier
CLAYTON & BELL
Glass Manufacturers, Painters & Enamellers
ROBERT COCKS & CO.
Music Sellers
COLLINGWOOD AND CO.
Goldsmiths, Silversmiths and Jewellers
P. & D. COLNAGHI
Art Printsellers and Publishers
P. & D. COLNAGHI & CO.
Printers, Publishers and Printsellers
JOHN G. CRACE AND SON
Decorators and Painters
GEORGE CROSS
Bookbinders
W.F. D'ALMAINE
Embroiderers and Gold Lacemen
THOMAS W. DAVIES
Carriers
DENT AND HELLYER
Sanitary Engineers

E. DENT & CO.
Chronometer, Clock & Watch Makers
M.F. DENT
Chronometer, Clock & Watch Makers
DICKINSON
Art Printsellers and Publishers
A.W. DIXEY
Opticians
W.A. DIXEY
Opticians
W. AND D. DOWNEY
Photographers
J.F. & J.F. DUGGIN, JUN.
Dyers and Cleaners
EDE AND SON
Robe Makers
BENJAMIN EDGINGTON
Tent Makers
GEORGE EDWARD & SONS
Goldsmiths, Silversmiths and Jewellers
EDWARDS AND SONS
Booksellers and Stationers
FREDERICK ELKINGTON
Goldsmiths, Silversmiths and Jewellers
S. & P. ERARD
Harp and Pianoforte Makers
EMILY FAITHFUL
Printers, Publishers and Printsellers
THOMAS FALL
Photographers
T. AND W. FARMILOE
Glass Manufacturers, Painters & Enamellers
M. FEETHAM AND CO.
Ironmongers and Stove Makers
MARGARET J. FLEISCHMANN
Plumassier
C.T. FOX
Cabinet Makers, Upholsterers & Carpet Manufacturers
CHARLES FRODSHAM & CO.
Chronometer, Clock & Watch Makers
JAMES GARDNER
Ornithologist
GARDNER AND TOLHURST
Embroiderers and Gold Lacemen
R. & S. GARRARD & CO.
Goldsmiths, Silversmiths and Jewellers

T.J. GAWTHORP
Craftsman in Metals
GILLOW & CO.
Cabinet Makers, Upholsterers Carpet Manufacturers
DAN GODFREY SONS
Musical Instrument Manufacturers
ALGERNON GRAVES
Art Printsellers and Publishers
WILLIAM GRIGGS
Chromo-Lithographer
WILLIAM H. GROVE
Photographers
GUNN AND STUART
Photographers
F. HAINES AND SONS
Picture Cleaners & Restorers
HAMBURGER ROGERS AND CO.
Embroiderers and Gold Lacemen
C.F. HANCOCK
Goldsmiths, Silversmiths and Jewellers
CHARLES HARRIS
Turners and Toymen
HARRISON AND SONS
Booksellers and Stationers
HARRISON AND SONS
Printers, Publishers and Printsellers
H.J. HATFIELD
Brass, Bronze & Ormolu Manufacturers
ALEXANDER L. HENDERSON
Photographers
ALEXANDER HENRY LTD.
Gunmakers
HILL BROTHERS
Tailors
JAMES HILL
Lock and Safe Makers
W. EBSWORTH HILL AND SONS
Violin and Bow Manufacturers
WILLIAM HILL AND SON
Organ Builders
HILLS AND SAUNDERS
Photographers
HOBBS, HART & CO.
Lock and Safe Makers
HOOPER STRUVE & CO.
Chemists

HORNE AND THORNTHWAITE
Opticians
HUNT & ROSKELL
Goldsmiths, Silversmiths and Jewellers
GEORGE HYDE
Booksellers and Stationers
IMHOF AND MUCKLE
Harp and Pianoforte Makers
GEORGE JACKSON & SONS
Decorators and Painters
JOHNSTONE, NORMAN & CO.
Cabinet Makers, Upholsterers Carpet Manufacturers
ALEXANDER JONES AND CO.
Booksellers and Stationers
WILLIAM JAMES KEED
Glover
HORATIO NELSON KING
Photographers
A.A. KLAFTENBERGER
Chronometer, Clock & Watch Makers
LAMBERT & CO.
Goldsmiths, Silversmiths and Jewellers
LE ROY ET FILS
Chronometer, Clock & Watch Makers
LEVER BROTHERS LTD.
Soap Manufacturers
LIBERTY AND CO. LTD.
Art Fabrics
WILLIAM LIST & SONS
Horse Hair Manufacturers
LONDON STEREOSCOPIC & PHOTOGRAPHIC
CO. LTD
Photographers
LONGMAN AND CO.
Engravers (Seal and Gem)
STANLEY LUCAS, WEBER, PITT & HATZFELD
Music Sellers
MACLURE AND COMPANY
Lithographers
MAPLE & CO.,
Cabinet Makers, Upholsterers Carpet Manufacturers
MAY AND WILLIAMS
Newsagents
THOMAS MCLEAN
Art Printsellers and Publishers

ISAAC P. MENDOZA
Art Printsellers and Publishers
JAMES A. MESSENGER
Boat Builders
MILLER & SONS
Lamp & Lustre Manufacturers
MINTON, HOLLINS AND CO.
Porcelain Tile Manufacturers
JOHN HAYNES MINTORN
Wax Flower Modeller
WILLIAM S. MITCHELL
Printers, Publishers and Printsellers
JOSIAH MOORE AND SONS
Ventilator Makers
MORANT & CO.
Decorators and Painters
FREDERICK MORTIMER
Tailors
ROBERT C. MURRAY
Scientific, Chemical & Physical Apparatus Manufacturers
L. & H. NATHAN
Costumiers
NEEDS AND CO.
Lock and Safe Makers
NEGRETTI AND ZAMBRA
Opticians
H.J. NICHOLL & CO.
Tailors
W.G. NIXEY
Blacklead Manufacturer
ORTNER AND HOULE
Engravers (Seal and Gem)
F. & C. OSLER
Glass Manufacturers, Painters & Enamellers
THE PATENT BORAX COMPANY
Borax Manufacturers
A. & F. PEARS
Soap Manufacturers
J. AND B. PEARSE & CO.
Clothiers and Cloth Merchants
PERRY & CO.
Lamp & Lustre Manufacturers
PHILLIPS BROTHERS AND SON
Goldsmiths, Silversmiths and Jewellers
HENRY POOLE AND CO.
Tailors

JAMES PURDEY
Gunmakers
JOSEPH RAYNER & CO.
Turners and Toymen
REDMAYNE AND CO.
Insignia Riband Makers
SIR CHARLES REED AND SONS
Type Founders
R. RIVIÈRE AND SON
Bookbinders
MISS CHARLOTTE ROBINSON
Home Art Decorator
RUSSELL AND SONS
Photographers
ANTONIO SALVIATI
Glass Manufacturers, Painters & Enamellers
SAVORY AND MOORE
Chemists
CONRAD WILLIAM SCHMIDT
Varnish and Enamel Manufacturer
SCHOTT & CO.
Music Sellers
SEARLE AND SONS
Boat Builders
SEGUIER AND SMART
Picture Cleaners & Restorers
AUGUST SIEGLE
Booksellers and Stationers
J. SIMMONS & SONS
Costumiers
SKEFFINGTON AND SON
Printers, Publishers and Printsellers
C. SMITH AND SON
Embroiderers and Gold Lacemen
GEORGE SMITH & CO.
Joiners
GEORGE SPENCER
Gymnastic Apparatus Maker
P.W. & A.H. SQUIRE
Chemists
EDWARD STANFORD
Geographers
STEINWAY & SONS
Harp and Pianoforte Makers
ALFRED STRATTON
Linen Drapers

SUTTON & CO.
Carriers
T.G. TAGG & SON
Boat Builders
A. AND G. TAYLOR
Photographers
JOHN THOMSON
Photographers
THURSTON AND CO. LTD.
Billiard Table Manufacturers
G. TROLLOPE AND SONS
Paperhangers
RAPHAEL TUCK AND SONS LTD.
Printers, Publishers and Printsellers
TURBERVILLE SMITH & SON
Cabinet Makers, Upholsterers Carpet Manufacturers
HENRY LEWIS TURNER & CO.
Goldsmiths, Silversmiths and Jewellers
TYPE WRITER COMPANY LTD.
Type Writer Machine Makers
JOHN UNITE
Tent Makers
MR. JOHN COLLARD VICKERY
Dressing Case and Bag Manufacturer
J.A. VINTER
Lithographers
WALERY LTD.
Photographers
JOHN WARD
Invalid Chair Maker
ROBERT WARNER
Brass, Bronze & Ormolu Manufacturers
GEORGE WAUGH & CO.
Chemists
R. WAYGOOD AND CO.
Lift Manufacturers
JOHN WELLS
Goldsmiths, Silversmiths and Jewellers
WILLIAM WHITELEY
Cabinet Makers, Upholsterers & Carpet Manufacturers
J.R. WILKINSON
Robe Makers
WILKINSON SWORD COMPANY LTD.
Sword Makers
WILSON AND SONS
Ironmongers and Stove Makers

WINSOR AND NEWTON
Artists' Colourmen
GEORGE WRIGHT AND SONS
Dyers and Cleaners

JAMES J.C. WYLD
Geographers

PROVINCIAL

ABEL AND SONS
Booksellers and Librarians
HENRY ABRAHAM
Goldsmiths, Silversmiths and Jewellers
PASCAL ATKEY AND SON
Ironmakers
ALFRED THOMPSON BARBER
Art Dealer
ALFRED E. BEKEN
Chemists and Druggists
BENJAMIN BENSON
Booksellers and Librarians
CHARLES BORELLI
Chronometer, Watch and Clock Makers
BRIGHT & MINNS
Dyers and Cleaners
BRISTOL GOLDSMITHS ALLIANCE &
MANUFACTURING CO.
Goldsmiths, Silversmiths and Jewellers
ROBERT BRODIE
Printers, Publishers and Printsellers
BROWN BARNES AND BELL
Photographers
WILLIAM BROWN
Silk Mercers
CALEY & SON
Linen Drapers
GEORGE P. CARTLAND
Photographers
CLAY AND ABRAHAM
Chemists and Druggists

WILLIAM CLEAVE
Cabinet Makers and Upholsterers
THOMAS R. COBDEN
Tailor
ALF COOKE
Chromo-Lithographer
GEORGE COOPER & SON
Decorators, Painters and Glaziers
DERBY CROWN PORCELAIN CO.
China and Glass Manufacturers
JAMES DIMMICK
Chronometer, Watch and Clock Makers
JAMES DUDLEY
Goldsmiths, Silversmiths and Jewellers
WILLIAM DYER
Chemists and Druggists
DYSON & SONS
Music Sellers
A.L. EMANUEL
Goldsmiths, Silversmiths and Jewellers
E. & E. EMANUEL
Goldsmiths, Silversmiths and Jewellers
EDWARD FARRELL
Carvers and Gilders
FERRISS AND CO.
Chemists and Druggists
GEORGE FLASHMAN
Cabinet Makers and Upholsterers
ELIZA FOUNTAIN
Statuary Mason

W.E. FRANKLIN
Booksellers and Librarians
F. LE GALLAIS
Cabinet Makers and Upholsterers
GALT AND CO.
Booksellers and Librarians
T.G. & W. GIBBONS
Chemists and Druggists
JOSEPH GILLOTT
Steel Pen Manufacturers
THOMAS D. GOERTZ
Cabinet Makers and Upholsterers
GRIFFIN AND CO.
Booksellers and Librarians
EDWARD GRISBROOK
Chemists and Druggists
WILLIAM J. GUBBINS
Booksellers and Librarians
W.T. GUBBINS & SON
Pianoforte Makers and Tuners
A. & F. HALLIDAY
Cabinet Makers, Upholsterers, Carvers and Gilders
S. HANNINGTON & SONS
Linen Drapers
HAYDON HARE
Printers, Publishers and Printsellers
WILLIAM J. HERBERT
Toys and Fancy Goods Makers
G.A. HILLYER
Soap Purveyors
HOPWOOD AND SON
Chemists and Druggists
HUGHES AND MULLINS
Photographers
WILLIAM JOHNSON
Electrical Engineer
MARY JONES
Stationer
JONES & WILLIS
Silk Mercers
EDWIN JOYCE
Carvers and Gilders
ROBERT THOMAS KNIGHT
Cabinet Makers and Upholsterers
LETTSOME AND SONS
Photographers

LEWIS & SON
Goldsmiths, Silversmiths and Jewellers
JAMES LINDSAY
Carvers and Gilders
CHARLES LUKE
Booksellers and Librarians
ERNEST MARSHALL
Printers, Publishers and Printsellers
GEORGE MARVIN
Cabinet Makers and Upholsterers
HENRY NICHOLAS MILLS
Antique Furniture Dealer
MINTONS
China and Glass Manufacturers
MINTON, HOLLINS AND CO.
China and Glass Manufacturers
JOHN MITCHELL
Steel Pen Manufacturers
MOORMAN AND SON
Cabinet Makers and Upholsterers
ANN MURRELL
Cabinet Makers and Upholsterers
GEORGE NEW
Booksellers and Librarians
LEOPOLD MURRAY NIXON
China and Glass Manufacturers
WILLIAM OLDHAM
Photographers
R. & F.W. OXLEY
Printers, Publishers and Printsellers
J.A. PURNELL
Cabinet Makers and Upholsterers
REDFERN & SONS
Silk Mercers
THOMAS REED
Goldsmiths, Silversmiths and Jewellers
REID & SONS
Goldsmiths, Silversmiths and Jewellers
HENRY F. ROBERTS
Pianoforte Makers and Tuners
ROBERTS & SON
Soap Purveyors
JOSEPH W. ROBERTS & SON
Pianoforte Makers and Tuners
JOHN ROBINSON
Decorators, Painters and Glaziers

THOMAS RODGERS & EDWIN DENYER
Linen Drapers
JOSEPH ROGERS & SONS
Cutlers
RUSSELL AND CO.
Chemists and Druggists
THOMAS ROBERT RUSSELL
Chronometer, Watch and Clock Makers
THOMAS P. SALT
Cutlers
HENRY SIMMS & SON
Music Sellers
SIMPSON BENZIE
Goldsmiths, Silversmiths and Jewellers
JAMES SMITH & SON
Pianoforte Makers and Tuners
TASKER SONS & CO.
Telephonic engineers
WILLIAM WAGLAND
Chronometer, Watch and Clock Makers

S.J. WARING & SONS
Cabinet Makers and Upholsterers
G. & E. WATTS
Decorators, Painters, Glaziers and Plumbers
HENRY JOSEPH WHITLOCK
Photographers
W. WILLIAMSON AND SONS
Cabinet Makers and Upholsterers
WOOD & HORSPOOL
Ironmongers
E. WOODYEAR & SONS
Linen Drapers
WORCESTER ROYAL PORCELAIN CO.
China and Glass Manufacturers
YATES AND CO.
Carpet Manufacturers
YELF BROS.
Printers, Publishers and Printsellers

SCOTLAND

JAMES AITCHISON
Goldsmiths, Silversmiths and Jewellers
DAVID ALLAN
Cabinet Makers and Upholsterers
RODERICK ANDERSON AND SONS
Fishing Tackle Manufacturers
T. AND R. ANNAN AND SONS
Photographers
J.B. BENNETT AND SONS
Decorators and Painters
BROOK AND SON
Goldsmiths, Silversmiths and Jewellers
BROWN & POLSON
Starch Manufacturers
ROBERT BRYSON AND SONS
Chronometer, Watch and Clock Makers

GEORGE COTTON
Snuff Manufacturer
WILLIAM COUTTS AND SONS
Decorators and Painters
JOHN AND JAMES COWAN
Stationers Etc.
DAVIDSON AND KAY
Chemists and Druggists
DOIG, WILSON AND WHEATLEY
Lithographers, Print Sellers and Printers
W. DUNNINGHAM AND CO.
Chronometer, Watch and Clock Makers
DUNCAN FLOCKHART AND CO.
Chemists and Druggists
JOHN FORD AND CO.
Glass Manufacturers

FRASER AND GREEN
Chemists and Druggists
JOHN FYFE & SON
Brushmakers
ALEXANDER GARDNER
Booksellers and Publishers
JAMES GRAY & SON
Ironmongers, Stovemakers, Etc.
HAMILTON AND INCHES
Chronometer, Watch and Clock Makers
HAY & LYALL
Carvers and Gilders
HENDERSON & BISSET
Bookbinder
HARVEY HILLIARD & SON
Surgical Instrument Makers
PETER AND JOHN IRVIN
Brushmakers
GEORGE JAMIESON AND SONS
Goldsmiths, Silversmiths and Jewellers
GEORGE HARVEY JOHNSTON
Geographer
W. AND A.K. JOHNSTON
Engravers
JAMES LUMSDEN
Stationers Etc.
ALEXANDER MACDONALD & CO.
Marble and Granite Manufacturers
GAVIN CAMPBELL MACDOUGALL
Bagpiper Maker
WALTER MACLEAN
Lithographers, Print Sellers and Printers
JAMES MCCLURE & SON
Carvers and Gilders
DAVID MCHARDY
Ironmongers, Stovemakers, Etc.
MARR, WOOD AND CO.
Pianoforte Makers
W. MARSHALL AND CO.
Goldsmiths, Silversmiths and Jewellers
THOMAS MEIN
Optician
METHVEN SIMPSON AND CO.
Music Sellers

MILLER AND RICHARD
Type Founder
MILNE LOW AND CO.
Clothiers, Hosiers and Glovers
ROBERT MILNE
Photographers
JAMES MUIRHEAD AND SONS
Chronometer, Watch and Clock Makers
HUGH PATON AND SONS
Carvers and Gilders
PETERSON AND SONS
Music Sellers
WILLIAM POLSON
Starch Manufacturers
JOHN PULLAR & SONS
Dyers and Cleaners
D.P. RAIT AND SONS
Goldsmiths, Silversmiths and Jewellers
JAMES SAINT & CO.
Drapers and Silk Mercers
JOHN SIBBALD AND SONS
Ironmongers, Stovemakers, Etc.
LEWIS SMITH AND SON
Booksellers and Publishers
SMITH AND SONS
Goldsmiths, Silversmiths and Jewellers
ROBERT STEWART
Goldsmiths, Silversmiths and Jewellers
TAYLOR & HENDERSON
Lithographers, Print Sellers and Printers
J. AND A.B. WHITE
Clothiers, Hosiers and Glovers
WHYTOCK REID AND CO.
Cabinet Makers and Upholsterers
CHARLES ALBERT WILSON
Photographers
PETER GEORGE WILSON
Goldsmiths, Silversmiths and Jewellers
JAMES WRIGHT AND SONS
Marble and Granite Manufacturers
D. WYLLIE AND SONS
Booksellers and Publishers

IRELAND

GEORGE ANDREWS
Linen and Damask
RICHARD ATKINSON AND CO.
Tabinet Manufacturers
CHANCELLOR AND SON
Photographers
JOHN EVANS
Chemists and Apothecaries
HENRY FIELDING
Poplin Manufacturer
EDMOND JOHNSON
Silversmiths and Jewellers
JAMES LAFAYETTE
Photographers

HAMILTON LONG AND CO.
Chemists and Apothecaries
FREDERICK PILKINGTON
Bookbinder
ROBINSON AND CLEAVER
Lace Manufacturers
FRANCIS DAVIS WARD
Leather Good Manufacturer
SAMUEL S. WATERHOUSE
Silversmiths and Jewellers
WEST AND SON
Silversmiths and Jewellers
S. WILSON AND CO.
Tent and Marquee Manufacturers

SPENCER PONSONBY-FANE
Comptroller of Accounts
Lord Chamberlain's Office, St. James's Palace
January 1, 1900

LIST OF TRADESMEN WHO HOLD WARRANTS OF APPOINTMENT FROM
THE MASTER OF THE HORSE, WITH AUTHORITY TO USE THE ROYAL ARMS

W. BAIN
Posting Masters
BARKER AND CO.
Coachmakers
BARTLEY AND SONS
Bootmakers
E. BLACKMAN
Dealers in Horses
J.V. BLAKE
Veterinary Surgeons
T. BRIGG AND SONS
Umbrella Makers
BROWN, SON AND LONG
Tailors
CAMPBELLS LTD.
Posting Masters
CHAMPION AND WILTON
Harness and Saddle Makers
R.B. CHEVERTON
Coachmakers
J.T. CLARK
Coachmakers
W. CLARK
Blacking Manufacturers
C.A. COBDEN
Tailors
COOK AND HOLDWAY
Coachmakers
W. COOPER, WILLIS AND WICKS
Harness and Saddle Makers
F. COUTTS
Posting Masters
CROALL AND CROALL
Coachmakers
T. DAVIES
Cooper
DAY AND MARTIN
Blacking Manufacturers

DEAR AND MORGAN
Corn Merchants
DEVEREUX AND SON
Hatters
H. DUNKLEY AND SON
Bootmakers
J.W. EDWARDS
Veterinary Surgeons
FIRMIN AND SONS LTD.
Button Manufacturers
FORDER AND CO. LTD.
Coachmakers
H. GOERTZ & SON
Upholsterers
C.A. GOOD
Veterinary Surgeons
F.E. GOUGH
Coachmakers
W. GREGORY AND SONS
Posting Masters
HACKER AND ROWELL
Tailors
H. HALL AND SON
Bootmakers
HAMBURGER, ROGERS AND SONS
Gold Lacemen
HAMMOND AND CO.
Leather Breeches Maker
C. HARRIS
Turners
J. HAWKINS
Farriers
J. HEINIGER
Posting Masters
HOBY AND CO.
Bootmakers
HOLMES AND CO.
Coachmakers

HOOPER AND CO. LTD.
Coachmakers
H. HUNTSMAN AND SONS
Tailors and Leather Breeches Maker
JEYES SANITARY COMPOUNDS CO. LTD.
Disinfectants
W. LANE AND SON
Builder
LATCHFORD AND CO.
Bit and Spur Makers
LAWRENCE AND SON
Dyers
J. & B. MARSH
Corn Merchants
MARTIN HORSE-SHOE COMPANY LTD.
Patent Horse-Shoes
L. MARY
Farriers
MAYHEW AND CO.
Harness and Saddle Makers
MEARNS AND CO.
Harness and Saddle Makers
S. MERRY AND CO.
Harness and Saddle Makers
J. MITCHELL
Farriers
J. MORGAN AND SONS
Tailors
MUSSON AND SON
Harness and Saddle Makers
NEWTON AND COOK
Sponge Merchants
W. NICHOLLS AND CO.
Turners
J. PASMORE AND SONS
Coachmakers
J. PECKOVER, PRICE, WHITTAKER AND CO.
Tailors
T. PETERS AND SONS
Coachmakers
C. PITT AND CO.
Button Manufacturers
R.W. AND J. PULLMAN
Leather Merchants

J.Y. ROOD AND CO.
Upholsterers
C.J. ROTHERHAM
Canine Surgeon
SCOTTS LTD.
Hatters
SHEATH BROTHERS
Patent Spoke-Brush Makers
T. SHORT
Dyers
S.W. SILVER & CO.
Waterproof Clothing
SIR H.L. SIMPSON
Veterinary Surgeons
JOHN SMART
Carrier
G. SMITH
Harness and Saddle Makers
W.J. SMITH
Dealers in Horses
J.I. SOWTER AND CO.
Harness and Saddle Makers
SPRATT'S PATENT LTD.
Purveyor of Dog Biscuits
STARLEY BROTHERS LTD.
Tricycle Manufacturers
E. STILLWELL AND SON
Gold Lacemen
SWAINE AND ADENEY
Whipmakers
J. TAYLOR
Wig and Curl Maker
R.C. TENNANT
Veterinary Surgeons
W. & F. THORN
Coachmakers
THRUPP AND MABERLY
Coachmakers
UNDERWOOD AND FARRANT
Cutlers
VEZEY AND CO.
Coachmakers
WELLS & SONS
Wheelwrights

WHIPPY, STEGGALL AND CO.
Harness and Saddle Makers
WILKINSON AND SON
Tailors

G. WILLIAMS
Veterinary Surgeons
WYBURN & CO.
Coachmakers

H. P. EWART
Crown Equerry
Master of the Horse's Office
Royal Mews, Pimlico, January 1, 1900

1946

LIST OF TRADESMEN WHO HOLD WARRANTS OF APPOINTMENT TO THE KING FROM THE KEEPER OF HIS MAJESTY'S PRIVY PURSE, WITH AUTHORITY TO DISPLAY THE ROYAL ARMS, BUT NOT TO FLY THE ROYAL STANDARD, NOR TO USE THE WORD "ROYAL"

ALBION MOTORS LTD.
Motor Lorry Manufacturers
JAMES ALLAN AND CO. (ABERDEEN) LTD.
House Furnishers
ALLOM BROTHERS LTD.
Makers of Electrical Fittings
W.J. ANDERSON LTD.
Works Contractors
ASHTON AND MITCHELL LTD.
Theatre and Concert Ticket Agents
ASHWELL & NESBIT LTD.
Manufacturers of Mechanical Stokers and
of Heating and Hot Water Equipment
ASPREY AND CO. LTD.
Silversmiths and Jewellers
BAMFORDS LTD.
Manufacturers of Agricultural Machinery
BEESTON BOILER CO. LTD.
Makers of Domestic Boilers
BENSON AND CLEGG LTD.
Tailors
JOSEPH BENTLEY LTD.
Suppliers of Horticultural Chemicals
HENRY BLACKLOCK & CO. LTD.
Publishers of Bradshaw's Guides
J.H.G. BORLAND
Seed Merchant
A. AND J. BOWKER
Corn and Cake Merchants
J.J. BRANTOM & CO. LTD.
Suppliers of Animal Feeding Stuffs
BRITISH GLUES AND CHEMICALS LTD.
Suppliers of Mineral Supplements
BRITISH LEGION POPPY FACTORY LTD.
British Legion Poppy Manufacturers
J. BROWN AND SON
Suppliers of Stock Game
S.S. BURLINGHAM LTD.
Clockmakers
JAMES BURNETT
Chemists
OSCAR CALLOW
Silversmiths

CALTHROPS LTD.
Suppliers of Animal Feeding Stuffs
CARRINGTON & CO. LTD.
Silversmiths
CARRON CO.
Ironfounders
CARTER'S TESTED SEEDS LTD.
Seedsmen
CARTIER LTD.
Jewellers and Goldsmiths
CATCHPOLE AND WILLIAMS LTD.
Silversmiths
ROBERT CHALMERS
Suppliers of Highland Dress Accessories
W.G. CLARKE & SONS (1929) LTD.
Suppliers of Dog and Game Food
CLIBRANS LTD.
Nurserymen and Seedsmen
T. CLOUGH AND SON
Gun and Cartridge Makers
COLAS PRODUCTS LTD.
Manufacturers of Bitumen Emulsion
R. COLLER AND SONS LTD.
Coal Merchants
COLLINGWOOD (JEWELLERS) LTD.
Jewellers and Silversmiths
COOPER, MCDOUGALL AND ROBERTSON LTD.
Suppliers of Sheep and Cattle Dips and Veterinary
Preparations
J.S. CRABTREE & CO. LTD.,
Suppliers of Lighting Switches
CRICHTON BROS.
Silversmiths
R. CRITTALL AND CO. LTD.
Engineers
A.L. CURTIS
Manufacturer of Fire Cement
DAIRY SUPPLY CO. LTD.
Makers of Dairy Appliances
DARE AND DOLPHIN LTD.
Hosiers
DAY AND SONS, CREWE LTD.
Suppliers of Animal Medicines

DAY, SON AND HEWITT LTD.
Suppliers of Animal Medicines
DENNIS BROS. LTD.
Motor Mower Manufacturers
ALEX. DICKSON AND SONS LTD.
Nurserymen and Seedsmen
DICKSON & ROBINSON LTD.
Seedsmen
DICKSONS AND CO.
Nurserymen and Seedsmen
A. DODMAN AND CO. LTD.
Engineers
GEORGE DONALD AND SONS LTD.
Decorators
DRAKE AND MOUNT LTD.
Suppliers of Animal Feeding Stuffs
ALFRED DUNHILL LTD.
Tobacconists
GEORGE DUNLOP AND SON
Suppliers of Game Foods
DUNNS FARM SEEDS LTD.
Seedsmen
M.W. DWIGHT
Suppliers of Stock Game
G. AND T. EARLE LTD.
Cement Manufacturers
EDE AND RAVENSCROFT
Robe Makers
EDISON-SWAN ELECTRIC CO. LTD.
Suppliers of Electric Lamps
ELECTRICAL INSTALLATIONS
Electrical Engineers
EXPRESS DAIRY CO. LTD.
Dairy Suppliers
R.W. FARMAN
Norfolk Reed Thatcher
FISONS LTD.
Makers of Chemical Fertilisers
FODENS LTD.
Motor Tractor Manufacturers
JOHN FORBES (HARWICK) LTD.
Nurserymen and Seedsmen
A.E. FOUNTAIN AND SONS
Agricultural Merchants
GARRARD AND CO. LTD.
Goldsmiths and Crown Jewellers
G.B. EQUIPMENTS LTD.
Manufacturers of Cinema Equipment

STANLEY GIBBONS LTD.
Philatelists
GIBSON AND MITCHAM LTD.
Seedsmen
GIEVES LTD.
Naval Outfitters
GILBERTSON AND PAGE LTD.
Dog Food Manufacturers
GIRLINGS FERO-CONCRETE CO. LTD.
Suppliers of Fero-Concrete Work
GOLDSMITHS AND SILVERSMITHS CO. LTD.
Silversmiths
G. GOMM LTD.
Forage and Coal Merchants
P.M. GOODCHILD
Photographer
JAMES GORDON
Coal Merchant
GRAMOPHONE CO. LTD.
Suppliers of Gramophones, Records and Radio Apparatus
THEODORE HAMBLIN LTD.
Opticians
HAMILTON & CO. LTD.
Jewellers and Silversmiths
HARBOROWS LTD.
Glovemakers
HARDY BROS. LTD.
Goldsmiths
JOHN G. HARDY LTD.
Mercers of Woollen Cloth
HARRISON AND SONS LTD.
Printers
HART ACCUMULATOR CO. LTD.
Makers of Accumulators
HATCHARDS LTD.
Booksellers
HAWES AND CURTIS LTD.
Shirt Makers and Hosiers
ALFRED HAYS LTD.
Suppliers of Music and Gramophones
HENRY HEATH LTD.
Hatters
ROBERT HEATH LTD.
Trunk Makers
WALLACE HEATON LTD.
Suppliers of Photographic Equipment
HEMING AND CO. LTD.
Silversmiths

HUMBER FISHING AND FISH MANURE CO. LTD.
Fish Fertiliser Manufacturers
HUNT AND ROSKELL LTD.
Silversmiths
A.J. IZOD LTD.
Shirtmakers
JERMYN AND SONS LTD.
Drapers and Furnishers
WALTER C. JOEL LTD.
Clockmakers
C.F. JOHNS AND PEGG
Military Tailors
W.H. JOHNSON AND SONS LTD.
Motor Engineers
PETER JONES
Suppliers of Furnishings
J.K. KING & SONS LTD.
Seedsmen
LAING AND MATHER LTD.
Seedsmen
JAMES LAMBERT AND SON LTD.
Ironmongers
E.G. LEHMANN
House Furnisher
LENYGON AND MORANT LTD.
Decorators
LILLYWHITES LTD.
Athletic Outfitters
LITTLE & BALLANTYNE LTD.
Nurserymen and Seedsmen
LOCKWOOD-BROWN AND CO. LTD.
Athletic Outfitters
ARCHIBALD MACDONALD
Decorator
SIR HERBERT MARSHALL & SONS LTD.
Piano Tuners
MASSEY-HARRIS CO. LTD.
Makers of Agricultural Implements
HENRY MAXWELL & CO. LTD.
Boot and Spur Makers
MERRYWEATHER AND SONS LTD.
Fire Engineers
MEYER AND MORTIMER LTD.
Military Outfitters
JOHN MILNE
Carrier and Coal Merchant
MILNS, CARTWRIGHT AND REYNOLDS LTD.
Livery Tailors

JOHN MOWLEM & CO. LTD.
Builders and Contractors
A. NELSON AND CO. LTD.
Chemists
CHAS. NISSEN AND CO. LTD.
Stamp Dealers
NUTT PRODUCTS LTD.
Pipe Makers
BERTRAM PARK
Photographer
PATTRICK AND THOMPSONS LTD.
Timber Merchants
PERMUTIT CO. LTD.
Suppliers of Water Treatment Equipment
H.H. PLANTE
Jeweller and Silversmith
PLOWRIGHT, PRATT AND HARBAGE LTD.
Ironmongers
C. AND V. POPKISS
Upholsterers
POWELL AND SON
Corn and Seed Merchants
CHARLES H. PUGH LTD.
Motor Mower Manufacturers
JAMES PURDEY AND SONS LTD.
Gun Makers
PURIMACHOS LTD.
Manufacturers of Refractory Cements
RANSOMES, SIMS AND JEFFERIES LTD.
Makers of Agricultural and Horticultural Machinery
JOHN RIGBY AND CO. (GUNMAKERS) LTD.
Rifle Manufacturers
RIVERSIDE GARAGE
Motor Engineers
A.B. ROBERTSON AND SON LTD.
Electrical Engineers
FRANK ROBINSON
Racehorse Plater
RICHARD SANKEY AND SON LTD.
Makers of Horticultural Pottery
H. SCOTT AND SONS
Suppliers of Horticultural Chemicals
SCOTTISH AGRICULTURAL INDUSTRIES LTD.
Suppliers of Agricultural Goods, Chemical Manures
and Seeds
ALEXANDER SHIMWELL AND CO.
Electrical Engineers

J.L. SHIRLEY AND SON
Suppliers of Cattle Feeding Stuffs
SHIRRAS LAING & CO. LTD.
Ironmongers
R. SILCOCK AND SONS LTD.
Suppliers of Animal Feeding Stuffs
EDWARD SMITH
Cap and Accoutrement Maker
GEORGE SMITH AND CO.
Sporting Outfitters
SPENCER AND CO.
Masonic Outfitters
SPINK AND SON LTD.
Medallists
SPRATT'S PATENT LTD.
Suppliers of Dog Foods
J. STEELE
Live Stock Carrier
STEPHENS BROTHERS LTD.
Hosiers
STEVENSON AND RUSSELL
Clockmakers
S. STRAKER AND SONS
Printers and Stationers
STRATSTONE LTD.
Motor Car Distributors
SUTTON AND SONS LTD.
Seedsmen
TAYLOR AND HENDERSON
Printers and Stationers
TELFORD, GRIER, MACKAY & CO. LTD.
Electrical Engineers
JOSEPH THORLEY LTD.
Makers of Cattle Foods
THRESHER & GLENNY LTD.
Tailors

TOOGOOD AND SONS LTD.
Seed Merchants
MISS GEORGINA M. TRUMPER
Hairdresser
RAPHAEL TUCK AND SONS LTD.
Fine Art Publishers
VACUUM OIL CO. LTD.
Suppliers of Lubricating Oils
VINCENTS OF READING LTD.
Motor Horse Box Makers
ROWLAND WARD LTD.
Naturalists
WARING BROS. LTD.
Dog and Game Food Manufacturers
WATERLOO MILLS CAKE AND WAREHOUSING
CO.LTD.
Animal Feeding Stuffs Manufacturers
BERNARD WEATHERILL LTD.
Breeches and Jodhpur Makers and Livery Tailors
EDWARD WEBB AND SONS (STOURBRIDGE)
LTD.
Seedsmen
D. AND J. WELBY LTD.
Silversmiths
WHITE HEATHER LAUNDRY (LONDON) LTD
Launderers and Cleaners
JOHN WILDER LTD.
Manufacturers of Agricultural Machinery
DOROTHY WILDING PORTRAITS LTD.
Photographers
WILLIAM WILLETT LTD.
Builders and Decorators
JAMES WILSON AND SON (ABERDEEN) LTD.
Suppliers of Animal Feeding Stuffs
WILLIAM WOOD AND SON LTD.
Garden Contractors and Horticultural Builders

ULICK ALEXANDER,
Keeper of the Privy Purse
Privy Purse Office, Buckingham Palace
1st January 1946

1946

LIST OF TRADESMEN IN THE DEPARTMENT OF HIS MAJESTY'S PRIVY PURSE, PERMITTED TO STYLE THEMSELVES "BY APPOINTMENT TO THE LATE KING GEORGE V", ENTITLING THEM TO DISPLAY THE ROYAL ARMS, BUT NOT TO FLY THE ROYAL STANDARD, NOR TO USE THE WORD "ROYAL"

AILSA CRAIG MOTOR CO. LTD.
Makers of Marine Motors
W. ANDERSON AND SONS LTD.
Tailors
BING AND GRONDAHL
Porcelain Manufacturers
G.M. BRIDGES AND SON LTD.
Scenic Artists and Decorators
BURBERRYS LTD.
Tailors
W. CALLAGHAN AND CO. LTD.
Opticians
CHARPENTIER LTD.
Booksellers
CLIBRANS LTD.
Nurserymen
J.C. CORDING AND CO. LTD.
Waterproofers
T. CRAPPER AND CO. LTD.
Sanitary Engineers
J. DANIELS AND CO. LTD.
Uniform Makers
DAVIDSON AND KAY LTD.
Chemists
DAVIES AND SON (LONDON) LTD
Tailors
E. DENT AND CO. LTD.
Watch and Clock Makers
DOBBIE AND CO. LTD.
Seedsmen
J. DUVELLEROY LTD.
Fan Makers
FELL AND CO. (HEXHAM) LTD.
Seedsmen and Nurserymen
J. FINDLAY
Taxidermist
FRASER, FERGUSON AND MACBEAN LTD.
Highland Ornament Makers
GILBERSON AND PAGE LTD.
Dog and Game Food Manufacturers

P. AND J. HAGGART
Tartan Manufacturers
HARMAN AND CO. LTD.
Silversmiths
J.F. HARPER
Posting Master
DAVID HEDGES AND SONS
Photographers
HENNINGHAM AND HOLLIS
Stationers
CAPTAIN S.E. HILL
Veterinary Surgeon
HOLLAND AND HOLLAND LTD.
Gun Makers
E. HYNER AND CO. LTD.
Motor Carriers
JARROLD AND SONS LTD.
Stationers
JOHNSON BROS. AND CO. LTD.
Iron Fencing Manufacturers
G.W. KING LTD.
Manufacturers of Dairy Equipment
LAVENDER AND BATEMAN LTD.
Roadstone Merchants
R.G. LAWRIE LTD.
Bagpipe Makers
SAMUEL LEE AND SON
Yachting Shoemakers
W. LOCK AND SON LTD.
Plumbers
MACKENZIE AND MONCUR LTD.
Hothouse Builders & Heating Engineers
MAGGS BROTHERS LTD.
Booksellers
PENNELL AND SONS
Seedsmen
PRATCHITT BROS. LTD.
Manufacturers of Pumping Machinery
RANDS AND JECKELL LTD.
Rick Cloths, Sacks and Tents Maker

SULLIVAN POWELL AND CO. LTD.
Tobacconists
JAMES TAGGART AND SON
Monumental Sculptors
DUNCAN WATSON LTD.
Electrical Engineers

WHITE ALLOM LTD.
Decorative Artists
ZAEHNSDORF LTD.
Bookbinders and Booksellers

ULICK ALEXANDER,
Keeper of the Privy Purse
Privy Purse Office, Buckingham Palace
1st January 1946

LIST OF TRADESMEN WHO HOLD WARRANTS OF APPOINTMENT TO THE KING IN THE
DEPARTMENT OF THE MASTER OF THE HOUSEHOLD, WITH AUTHORITY TO USE THE ROYAL
ARMS. THESE WARRANTS DO NOT CARRY THE RIGHT TO FLY THE ROYAL STANDARD,
OR TO USE THE WORD "ROYAL"

ARDATH TOBACCO CO. LTD.
"State Express" Cigarette Manufacturers
THE ARTISTIC BLIND CO. LTD.
Blindmakers
J. AND E. ATKINSON LTD.
Perfumers
JOHN BAILEY & SON (POULTERERS) LTD
Purveyors of Poultry and Game
J.W. BAKER (CHINA AND GLASS) LTD.
China and Glass Merchants
J. BENNETT (BILLINGSGATE) LTD.
Fishmongers
BENSON AND HEDGES LTD.
Tobacconists
BERRY BROS. AND RUDD LTD.
Wine Merchants

BINNS LTD.
House Furnishers
BOILERINE LTD.
Manufacturing Chemists
BOOTH'S DISTILLERIES LTD.
Gin Distillers
BOOTS PURE DRUG CO. LTD.
Suppliers of First Aid Dressings & Soap
CHARLES BORELLI AND SONS
Clockmakers
BOVRIL LTD.
Suppliers of Bovril
BRAND AND CO. LTD.
Suppliers of Meat Essence
BRICKWOOD AND CO. LTD.
Brewers

JOHN BROADWOOD AND SONS LTD.
Pianoforte Tuners
C.T. BROCK AND CO.'S "CRYSTAL PALACE"
FIREWORKS LTD.
Pyrotechnists
H. BRONNLEY AND CO. LTD.
Toilet Soap Makers
BROWN AND POLSON LTD.
Cornflour Manufacturers
BRYANT AND MAY LTD.
Match Manufacturers
JAMES BUCHANAN AND CO. LTD.
Scotch Whisky Distillers
WILLIAM BUDDLES AND CO.
Chemists
BUDGEN AND CO. LTD.
Grocers
BULLOCK, LADE & CO. LTD.
Whisky Distillers
H.P. BULMER AND CO. LTD.
Cider Makers
P.B. BURGOYNE AND CO. LTD.
Empire Wine Makers
BURROUGHS & WATTS LTD.
Billiard Table Makers
W. AND J. BURROW LTD.
Suppliers of Malvern Water
CADBURY BROTHERS LTD.
Chocolate and Cocoa Manufacturers
CADBURY, PRATT AND CO. LTD.
Provision Merchants
R. CADISCH AND SONS
Suppliers of Household Cleaning Requisites
A.J. CALEY LTD.
Mineral Water Manufacturers
STEWARD CALLARD AND WATT LTD.
Bakers
CAMPBELL BROTHERS
Meat and Poultry Purveyors
CAMPBELL, HOPE AND KING, ARCHIBALD LTD.
Brewers
CANTRELL AND COCHRANE LTD.
Mineral Water Manufacturers
T.B. CARLIN LTD.
Cigar Merchants

E.J. CARPENTER LTD.
Carriers
CARPET MANUFACTURING CO. LTD.
Carpet Manufacturers
CEREBOS LTD.
Table Salt Manufacturers
CHARLIE, RICHARDS AND CO. LTD.
Wine Merchants
CHARLES
Fishmongers and Poulterers
CHARRINGTON, GARDNER, LOCKET
AND CO. LTD.
Coal and Coke Merchants
CHIVAS BROS. LTD.
Purveyors of Provisions and Whisky
CHIVERS AND SONS LTD.
Purveyors of Jams, Jellies, Canned Fruit and Vegetables
CHRISTOPHER AND CO. LTD.
Wine Merchants
ANDREW COLLIE AND CO. LTD
Grocers
COOPER AND CO.'S STORES LTD.
Grocers
FRANK COOPER LTD.
Oxford Marmalade Makers
CORNEY AND BARROW LTD.
Wine Merchants
GEORGE COTTON AND SON
Cigar Merchants
JAMES COWAN AND SONS LTD.
Launderers
WILLIAM CRAWFORD AND SONS LTD.
Biscuit Manufacturers
JOSEPH CROSFIELD AND SONS LTD.
Soap Manufacturers
CROSSE AND BLACKWELL LTD.
Purveyors of Preserved Provisions
JOHN CURTIS
Purveyors of Kippers
DARVILLE & SONS LTD.
Wine Merchants
W.S. DAVIDSON
Purveyors of Meat and Poultry
DAVIES BOTTLED FRUITS LTD.
Purveyors of Bottled Fruits

DAVIS AND SON, DYERS, LONDON LTD.
Dyers and Cleaners
RICHARD DAVIS LTD.
Mineral Water Manufacturers
DEBENHAM AND FREEBODY
Linen Drapers
J.A. DEVENISH AND CO. LTD.
Brewers
JOHN DEWAR AND SONS LTD.
Scotch Whisky Distillers
J.T. DOBBINS LTD.
Suppliers of Household Cleaning Materials
JOHN DONALD AND CO. (CHINA MERCHANTS) LTD.
Glass Manufacturers & China Merchants
DONALDSONS
Suppliers of Fish and Ice
DYSON & SONS LTD.
Clockmakers, Gold and Silversmiths
EASTMAN AND SON
Dyers and Cleaners
ELECTROLUX LTD.
Refrigerator Makers
EMU WINE CO. LTD.
Australian Wine Merchants
ERASMIC CO. LTD.
Toilet Soap Makers
W. FENN
Poulterer
FINDLATER MACKIE TODD AND CO. LTD.
Wine and Spirit Merchants
FITCH AND SON LTD.
Provision Merchants
J. FLORIS
Perfumers
JOHN FORD AND CO.
Suppliers of China and Glass
FORTNUM AND MASON LTD.
Grocers
JOHN FOSTER AND CO. LTD.
Suppliers of Furnishing Fabrics
GEORGE FOWLER, LEE & CO. LTD.
Suppliers of Fruit Preserving Appliances
J.S. FRY AND SONS LTD.
Cocoa and Chocolate Manufacturers

ROBERT GARROW LTD.
Fishmongers
J.R. GAUNT AND SON LTD.
Medallists and Button Makers
WILLIAM GAYMER AND SON LTD.
Cyder Manufacturers
R. AND T. GIBSON LTD.
Grocers
GILLARD AND CO. LTD.
Sauce and Pickle Manufacturers
GLADWIN LTD.
Manufacturers of Electro Plate & Cutlery
GONZALEZ, BYASS AND CO. LTD.
Sherry Merchants
THOMAS GOODE AND CO. (LONDON) LTD.
China and Glass Manufacturers
EDWARD GOODYEAR
Florists
LUIS GORDON AND SONS LTD.
Domecq's Sherry Merchants
GOSLIN AND CO. LTD.
Purveyors of Meat and Poultry
JAMES GRAY AND SON IRONMONGERS AND ELECTRICIANS LTD.
Ironmongers
GROSVENOR ELECTRICAL CO.
Suppliers of Electrical Fittings
HALL AND SONS (BUTCHERS) LTD.
Suppliers of Meat
HANKEY, BANNISTER AND CO.
Wine Merchants
C. AND T. HARRIS (CALNE) LTD.
Bacon Curers
HARRISON BROS. AND HOWSON
Silversmiths and Cutlers
HARRODS LTD.
Grocers and Provision Merchants
JOHN HARVEY AND SONS LTD.
Wine Merchants
HATCH, MANSFIELD AND CO. LTD.
Wine Merchants
HEDGES AND BUTLER LTD.
Wine Merchants
PETER F. HEERING
Purveyors of Cherry Brandy

RICHARD HICKS (COVENT GARDEN) LTD.
Fruiterers and Greengrocers
HILL, THOMSON AND CO. LTD.
Wine and Spirit Merchants
HOOPER STRUVE AND CO. LTD.
Mineral Water Manufacturers
HOOVER LTD.
Manufacturers of Electric Suction Sweepers
HORLICKS LTD.
Purveyors of Malted Milk
J. HOWSE AND CO.
Suppliers of Brushwood
HUNTLEY AND PALMERS LTD.
Biscuit Manufacturers
IDRIS LTD.
Manufacturers of Mineral Water and Fruit Beverages
IND COOPE & ALLSOPP LTD.
Brewers
JACKSON, R., AND CO. LTD.
Grocers
W. AND R. JACOB AND CO. (L'POOL) LTD.
Biscuit Manufacturers
JUDD, BUDD LTD.
Coal Merchants
JUSTERINI AND BROOKS LTD.
Wine Merchants
G.H. KEEN LTD.
Furnishers and Upholsterers
JAMES KEILLER & SON LTD
Purveyors of Dundee Marmalade, Mincemeat and
Shortbread
KELLY'S DIRECTORIES LTD.
Suppliers of Directories
G.B. KENT & SONS LTD
Brushmakers
GEORGE KENT LTD.
Knife Cleaning Machine Makers
KIA-ORA LTD.
Suppliers of Fruit Beverages
JOHN KNIGHT LTD.
Soap Manufacturers
W.J. LATCHFORD AND SONS
Timber Merchants
LEA AND PERRINS LTD.
Purveyors of Worcestershire Sauce

GEORGE LEITH AND SON
Bakers
LEVER BROS. (PORT SUNLIGHT) LTD.
Soap and Soap Powder Manufacturers
JOHN LINE AND SONS LTD.
Suppliers of Wallpaper and Paint
LONDON ESSENCE CO. LTD.
Suppliers of Cleaning Compound
JOHN LUSTY LTD.
Purveyors of Turtle Soup
J. LYONS AND CO. LTD.
Purveyors of Bread, Rolls and Cakes
MACFARLANE LANG AND CO. LTD.
Biscuit Manufacturers
A. AND J. MACNAB LTD.
Dyers and Cleaners
MACVITIES GUEST AND CO. LTD.
Bakers and Confectioners and Purveyors
J. MANLEY
Gilder and Picture Frame Maker
MANSELL, HUNT, CATTY AND CO. LTD.
Table Stationers
MCCALLUM AND CRAIGIE LTD.
Manufacturers of "Lan-Air-Cel" Blankets
WILLIAM MCEWAN AND CO. LTD.
Brewers
MCVITIE AND PRICE LTD.
Biscuit Manufacturers
MELTONIAN (E. BROWN AND SON) LTD.
Meltonian Cream
MINEAR AND MUNDAY
Fruiterers and Greengrocers
MITCHELL AND MUIL LTD.
Biscuit Manufacturers
JAMES MORLEY
Purveyors of Potted Shrimps
MOYSES STEVENS LTD.
Florists
CHARLES MUMBY AND CO. LTD.
Mineral Water Manufacturers
NAIROBI COFFEE AND TEA CO.
Coffee Merchants
NEW SHEPLEY LINOLEUM CO. LTD.
Linoleum Manufacturers
NUNN & CO.
Livery Tailors

WILLIAM ORR LTD.
Purveyors of Meat
OXLEY AND SON (WINDSOR) LTD.
Stationers and Printers
OXO LTD.
Purveyors of Oxo
A. AND F. PEARS LTD.
Toilet Soap Manufacturers
JOHN PECK AND CO. LTD.
Overalls Makers
PEEK, FREAN & CO. LTD.
Biscuits & Vitawheat Crispbread Mfrs.
GEORGE PEGLER AND CO. LTD.
Fruiterers and Greengrocers
W. PINK AND SONS LTD.
Grocers
J.P. PRATT AND SON
Hardware Merchants
PRIDMORE BROS.
Purveyors of Meat
J. PULLAR AND SONS LTD.
Dyers and Cleaners
H.D. RAWLINGS LTD.
Mineral Water Manufacturers
RECKITT AND COLMAN LTD.
Suppliers of Mustard, Blue, Metal Polish, Blacklead
REDFERN'S RUBBER WORKS LTD.
Suppliers of Rubber Mats and Flooring
C. REEVES AND SONS LTD.
Purveyors of Meat
ALEXANDER RIDDLE AND CO. LTD.
Suppliers of Stowers Fruit Cordials
RIDGWAYS LTD.
Tea Merchants
ROBERTS WINDSOR SOAP CO. LTD.
Toilet Soap Manufacturers
JAMES ROBERTSON AND SONS (P.M.) LTD.
Marmalade Manufacturers
ROBINSON AND CLEAVER LTD.
Suppliers of Linen
CHAMPAGNE LOUIS ROEDERER
Purveyors of Champagne
ROGERS AND COOK LTD.
Launderers, Cleaners and Dyers
A. ROMARY AND CO. LTD.
Biscuit Manufacturers

RONUK LTD.
Sanitary Polish Manufacturers
THE RYVITA CO. LTD.
Ryvita Manufacturers
S.A.B.D. LTD
Brandy Distillers
GEO. G. SANDEMAN SONS AND CO. LTD.
Wine Merchants
WILLIAM SANDERSON AND SON LTD.
Scotch Whisky Distillers
G.A. SAWYER LTD.
Furnishers and Decorators
B. SAYERS
Bootmaker
SCHWEPPES LTD.
Mineral Water Manufacturers
SCRUBB AND CO LTD.
Suppliers of Scrubb's Ammonia
H. AND G. SIMONDS LTD.
Brewers
SINGER SEWING MACHINE CO. LTD.
Sewing Machine Manufacturers
SLUMBERLAND LTD.
Bed Manufacturers
H. ALLEN SMITH
Wine Cooper and Merchant
SOLOMON BROTHERS LTD.
Furnishers
CHARLES SOUTHWELL AND CO. LTD.
Confectioners etc.
F. SQUIRE AND SONS LTD.
Contractors for Removal of Kitchen Waste
STAPLES AND CO. LTD.
Beds and Wire Mattress Manufacturers
STEVENSON BROS (DUNDEE) LTD.
Launderers
STEWARD AND PATTESON LTD.
Brewers
J. AND G. STEWARD LTD.
Scotch Whisky Distillers
TANQUERAY, GORDON AND CO. LTD.
Suppliers of Gin
TATE AND LYLE LTD.
Sugar and Golden Syrup Merchants
TEMPLE AND CROOK LTD.
Turners and Brushmakers

THERMOS (1925) LTD.
Manufacturers of Thermos Vacuum Vessels
TOZER AND SONS
Coal and Coke Merchants
TULL AND SON
Bakers
R. TWINING AND CO. LTD.
Tea and Coffee Merchants
UNITED DAIRIES (LONDON) LTD.
Suppliers of Dairy Produce
D. VIGO AND SONS (1929) LTD.
Fishmongers and Poulterers
VINOLIA CO. LTD.
Soap Manufacturers
WAITROSE & CO. LTD.
Suppliers of Groceries and Cleaning Materials
HIRAM WALKER AND SONS LTD.
Suppliers of "Canadian Club" Whisky
WALPOLE BROS. (LONDON) LTD.
Linen Manufacturers
A. WANDER LTD.
Ovaltine Manufacturers
WARNER AND SONS LTD.
Silk Manufacturers
WATNEY, COMBE, REID AND CO. LTD.
Brewers

WESTBURN SUGAR REFINERIES LTD.
Sugar Merchants
GEO. M. WHILEY LTD.
Suppliers of Gold Leaf
WHITE HORSE DISTILLERS LTD.
Scotch Whisky Distillers
WHYTOCK AND REID
Decorators and Furnishers
WILKIN AND SONS LTD.
Jam Merchants
J. WILLIAMSON AND SON
Purveyors of Meat and Poultry
WILLS AND SEGAR LTD.
Florists
WISBECH PRODUCE CANNERS LTD.
Suppliers of Canned and Bottled Fruit and Vegetables
WOLSEY LTD.
Hosiery Manufacturers
WOOD BROTHERS
Purveyors of Meat
WOODROW AND SONS LTD.
Hatters
WYLIE AND LOCHHEAD LTD.
Cabinet Makers and Upholsterers
"X" CHAIR PATENTS CO. LTD.
House and Garden Furnishers

CLARENDON, Lord Chamberlain
Buckingham Palace
1st January 1946

LIST OF TRADESMEN IN THE DEPARTMENT OF THE MASTER OF THE HOUSEHOLD PERMITTED TO STYLE THEMSELVES "BY APPOINTMENT TO THE LATE KING GEORGE V", ENTITLING THEM TO DISPLAY THE ROYAL ARMS, BUT NOT TO FLY THE ROYAL STANDARD, NOR TO USE THE WORD "ROYAL"

R.F. AND J. ALEXANDER AND CO. LTD.
Manufacturers of Cotton Thread
ANGLO-RHODESIAN TOBACCO CO. LTD.
Tobacconists
ANGOSTURA BITTERS (DR. J.G.B. SIEGERT & SONS) LTD.
Angostura Bitters Merchants
APOLLINARIS CO. LTD.
Suppliers of Natural Mineral Waters
ATKEY, PASCALL AND SON LTD.
Suppliers of Ironmongery & Yacht Fittings
BASS, RATCLIFF AND GRETTON LTD.
Brewers
BEAL, FRENCH AND SON
Suppliers of Wine Corks
CHARLES BEASLEY LTD.
Brewers
JOHN BEGG LTD.
Whisky Distillers
BENHAM AND SONS LTD.
Suppliers of Braziery
BEWLEY, SONS AND CO. LTD.
Grocers
BICKEL LTD.
Fishmongers
F. BLACKLEY
Bakers
BLOCK, GREY AND BLOCK LTD.
Wine and Spirit Merchants
BOLLANDS LTD.
Confectioners
WILLIAM BOWEN
Suppliers of Brushwood
THE BRITISH-AMERICAN TOBACCO CO. LTD.
Cigar Merchants
W. BROOKS AND SON
Fruiterers
BUCKLAND AND SONS
Auctioneers
BUCKLEYS BREWERY LTD.
Brewers
JOHN BURGESS AND SON LTD.
Suppliers of Fish Sauce

BUTLER, MCCULLOCH AND CO. LTD.
Florists
JAMES CARTLAND AND SON LTD.
Brassfounders
CATER, STOFFELL AND FORTT LTD.
Caterers
H. CAWS AND SON
Purveyors of Meat
A. AND T. CHANNON
Bakers
CHILD AND CO.
Cider Manufacturers
COCKBURN AND CO. (LEITH) LTD.
Wine Merchants
G.J. COCKERELL AND CO.
Coal Merchants
COLLIER AND CO.
Wine Merchants
W.T. COPELAND AND SONS LTD.
China Manufacturers
WILLIAM COULSON AND SONS
Suppliers of Damask Table Linen
DANIEL BROS. LTD.
Seedsmen
DEAR AND MORGAN LTD.
Grocers
JOHN DOBELL AND CO. LTD.
Wine Merchants
DOMECQ, PEDRO Y CIA OF JEREZ AND PETER DOMECQ AND CO. OF LONDON
Sherry, Brandy and Wine Merchants
JOHN DUNCAN AND SON LTD.
Auctioneers
EDINBURGH & DUMFRIESSHIRE DAIRY CO. LTD.
Suppliers of Milk and Cream
ELLIS AND CO. (RICHMOND) LTD.
Wine Merchants
EN-TOUT CAS CO. LTD.
Hard Lawn Tennis Court Makers
FARROW AND JACKSON LTD.
Suppliers of Cellar Implements

ALEX FERGUSON LTD.
Suppliers of Edinburgh Rock
FISHER, SON AND SIBRAY LTD.
Suppliers of Trees and Seeds
FLETCHER AND SONS (WINDSOR) LTD.
Livery Tailors
CHARLES FRANKLIN
Coal Merchants
GIRDHAR DAS, JAGMOHAN DAS
Jewellers
GIRDHAR DAS, HARI DAS, RAGHUNATH DAS
Jewellers
GOODALL, BACKHOUSE AND CO. LTD.
Sauces and Pickle Manufacturers
ARTHUR GUINNESS SON AND CO. LTD.
Brewers
JOHN HAIG AND CO. LTD.
Whisky Distillers
EDWARD HAMER AND CO.
Suppliers of Welsh Mutton
C. HATCH
Florist
HAWKER AND BOTWOOD LTD.
Suppliers of Corvusine D.G.
JOSEPH HAZELL AND CO.
Coal Merchants
HEAL AND SON LTD.
Beds and Bedding Makers
RICHARD HEMSLEY LTD.
Jewellers
ALFRED HUGHES AND SONS LTD.
Cake and Biscuit Manufacturers
W. & R. JACOB AND CO. LTD.
Biscuit Manufacturers
JEWSBURY AND BROWN LTD.
Mineral Water Manufacturers
JOHNSTON, GREEN LTD.
Fishmongers and Poulterers
KESTON FOREIGN BIRD FARM LTD.
Aviculturists
KINGSTON, MILLER AND CO. LTD.
Confectioners
G.J. KITE
Chimney Sweep
JOHN KNOWLES AND SONS
Watchmakers and Jewellers
LAMPORT AND CO. LTD.
Purveyors of Meat

LEESINGS
Purveyors of Pork
LEFTWICH LTD.
Suppliers of Ice
LETHEBY AND CHRISTOPHER LTD.
Refreshment Contractors
LIPTON LTD.
Tea Merchants
LUMSDEN AND GIBSON
Grocers
A.P. LUNDBERG AND SONS LTD.
Suppliers of Electrical Accessories
MANLOVE, ALLIOT AND CO. LTD.
Makers of Laundry Machinery
MARSHALL AND SNELGROVE
Linen Drapers
SAMUEL MCGREDY AND SON
Nurserymen, Seedsmen and Florists
MELROSES LTD.
Tea and Coffee Merchants
MEREDITH AND DREW LTD. AND WRIGHT AND
SON LTD.
Biscuit Manufacturers
MINTONS LTD.
Earthenware and China Manufacturers
HIRAM MORECROFT
Removal Contractor
JOHN MORGAN AND SONS LTD.
Wine Merchants
MURCHIE'S CREAMERIES LTD.
Purveyors of Milk and Cream
MURPHY AND ORR LTD.
Linen Drapers
MUSK AND CO.
Purveyors of Meat
NATIONAL FLOORING CO. LTD.
Parquet Flooring Manufacturers
NEWMAN SMITH AND NEWMAN (QUILTS) LTD.
Suppliers of Quilts and Bedspreads
S. OSMOND AND SON
Purveyors of Meat
J.W. PARKER AND SON
Grocer
JOHN PEED AND SON
Suppliers of Plants and Seeds
C. PLAYFORD
Bakers

JOHN POWER AND SON LTD.
Whisky Distillers
C.J. PRATT
Fireplace Furnisher
PUGH AND CO.
Coal Merchants
PULHAM AND SON LTD.
Rockworkers and Makers of Terracotta
RANKINS' FRUIT MARKETS LTD.
Fruiterers and Greengrocers
JOHN AND FRANCIS RESTANO
Purveyors of Meat
JOSEPH RODGERS AND SONS LTD.
Cutlers
JOHN ROOTH LTD.
Purveyors of Meat
ROYAL ATHENAEUM LTD.
Refreshment Contractors
THE ROYAL LAUNDRY, SOUTHSEA
Launderers
ST. JAMES'S DAIRY
Purveyors of Milk and Cream
SAMS AND CO.
Purveyors of Milk
SANDERS (ST. ALBANS) LTD.
Nurserymen
ARTHUR SANDERSON AND SONS LTD.
Suppliers of Wallpaper and Paint
H.L. SAVORY AND CO.
Tobacconists
SHIRRAS, LAING AND CO. LTD.
Ironmongers
SILVA AND COSENS LTD.
Wine Merchants
SMETHURST AND CO.
Wax Manufacturers
TOM SMITH AND CO. LTD.
Suppliers of Christmas Crackers
LEWIS SOLOMON LTD.
Fruiterers
A. SPRINGETT
Signwriter and Decorator
THOS. STEVENS CONFECTIONER LTD.
Confectioners

STEVENS AND WILLIAMS LTD.
Glass Manufacturers
R. STEVENSON, TAYLOR AND CO. LTD.
Whisky Distillers
SUPEX LTD.
Chocolate Manufacturers
HUMPHREY TAYLOR AND CO. LTD.
Liqueur Distillers
WILLIAM THOMAS (ABERDEEN) LTD.
Mineral Water Manufacturers
J.G. THOMSON AND CO. LTD.
Wine Merchants
A. AND R. THWAITES AND CO. LTD.
Mineral Water Manufacturers
THOMAS TURNER AND CO. (SHEFFIELD) LTD.
Cutlers
ALLIBHOY VALLIJEE AND SONS LTD.
Suppliers of Despatch Boxes
W.P. VINE
Bakers
VINER'S LTD.
Cutlers and Silversmiths
WAITE AND SON LTD.
Suppliers of Lamp Shades and Fittings
WARRINGTON AND CO.
Engravers
WATSON AND SONS (ELECTRO-MEDICAL) LTD.
Manufacturers of Electro-Medical Apparatus
WHITSTABLE OYSTER FISHERY CO.
Purveyors of Oysters
WHYTE AND SONS LTD.
Glass and China Manufacturers
C. WILSON AND SONS LTD.
Purveyors of Meat
WOODFORD, BOURNE AND CO. LTD.
Wine Merchants
WORCESTER CHINA CO. LTD.
Porcelain Manufacturers
WORTHINGTON AND CO. LTD.
Brewers
WM. YOUNGER AND CO. LTD.
Brewers

CLARENDON, Lord Chamberlain
Buckingham Palace
1st January 1946

LIST OF TRADESMEN IN THE DEPARTMENT OF THE MASTER OF THE HOUSEHOLD PERMITTED TO STYLE THEMSELVES "BY APPOINTMENT TO THE LATE KING EDWARD VII", ENTITLING THEM TO DISPLAY THE ROYAL ARMS, BUT NOT TO FLY THE ROYAL STANDARD, NOR TO USE THE WORD "ROYAL"

G. AND J. BRAMPTON
Butchers

JAMES SMITH AND SONS
Nurserymen

CLARENDON, Lord Chamberlain
Buckingham Palace
1st January 1946

LIST OF TRADESMEN IN THE DEPARTMENT OF THE MASTER OF THE HOUSEHOLD PERMITTED TO STYLE THEMSELVES "BY APPOINTMENT TO THE LATE QUEEN VICTORIA", ENTITLING THEM TO DISPLAY THE ROYAL ARMS, BUT NOT TO FLY THE ROYAL STANDARD, NOR TO USE THE WORD "ROYAL"

BROUGHTON AND PLAS POWER COAL CO.
Coal Merchants
JAMES GREEN AND NEPHEW LTD.
China and Glass Merchants

HODGES AND SONS LTD.
Ironmongers

CLARENDON, Lord Chamberlain
Buckingham Palace
1st January 1946

LIST OF TRADESMEN WHO HOLD WARRANTS OF APPOINTMENT TO THE KING IN THE LORD CHAMBERLAIN'S OFFICE, WITH AUTHORITY TO DISPLAY THE ROYAL ARMS, BUT NOT TO FLY THE ROYAL STANDARD, NOR TO USE THE WORD "ROYAL"

JOHN AND EDWARD BUMPUS LTD.
Booksellers
CHAPMAN BROTHERS (CHELSEA) LTD.
Suppliers of Gold Leaf etc.
CHUBB AND SONS LOCK AND SAFE CO. LTD.
Patent Lock and Safe Makers
PERCY VERE COLLINGS
Heraldic Painter
J. COMPTON SONS AND WEBB LTD.
Uniform Makers
EDWARD COOK AND CO. LTD.
Soap Manufacturers
C.W. DIXEY AND SON LTD.
Opticians
ELKINGTON AND CO. LTD.
Goldsmiths, Silversmiths & Bronze Manufacturers
CHARLES FARRIS LTD.
Chandlers
CHARLES FRODSHAM AND CO. LTD.
Clock and Watch Makers
WM. HILL AND SON AND NORMAN AND BOARD LTD.
Organ Builders
HILLS AND SAUNDERS
Photographers

FRANCIS C. INGLIS AND SON
Photographers
MACKENZIE AND CO.
Chemists
MAY AND WILLIAMS
Newsagents
THOMAS H. PARKER LTD.
Picture Dealers
SAVORY AND MOORE LTD.
Chemists
SILVER AND EDGINGTON LTD.
Tent and Flag Makers
SQUIRE AND SONS LTD.
Chemists and Druggists
J.W. WALKER AND SONS LTD.
Organ Builders
WALKER'S GALLERIES LTD.
Picture Dealers
WATKINS AND WATSON LTD.
Organ Blower Manufacturers
W.H. WHEELER AND SONS
Furnishing Upholsterers
WILKINSON SWORD CO. LTD.
Sword Cutlers
WOOD'S PHARMACY LTD.
Purveyors of Photographic Materials

CLARENDON, Lord Chamberlain
St. James's Palace
1st January 1946

LIST OF TRADESMEN IN THE LORD CHAMBERLAIN'S OFFICE PERMITTED TO STYLE THEMSELVES
"BY APPOINTMENT TO THE LATE KING GEORGE V", ENTITLING THEM TO DISPLAY THE ROYAL
ARMS, BUT NOT TO FLY THE ROYAL STANDARD, NOR TO USE THE WORD "ROYAL"

THOMAS AGNEW AND SONS LTD.
Fine Art Publishers
G. BAILEY AND SONS LTD.
Carriers
BARBER AND SONS
Purveyors of Works of Art
BAR-LOCK TYPEWRITER CO.
Typewriter Manufacturers
W. BARRETT AND SON LTD.
Brush and Leather Goods Manufacturers
JOHN BARTHOLOMEW AND SONS LTD.
Cartographers
BEKEN AND SON
Chemists and Druggists
SIMPSON BENZIE
Jeweller
JOSEPH BOX LTD.
Bootmaker
BRITISH PENS LTD.
Steel Pen Manufacturers
BROMSGROVE GUILD LTD.
Metal Workers
CAESAR BROTHERS LTD.
Builders and Decorators
CARTERS (J. AND A.) LTD.
Invalid Furniture Manufacturers
CHAPPUIS REFLECTORS LTD.
Daylight Reflector Manufacturers
CLAYTON AND BELL
Glass Painters
WILLIAM CREAK LTD.
Outfitters and Furnishers
CHARLES DEACON AND SON
Wood Carvers
DENT AND·HELLYER LTD.
Sanitary Engineers
DOIG, WILSON AND WHEATLEY
Picture Restorers, Printsellers & Publishers
DOULTON AND CO. LTD.
Potters

DUSMO CO. LTD.
Sweeping Powder Manufacturers
DYSON AND SONS (MUSIC STORES) LTD.
Pianoforte Tuners
RICHARD ELLIS
Photographer
GARRET AND HAYSOM
Marble and Stone Workers
GILLETT AND JOHNSTON LTD.
Clock Manufacturers and Bell Founders
JOSEPH GILLOTT AND SONS LTD.
Penmakers
ALFRED GOSLETT AND CO. LTD.
Suppliers of Plate Glass
HALL AND ANDERSON LTD.
General Furnishers
W.T. HAMBLIN AND CO.
Upholsterers
HAMILTON AND INCHES
Chronometer, Clock and Watch Makers
HAZELL, WATSON AND VINEY LTD.
Printers
HERZOG AND HIGGINS
Photographers
W.H. HEYWOOD AND CO. LTD.
Roofing Engineers
HOBBS, HART AND CO. LTD.
Strong Room Door & Lock & Safe Makers
HOBY AND CO.
Boot Makers
IDEAL BOILERS AND RADIATORS LTD.
Radiator Manufacturers
IMPERIAL TYPEWRITER CO. LTD.
Typewriter Manufacturers
INGLESANTS
Upholsterers
G. JACKSON AND SONS LTD.
Decorators in Relief
JENNERS (PRINCES STREET, EDINBURGH) LTD.
Linen Drapers

JOHNSTON, UMBRELLAS LTD.
Stick and Umbrella Makers
KANJIMULL AND SONS
Jewellers
WILLIAM KEMP AND CO. LTD.
Ironmongers
WILLIAM U. KIRK AND SON
Photographers
LEGGATT BROTHERS
Print Sellers
LE ROY ET FILS
Watch and Clock Makers
WILLIAM LIST AND SONS LTD.
Horse Hair Manufacturers
MAPLE AND CO. LTD.
Upholsterers and Decorators
MAPPIN AND WEBB LTD.
Silversmiths
MEDICI SOCIETY LTD.
Art Publishers
MILLAR AND BEATTY LTD.
House Furnishers
JOHN MITCHELL
Steel Pen Manufacturers
JOHN MORGAN AND SONS (COWES AND
SOTON) LTD.
Tailors
NEWTON AND CO.
Opticians
P. ORR AND SONS LTD.
Jewellers
JAMES PAIN AND SONS LTD.
Pyrotechnists
PARIPAN LTD.
Enamel and Varnish Manufacturers
PEAL AND CO.
Boot and Shoe Makers
J.W. ROBERTS AND SON
Pianoforte Tuners
WILLIAM RODMAN AND CO. LTD.
Stationers

GEORGE ROWNEY AND CO. LTD.
Manufacturers of Black Lead Pencils
ROYAL SOVEREIGN PENCIL CO. LTD.
Manufacturers of Black Lead Pencils
RUSSELL AND CO.
Chemists
SALT AND SON LTD.
Cutlers
THE SANITAS CO. LTD.
Disinfectant Manufacturers
W.F. SEDGWICK LTD.
Photographic Engravers
SHALIMAR PAINT, COLOUR AND VARNISH
CO. LTD.
Paint and Varnish Makers
ROBERT AND WILLIAM SORLEY LTD.
Jewellers
STEINWAY AND SONS
Pianoforte Manufacturers
G. STREET AND CO. LTD.
Newsagents
THURSTON AND CO. LTD.
Billiard Table Manufacturers
TIFFANY AND CO.
Jewellers
JOHN TIMS AND SONS
Board Builders
VACHER AND SONS LTD.
Stationers
WARING AND GILLOW LTD.
Upholsterers and Decorators
EDWARD WATTS AND SONS LTD.
House and Yacht Plumbers and Decorators
THOMAS WHITE AND CO. LTD.
Upholsterers and Military Outfitters
H.J. WHITLOCK AND SONS LTD.
Photographers
WILKINSON AND SON
Robe Makers and Tailors

CLARENDON, Lord Chamberlain
St. James's Palace
1st January 1946

LIST OF TRADESMEN IN THE LORD CHAMBERLAIN'S OFFICE PERMITTED TO STYLE THEMSELVES "BY APPOINTMENT TO THE LATE KING EDWARD VII", ENTITLING THEM TO DISPLAY THE ROYAL ARMS, BUT NOT TO FLY THE ROYAL STANDARD, NOR TO USE THE WORD "ROYAL"

BRITISH VACUUM CLEANER AND ENGINEERING CO. LTD.
Vacuum Cleaners

W.W. ROUCH AND CO.
Photographers

CLARENDON, Lord Chamberlain
St. James's Palace
1st January 1946

LIST OF TRADESMEN IN THE LORD CHAMBERLAIN'S OFFICE PERMITTED TO STYLE THEMSELVES "BY APPOINTMENT TO THE LATE QUEEN ALEXANDRA", ENTITLING THEM TO DISPLAY HER LATE MAJESTY'S ARMS, BUT NOT TO FLY HER LATE MAJESTY'S STANDARD, NOR TO USE THE WORD "ROYAL"

CHILVERS AND SON
Nurserymen
THOMAS DUNCAN AND CO.
Bootmakers
J. FOOT AND SON LTD.
Adjustable Chair Makers
GREENS (NURSERIES) LTD.
Nurserymen
FREDERICK WILLIAM HARTLEY
Jeweller and Silversmith
ROBERT HEATH LTD.
Hatters

JOHN MACKINTOSH AND SONS LTD.
Purveyors of Confectionery
PENNELL AND SONS LTD.
Seedsmen
DINA SCHULDT AND CO.
Florist
EDWARD SHARP AND SONS LTD.
Manufacturing Confectioners
R. WALLACE AND CO.
Nurserymen & Purveyors of Hardy, Alpine and Aquatic Plants
W. WILLIAMSON AND SONS
Silk Mercers

CLARENDON, Lord Chamberlain
St. James's Palace
1st January 1946

LIST OF TRADESMEN IN THE LORD CHAMBERLAIN'S OFFICE PERMITTED TO STYLE THEMSELVES "BY APPOINTMENT TO THE LATE QUEEN VICTORIA", ENTITLING THEM TO DISPLAY THE ROYAL ARMS, BUT NOT TO FLY THE ROYAL STANDARD, NOR TO USE THE WORD "ROYAL"

T. AND R. ANNAN AND SONS
Photographers and Photographic Engravers
J. FYFE AND SON
Brushmakers

G.A. HILLYER
Soap Purveyors

CLARENDON, Lord Chamberlain
St. James's Palace
1st January 1946

LIST OF TRADESMEN WHO HOLD WARRANTS OF APPOINTMENT TO THE KING IN THE ROYAL MEWS DEPARTMENT, WITH AUTHORITY TO DISPLAY THE ROYAL ARMS, BUT NOT TO FLY THE ROYAL STANDARD NOR TO USE THE WORD "ROYAL"

ANGLO-AMERICAN OIL CO. LTD.
Purveyors of Motor Spirit
ANSTEE AND CO. LTD.
Forage Merchants
BARTLEY AND SONS
Bootmakers
BARTON-GILLETTE CLIPPER CO. LTD.
Manufacturers of Clipping Machines
MARY ANNE BENNETT
Broom Maker
ASSOCIATION FOR PROMOTING THE GENERAL WELFARE OF THE BLIND
Suppliers of Stable Mats etc., and Renovators of Mattresses
BRITISH MALT PRODUCTS CO. LTD.
Purveyors of Horse Malt
BUNTING
Bootmakers
CHAMPION AND WILTON
Saddlers and Harness Makers

JOHN CROALL AND SONS LTD.
Motor Car Hirers and Garage Proprietors
DAIMLER CO. LTD.
Motor Car Manufacturers
DAIMLER HIRE LTD.
Motor Car Hirers
ALFRED DALES AND CO. LTD.
Horseshoe-pads Manufacturers
H.E. DAVIES
Horse Milliner
DENMAN AND GODDARD LTD.
Livery Tailors
W.B. DICK AND CO. LTD.
Purveyors of Motor Lubricants
DUNLOP RUBBER CO. LTD.
Motor Car Tyres Manufacturers
FORD MOTOR CO. LTD.
Motor Vehicle Manufacturers
GLOVER, WEBB AND LIVERSIDGE LTD.
Coach Builders

W. HARLAND AND SON
Manufacturers of Paints and Varnishes
HONEYBONE AND SON
Harness and Saddle makers
HOOPER AND CO. (COACHBUILDERS) LTD.
Coachbuilders and Motor Body Builders
HUMBER LTD.
Motor Car Manufacturers
HYGENOL CO. LTD.
Manufacturers of Cleaning, Polishing and
Disinfecting Materials
H. JENKS LTD.
Purveyors of Motor Car Accessories
JEYES' SANITARY COMPOUNDS CO. LTD.
Manufacturers of Disinfectants
LANCHESTER MOTOR CO. LTD.
Motor Car Manufacturers
LEYLAND MOTORS LTD.
Manufacturers of Motor Lorries and Vans
LINCOLN, BENNETT AND CO. LTD.
Hat Makers
OFFORD AND SONS LTD.
(INCORPORATING PETERS AND SONS)
Coach Builders
HENRY POOLE AND CO.
Livery Tailors
PRIDAY AND CO.
Suppliers of Bedding
PROPERT LTD.
Suppliers of Leather Dressings
R. AND J. PULLMAN LTD.
Chamois Leather Manufacturers

H. E. RANDALL LTD.
Bootmakers
REDLINE-GLICO LTD.
Purveyors of Motor Spirit
CHARLES RICHARDS LTD.
Road Transport Contractors
ROSSLEIGH LTD.
Motor Engineers
ROYAL ALBERT LAUNDRY LTD.
Launderers
SCOTTS LTD.
Makers of Hats
W.J. SMITH LTD.
Horse Dealers
STEDALL AND CO. LTD.
Manufacturers of Horseshoe Iron and Farrier Tools
SWAINE, ADENEY, BRIGG & SONS LTD.
Whip and Glove Makers
J. TAYLOR AND SONS LTD.
Corn and Hay Merchants
TURNER, BYRNE AND JOHN INNS LTD.
Forage Merchants
C. C. WAKEFIELD AND CO. LTD.
Purveyors of Moor Lubricants
WARREN BROTHERS
Grocers and General Stores
WILLIAM WILLOX AND SON
Motor Engineers
WINDOVERS LTD.
Coach Builders
WILLIAM WREN LTD.
Boot Polish Manufacturers

CLARENDON, Lord Chamberlain
Buckingham Palace
1st January 1946

LIST OF TRADESMEN IN THE ROYAL MEWS DEPARTMENT PERMITTED TO STYLE THEMSELVES "BY APPOINTMENT TO THE LATE KING GEORGE V", ENTITLING THEM TO DISPLAY THE ROYAL ARMS, BUT NOT TO FLY THE ROYAL STANDARD, NOR TO USE THE WORD "ROYAL"

ALDERSHOT AND DISTRICT TRACTION CO. LTD.
Road Transport Contractors

CROSSLEY MOTORS LTD.
Manufacturers of Motor Cars

CURTISS AND SONS LTD.
Forwarding Agents

DAY AND MARTIN
Boot Polish Manufacturers

C.F. ELLIS
Harness and Saddle Maker

FIRMIN AND SONS LTD.
Button Makers

D. AND W. GIBBS LTD.
Soap Manufacturers

F. GORRINGE LTD.
Linen Drapers

GRAY HORSESHOE PAD CO. LTD.
Patent Horseshoe Pad Manufacturers

J. HACKER AND SONS
Livery Tailors

HEADINGTON AND SON
Forage Merchants

JAMES HENDERSON LTD.
Carriage Hirers

THE JAEGER CO. LTD.
Purveyors of Horse Clothing

KEITH AND BOYLE (LONDON) LTD.
Motor Transport Contractors

LIQUID MEASUREMENTS LTD.
Suppliers of Petrol Pumps

MANDER BROTHERS LTD.
Manufacturers of Varnish and Colours

MUSGRAVE AND CO. LTD.
Manufacturers of Stable Fittings

NEWTON AND COOK
Sponge Merchants

CHARLES PITT AND CO. LTD.
Button Makers

ROGERS AND CO. (MILITARY OUTFITTERS) LTD.
Livery Tailors

M. SEGEREN AND SON
Horse Dealers

SHEATH BROTHERS
Patent Spoke Brush Manufacturers

SIMPSON AND CO. LTD.
Coachbuilders

SIMPSON AND SON (LIVERY OUTFITTERS) LTD.
Livery Tailors

S. SMITH AND SONS (MOTOR ACCESSORIES) LTD.
Manufacturers of Motor Car Watches And Speedometers

J.I. SOWTER AND CO.
Harness and Saddle Makers

E. STILLWELL AND SON LTD.
Gold Lace Manufacturers

MATHEW WELLS AND CO. LTD.
Purveyors of Motor Lubricants

WHITBREAD AND CO. LTD.
Brewers

CLARENDON, Lord Chamberlain
Buckingham Palace
1st January 1946

LIST OF TRADESMEN WHO HOLD WARRANTS OF APPOINTMENT TO THE QUEEN, FROM THE
LORD CHAMBERLAIN TO HER MAJESTY, WITH AUTHORITY TO DISPLAY HER MAJESTY'S ARMS,
BUT NOT TO FLY HER MAJESTY'S STANDARD, NOR TO USE THE WORD "ROYAL"

MARCUS ADAMS LTD.
Photographers
JAMES ALLAN AND SON LTD.
Shoemakers
R.L. BOULTON & SONS
Sculptors, Carvers and Modellers
C.H. BRANNAM LTD.
Pottery Makers
BRITISH LEGION DISABLED MEN'S
INDUSTRIES LTD.
Makers of Leather and Fancy Goods
CARRINGTON & CO. LTD.
Jewellers and Silversmiths
CATCHPOLE & WILLIAMS LTD.
Jewellers and Silversmiths
CHAD VALLEY CO. LTD.
Manufacturers of Dolls, Toys,Educational Playthings etc.
CHIVERS & SONS LTD.
Purveyors of Christmas Puddings
COLLINGWOOD (JEWELLERS) LTD.
Jewellers
COOPER, BOYD
Makers of Nurses' Uniforms
CRICHTON BROS.
Silversmiths
DONALD BROS. LTD.
Makers of Old Glamis Furnishing and
Embroidery Fabrics
JOHN DOUGLAS SONS & CO. LTD.
Manufacturers of Handbags
CYRIL EASTMAN (LONDON) LTD.
Dyers and Cleaners
EDE & RAVENSCROFT
Robemakers
EMILE LTD.
Hairdressers
FORTNUM & MASON LTD.
Suppliers of Leather, Glass & Fancy Goods
FREDERICK GORRINGE LTD.
Drapers

P. & J. HAGGART
Tartan and Woollen Manufacturers
HANDLEY-SEYMOUR LTD.
Dressmakers
D.R. HARRIS & CO.
Chemists
HARRODS LTD.
Suppliers of China, Glass & Fancy Goods
NORMAN HARTNELL LTD.
Dressmakers
HARVEY NICHOLS & CO. LTD.
Drapers
HATCHARDS LTD.
Booksellers
W. HAYFORD & SONS
Glove Makers
ROBERT HEATH LTD.
Trunk Makers
HILLIER & SONS
Nurserymen and Seedsmen
INCORPORATED SOLDIERS', SAILORS AND
AIRMEN'S HELP SOCIETY (LORD ROBERTS'
MEMORIAL WORKSHOPS FOR DISABLED
SOLDIERS AND SAILORS AND AIRMEN)
Furniture Makers
JACK JACOBUS LTD.
Shoemakers
JOHN KNOWLES & SONS
Watchmakers and Jewellers
LEGGATT BROS.
Fine Art Dealers
MADAME MARCYLE
Corsetiere
MARSHALL & SNELGROVE
Drapers
MOYSES STEVENS LTD.
Florists
NEWEY BROS. LTD.
Manufacturers of Hooks and Eyes

JAMES NEWMAN LTD.
Manufacturers of Artists' Colours and Materials
PAINTED FABRICS LTD.
Printed and Painted Frabric Makers
THE PAPWORTH INDUSTRIES
Trunk and Cabinet Makers
PARAGON CHINA LTD.
China Manufacturers
JAMES PASCALL LTD.
Confectioners
J.P. PRATT & SON (ETON) LTD.
Suppliers of China, Glass & Fancy Goods
REVILLON LTD.
Fur Cold Storage
M. RITA
Milliner
GORDON RUSSELL LTD.
Suppliers of Furniture, Furnishings, Antiques

THE SCOTTISH SEED HOUSE
Seedsmen
SQUIRE & SONS LTD.
Chemists and Druggists
SWAINE, ADENEY, BRIGG & SONS LTD.
Umbrella Makers
D.F. TAYLER & CO. LTD.
Pin Makers
RAPHAEL TUCK & SONS LTD.
Fine Art Publishers
VALENTINE & SONS LTD.
Fine Art Publishers
WARTSKI
Jewellers
WHITE HEATHER LAUNDRY (LONDON) LTD.
Launderers and Cleaners
PETER YAPP LTD.
Shoemakers

AIRLIE, Lord Chamberlain to The Queen
Buckingham Palace
1st January 1946

LIST OF TRADESMEN WHO HOLD WARRANTS OF APPOINTMENT TO QUEEN MARY, FROM THE
LORD CHAMBERLAIN TO HER MAJESTY, WITH AUTHORITY TO DISPLAY HER MAJESTY'S ARMS,
BUT NOT TO FLY HER MAJESTY'S STANDARD NOR TO USE THE WORD "ROYAL"

ARTHUR ACKERMANN AND SON LTD.
Fine Art Dealers
JAMES ALLAN AND SON LTD.
Boot and Shoe Makers
ALBERT AMOR LTD.
Fine Art Dealers
ANGLO-AMERICAN OIL CO. LTD.
Purveyors of Motor Spirit
ASHTON AND MITCHELL LTD.
Theatre and Concert Agents
J. AND E. ATKINSON LTD.
Suppliers of Perfumery
RICHARD ATKINSON AND CO.
Irish Poplin and Lace Manufacturers
W. BARRETT & SON LTD.
Goldsmiths and silversmiths
BARRINGER, WALLIS AND MANNERS LTD.
Fancy Metal Box Manufacturers
B.T. BATSFORD LTD.
Booksellers and Publishers
GEORGE BAYNTUN
Bookseller
HERBERT SIMPSON BENZIE
Jeweller
OSCAR BLACKFORD
Printer
C.H. BRANNAM LTD.
Manufacturers of the Royal Barum Ware Art Pottery
JOHN BROADWOOD AND SONS LTD.
Pianoforte Manufacturers
CADBURY BROS. LTD.
Cocoa and chocolate Manufacturers
CADBURY, PRATT AND CO. LTD.
Provision Merchants
A.J. CALEY AND SON LTD.
Chocolate, Confectionery and Cracker Manufacturers
CALEYS LTD.
Ladies and Childrens' Outfitters

W. CALLAGHAN AND CO. LTD.
Opticians
CAMEO CORNER
Dealers in Antiques
ALBERT CARTER
Silversmith
CARRINGTON AND CO. LTD.
Jewellers
CATCHPOLE AND WILLIAMS LTD.
Jewellers and Silversmiths
THE CAULDON POTTERIES LTD.
China and Earthenware Manufacturers
MANICK CHAND
Shawl Merchants
CHARLES
Fishmongers
CHIVERS AND SONS LTD.
Purveyors of Jams, Jellies, Canned English Fruits
and Canned Vegetables
COLLINGWOOD (JEWELLERS) LTD.
Jewellers
W.T. COPELAND AND SONS LTD.
Purveyors of China
COWTAN AND SONS LTD.
Decorators and Upholsterers
CRICHTON BROTHERS
Silversmiths
DAIMLER AND CO. LTD.
Motor Car Manufacturers
DEBENHAM AND FREEBODY
Costumiers and Linen Drapers
F.G. DE FAYE LTD.
Perfumers
E. DENT AND CO. LTD.
Chronometer, Clock and Watchmakers
DICKINS AND JONES LTD.
Silk Mercers
C.W. DIXEY AND SON LTD.
Opticians

DREWETT'S STORES
Grocers and Provision Merchants
J. DUVELLEROY LTD.
Fan Makers
EASTMAN AND SON
Dyers, Cleaners and Upholsterers
EDE AND RAVENSCROFT
Robe Makers
ELECTROLUX LTD.
Suction Cleaner & Refrigerator Mftrs.
ELKINGTON AND CO. LTD.
Jewellers and Silversmiths
C.W. FAULKNER AND CO. LTD.
Art Publishers and Printers
FINE ART SOCIETY LTD.
Printsellers
FORTNUM AND MASON LTD.
General Purveyors
FOSTER AND CO.
Robe Makers
MRS. FOWLER
Lace Maker
CHARLES FRODSHAM AND CO. LTD.
Watch and Clockmakers
J.S. FRY AND SONS LTD.
Chocolate and Cocoa Manufacturers
GALE AND POLDEN LTD.
Publishers and Printerss
A.W. GAMAGE LTD.
Sports and Athletic Outfitters
GANESHI, LAL AND SON
Jewellers and Embroiderers
GARRARD AND CO. LTD.
Goldsmiths and Jewellers
W. GAYMER AND SON LTD.
Cyder Makers
GENERAL ACCIDENT FIRE AND LIFE
ASSURANCE CORPORATION LTD.
Insurers of Motor Cars
GIRDHAR DAS JAGMOHAM DAS
Jewellers and Embroiderers
GIRDHAR DAS, HARI DAS, RAGHUNATH DAS
Jewellers and Embroiderers
GOLDSMITHS AND SILVERSMITHS CO. LTD.
Jewellers

THOMAS GOODE AND CO. (LONDON) LTD.
Purveyors of China and Glass
EDWARD GOODYEAR
Florist
FREDERICK GORRINGE LTD.
Silk Mercers
GRAMOPHONE CO. LTD.
Manufacturers of Gamophones & Records
THE GROSVENOR ELECTRICAL CO.
Electrical Contractors
GROUT AND CO. LTD.
Silk Manufacturers
P. AND J. HAGGART
Woollen Manufacturers
HALL AND SONS (BUTCHERS) LTD.
Butchers
THEODORE HAMBLIN LTD.
Opticians
HAMLEY BROTHERS LTD.
Toy and Sports Merchants
HANDLEY-SEYMOUR LTD.
Court Dressmakers
HARMAN AND CO. LTD.
Dealers in Silver and Jewellery
HARRISON AND SONS LTD.
Printers and Booksellers
HARRODS LTD.
Drapers and Furnishers
HARVEY NICHOLS AND CO. LTD.
General Drapers
HATCHARD LTD.
Booksellers
HATCH, MANSFIELD AND CO. LTD.
Wine and Spirit Merchants
W. HAYFORD AND SONS
Outfitters
HERZOG AND HIGGINS
Photographers
HOOPER AND CO. (COACHBUILDERS) LTD.
Coachbuilders and Motor Body Makers
HOOPER, STRUVE AND CO. LTD.
Mineral Water Manufacturers
HOOVER LTD.
Electric Suction Sweeper Manufacturers
IDRIS LTD.
Mineral Waters

ROBERT JACKSON AND CO. LTD.
Grocers
JOLLY AND SON LTD.
Silk Mercers
JAMES KEILLER AND SON LTD.
Chocolate Manufacturers
KISHAND CHAND AND SONS
Embroidery Manufacturers and Shawl Merchants
LEGGATT BROTHERS
Fine Art Dealers
F. LEWIS (PUBLISHERS) LTD.
Booksellers and Publishers
LIBERTY AND CO. LTD.
Silk Mercers
MACKAY AND CHISHOLM LTD.
Goldsmiths and Silversmiths
MACMICHAELS LTD.
Stationers
MALLETT AND SON LTD.
Antique Dealers
J. MANLEY
Gilder and Picture Frame Maker
MAPLE AND CO. LTD.
Cabinet Makers and Decorators
MARSHALL AND SNELGROVE
Silk Mercers
MCVITIE AND PRICE LTD.
Biscuit Manufacturers
W. MOORCROFT LTD.
Potters
NEWEY BROTHERS LTD.
Manufacturers of Hooks and Eyes
MAISON NICOL LTD.
Hairdressers and Perfumers
OVERTON LTD.
Fishmongers
PARAGON CHINA LTD.
China Manufacturers
J. PARKES
Jewellers and Silversmith
FRANK PARTRIDGE AND SONS LTD.
Fine Art Dealers
FRANK PARTRIDGE INC.
Fine Art Dealers
JAMES PASCALL LTD.
Manufacturers of Chocolates & Confectionery

PATERSON, SONS AND MARR WOOD LTD.
Pianoforte Makers and Music Dealers
A. AND F. PEARS LTD.
Soap Manufacturers
H.H. PLANTE
Jeweller and Silversmith
PUGH AND CO.
Coal and Coke Merchants
THE RAFFAELE SHOE GALLERIES (WEAVER & WEAVER LTD.)
Boot and Shoe Manufacturers
H. AND M. RAYNE LTD.
Shoe Makers
REVILLE LTD.
Court Dressmakers
REVILLON LTD.
Furriers
ROBINSON AND CLEAVER LTD.
Linen Manufacturers
J. THOMAS ROCHELLE
Dealers in Works of Art
S.J. ROOD AND CO. LTD.
Diamond Merchants
ROWNTREE AND CO. LTD.
Makers of Cocoa, Chocolate & Confectionery
ERNEST G.V. RUNTING
Chiropodist
RUSSELL AND SONS
Photographers
FREDERICK SAGE AND CO. LTD.
Showcase Makers
B. SAYERS
Livery Boot Maker
SCOTT ADIE LTD.
Manufacturers of Scotch Tartan
SINGER SEWING MACHINE CO. LTD.
Sewing Machine Merchants
SKINNER AND CO.
Jewellers and Silversmiths
S. SMITH AND SONS
(MOTOR ACCESSORIES) LTD.
Clock and Speedometer Makers
TOM SMITH AND CO. LTD.
Manufacturers of Christmas Crackers
W.H. SMITH AND HOOK KNOWLES LTD.
Boot Makers

SOLDIERS' & SAILORS' HELP SOCIETY
(INCORPORATED)
Basket and Cabinet Makers
LEWIS SOLOMON LTD.
Fruiterers and Greengrocers
JOHN SPARKS LTD.
Antiquaries of Chinese Art
SQUIRE AND SONS LTD.
Chemists and Druggists upon the
Establishment in Ordinary
STEINWAY AND SONS
Pianoforte Manufacturers
SUPEX LTD.
Chocolate Manufacturers
SWAINE ADENEY BRIGG AND SONS LTD.
Glove Makers and Umbrella Manufacturers
THRESHERS LTD.
Tropical Outfitters and Dressmakers
TUCK, RAPHAEL AND SONS LTD.
Fine Art Publishers
R. TWINING AND CO. LTD.
Tea and Coffee Merchants
D. VIGO AND SONS (1929) LTD.
Fishmonger
VINOLIA CO. LTD.
Soap Makers

WALKER'S GALLERIES LTD.
Picture Dealers
WARNER AND SONS LTD.
Suppliers of Silks and Furnishing Fabrics
WARREN BROTHERS
Grocers
WAY AND SONS LTD.
Silversmiths & Vendors of Objects of Art
BERNARD WEATHERILL LTD.
Livery Tailors
D. AND J. WELLBY LTD.
Jewellers and Silversmiths
WHITE ALLOM LTD.
Decorative Artists
WHITE HEATHER LAUNDRY (LONDON) LTD.
Launderers
WILKINSON AND SON LTD.
Robe Makers
WILLS AND SEGAR
Florists
WRIGHTSON, HAY LTD.
Photographers
YARDLEY AND CO. LTD.
Perfumers

ANGLESEY, Lord Chamberlain to H.M. Queen Mary
Marlborough House
1st January, 1946

LIST OF TRADESMEN WHO HOLD WARRANTS OF APPOINTMENT ISSUED BY HIS ROYAL HIGHNESS THE DUKE OF WINDSOR, WHEN PRINCE OF WALES, PERMITTED TO STYLE THEMSELVES "BY APPOINTMENT" IN CONJUNCTION WITH THE RELEVANT DATES, AND ENTITLING THEM TO DISPLAY THE PRINCE OF WALES' ARMS, BUT NOT TO FLY HIS ROYAL HIGHNESS'S STANDARD, NOR TO USE THE WORD "ROYAL"

AHAMED BROTHERS
Outfitters
AQUASCUTUM LTD.
Waterproofers
CHARLES ARNOLD
Athletic Outfitter
ASSOCIATED HOTELS OF INDIA LTD.
Caterers
ASSOCIATED SCREEN NEWS LTD.
Photographers
WALTER BARNARD AND SON
Hat and Cap Makers
W. BARRETT AND SON LTD.
Silversmiths and Brush and Leather Goods Manufacturers
BEHARI LAL GHASI RAM
Makers of Preserved Fruits
SIMPSON BENZIE
Silversmith
HENRY BIRKS AND SONS LTD.
Silversmiths
BOUCHERON, RADIUS AND CO.
Jewellers
BOWYERS (WILTSHIRE BACON) LTD.
Bacon Curers
BOYES, BASSETT AND CO.
Silversmiths
BRITISH LEGION DISABLED MEN'S INDUSTRIES LTD.
Disabled Men's Industries
BRITISH PRODUCE STORES
Grocers
BRYDGES
General Upholsterer
MORRIS BULL, F.W.C.F.
Farrier
WALTER BUSHNELL LTD.
Opticians

CAMPBELL AND CO.
Suppliers of Highland Tweeds
TOM CAMPBELL CO. LTD.
Hatters
CHARPENTIER LTD.
Booksellers
E.J. CHURCHILL (GUNMAKERS) LTD.
Gunmakers
ARTHUR COZENS
Electrical Contractor
CROSSLEY MOTORS LTD.
Motor Car Manufacturers
CURRY & PAXTON LTD.
Opticians
CURTISS AND SONS LTD.
Cartage Contractors
DAVIES AND SON (LONDON) LTD.
Tailors
DAVIS (PICCADILLY) LTD.
Travelling Bag Makers
DE HAVILLAND AIRCRAFT CO. LTD.
Aircraft Manufacturers
E. DENT AND CO. LTD.
Watch and Clock Makers
JOHN DRAKE AND CO.
Ironmongers
DYSON AND SONS
Piano Makers
ELLISTON AND CAVELL LTD.
Furnishers
FORSTER AND SON LTD.
Tailors
FRAZERS OF PERTH LTD.
Hosiers
CHARLES GILLING
Chemist
GIRDHARDAS, HARIDAS, RAGHUNATHDAS
Brocade and Silk Manufacturers

HALL BROTHERS LTD.
Tailors and Hosiers
HALSBY AND CO. LTD.
Suppliers of Protectograph Cheque Writers
HAMILTON AND CO. LTD.
Silversmiths
HARDY BROTHERS (ALNWICK) LTD.
Fishing Tackle Makers
ALFRED HAYS LTD.
Musical Instrument Dealers
ALFRED HUGHES AND SONS LTD.
Biscuit Manufacturers
KOLYNOS INCORPORATED
Dental Cream Manufacturers
LEFTWICH LTD.
Ice Merchants
ROBERT LEWIS (ST. JAMES'S) LTD.
Tobacconists
JAMES LOCK AND CO. LTD.
Hatters
MAGGS BROTHERS
Booksellers
MAPLE AND CO. LTD.
Furnishers
MAPPIN AND WEBB LTD.
Silversmiths
V. MARCH AND CO.
Cigarette Makers
MAYFAIR WINDOW CLEANING CO. LTD.
Window Cleaners
MORRIS COMMERCIAL CARS LTD.;
MORRIS MOTORS LTD.;
Motor Car Manufacturers
MUSK AND CO.
Sausage Manufacturers
J.G. NUTTING AND CO. LTD.
Motor Body Builders
ORIGINAL HELFORD OYSTERAGE & FISHING
CO. LTD.
Oyster Purveyors
PAGE, KEEN AND PAGE LTD.
Silversmiths
PAXTON AND WHITFIELD
Provision Merchants
PEAL AND CO.
Bootmakers

PUGH AND CO.
Coal and Coke Merchants
WALLACE S.R. PUGSLEY
Beer and Cider Merchant
HUGH REES LTD.
Booksellers
REVELATION SUITCASE CO. LTD.
Revelation Suitcase Makers
J. RIMELL AND SON LTD.
Dealers in Old Books and Engravings
ROLLS-ROYCE LTD.
Motor Car Manufacturers
ROOTES LTD.
Motor Car Suppliers
ROWELL AND SON LTD.
Silversmiths
ROWELL AND SONS
Livery Boot Makers
J. RUSSELL AND SONS
Photographers
RYMAN AND CO. LTD.
Printsellers
F.P. SCHOLTE LTD.
Tailors
SIFTON, PRAED AND CO. LTD.
Map and Booksellers
SKINNER AND CO.
Silversmiths
L.C. SMITH AND CORUNA TYPEWRITERS LTD.
Typewriter Manufacturers
SODASTREAM LTD.
Soda Water Machine Makers
G. STREET AND CO. LTD.
Press Cutting Agents
SULLIVAN POWELL AND CO. LTD.
Tobacconists
SUNNINGDALE MOTORS LTD.
Motor Car Accessories Dealers
TODHOUSE, REYNARD AND CO. LTD.
Tailors
TYLER AND CO. LTD.
Grocers and Wine Merchants
A.M.A. VIVIAN
Laundress
WALFORD AND SPOKES
Dealers in Antiques

WHITBREAD AND CO. LTD.
Brewers
WOLSELEY MOTORS (1927) LTD.
Motor Car Manufacturers

YARDLEY AND CO. LTD.
Perfumers and Fine Soap Manufacturers

ULICK ALEXANDER
Keeper of the Privy Purse
Privy Purse Office, Buckingham Palace
1st January, 1946

2001 Royal Warrant Holders

Grantor: HM The Queen - Privy Purse

ABBEY ROSE GARDENS
Rose Growers & Nurserymen
ABERDEEN LANDSCAPES & SPECIALIST TREE
SERVICES
Tree Surgeons
ACCESS PLUS
Printing Designers & Suppliers
AGCO LTD.
Manufacturers of Agricultural Machinery
AINSWORTHS HOMOEOPATHIC PHARMACY
Chemists
ALBA TREES PLC
Woodland Tree and Shrub Nurserymen
F.G. ALDEN LTD.
Building Services Engineers
ALISTAIR CASSIE
Television Supplier & Engineer
CHAS. D. ALLFLATT LTD.
Building Contractor
ALLIANCE TIMBER PRESERVATION (NORTH)
LTD.
Damp Proofing and Timber Preservation Specialists
ALBERT AMOR LTD.
Suppliers of 18th Century Porcelains
ANELLO & DAVIDE (BESPOKE AND
THEATRICAL) LTD.
Bespoke Shoe Manufacturer
ANGUS CHAIN SAW SERVICE
Horticultural Engineers
APEX LIFT & ESCALATOR ENGINEERS LTD.
Manufacturers & Suppliers of Passenger Lifts
AQUAZUR LTD.
Specialists in Water Treatment Services,
JAMES L. ARCHIBALD & SONS LTD.
Cabinetmakers & Upholsterers

ARMITAGE BROTHERS PLC
Pet Food Manufacturers
ASD NORFOLK STEEL
Suppliers of Steel Products
ASPREY LONDON LTD.
Jewellers, Goldsmiths and Silversmiths
THE "AT-A-GLANCE" CALENDAR CO. LTD.
Calendar Manufacturers
ATCO-QUALCAST LTD.
Manufacturers of Motor Mowers
AVENTIS CROPSCIENCE
Manufacturers of Agricultural Chemicals
B.H. LEATHER LTD.
Manufacturers of Royal Maundy Purses
BACO-COMPAK (NORFOLK) LTD.
Waste Disposal Contractors
A.C. BACON ENGINEERING LTD.
Manufacturer of Steel-Framed Buildings
C.H. &. E.I. BAMBRIDGE AND SONS
Purveyor of Oven Ready Game Produce
J.C. BAMFORD EXCAVATORS LTD.
Manufacturers of Construction & Agricultural Equipment
SIDNEY C. BANKS PLC
Suppliers of Agricultural Fertlizers
J. BARBOUR & SONS LTD.
Manufacturers of Waterproof & Protective Clothing
BARNHAMS ELECTRICAL CO LTD. T/A KINGS &
BARNHAMS ELECTRICAL CONTRACTORS
Electrical Contractor
THE F.A. BARTLETT TREE EXPERT CO. LTD.
T/A SOUTHERN TREE SURGEONS
Tree Surgeons
BARTRAM MOWERS LTD.
Supplier of Horticultural Equipment
JC BATEMAN
Servicing and Repair of Domestic Appliances

L.M. BATEMAN & CO. LTD.
Manufacturers of Livestock Equipment
BBC FIRE PROTECTION LTD.
Fire Protection Systems
H. & C. BEART LTD.
Manufacturers of Animal Feeds
J BECKETT & SONS LTD.
Painters and Decorators
JOHN BELL & CROYDEN LTD.
Chemists
VALERIE M. BENNETT-LEVY
Suppliers of Nosegays
BENNEY
Gold and Silversmiths
BERTHOUD SPRAYERS
Agricultural Crop Sprayers
BESTOBELL SERVICE
Maintenance Engineers
BILL AND BEN'S GREENHOUSE LTD.
Supplier of Flowers and Tropical Plants
BILSTON & BATTERSEA ENAMELS PLC
Manufacturers of Enamels
MARK BISHOP
Mechanical Engineer
BLUEBELL CATERING
Caterers
BOCM PAULS
Manufacturers of Animal Feeding Stuffs
BOULTER BOILERS LTD.
Boiler Manufacturer
M.D. BOWDEN
Newsagent
BP OIL UK LTD.
Purveyors of Motor Spirit
BRANDSHILL LIGHTING SERVICES
Supplier of Lighting Fittings & Allied Components
BRITISH GAS SERVICES
Repair & maintenance of gas lamp lighting
ANTHONY BUCKLEY & CONSTANTINE LTD.
Photographer
J & H BUNN LTD.
Manufacturers of Agricultural Fertilisers
BURBERRY LTD.
Weatherproofers
BEN BURGESS & CO.
Suppliers of Agricultural Machinery

JAMES BURN INTERNATIONAL
Suppliers of Office Binding Equipment
LW BURROWS & SON
Underground Pipework Specialists
H.C. BYNOTH
Roofing Contractor
CALDERS AND GRANDIDGE
Suppliers of Preserved Timber Fencing
CALEYS (WINDSOR)
Suppliers of Household & Fancy Goods
CALOR GAS LTD.
Suppliers of Liquefied Petroleum Gas
CAMPBELL, SMITH & CO LTD.
Decorators
CARADON PLUMBING SOLUTIONS
Manufacturer of Bathroom & Washroom Fittings
CARTERS TESTED SEEDS LTD.
Seedsmen
CASE UNITED KINGDOM LTD.
Manufacturers of Agricultural Machinery
CASTLE PLANT (DEESIDE) LTD.
Plant Hire Contractors
CATHEDRAL WORKS ORGANISATION
(CHICHESTER) LTD.
Stonemasonary & Restoration Contractors
CHARBONNEL ET WALKER LTD.
Chocolate Manufacturers
A.J. CHARLTON & SONS LTD.
Manufacturers of Timber Gates
CHARRINGTONS FUELS LTD.
Suppliers of Fuel Oils
A.A. CLARK LTD.
Automobile Engineers
CLARK & BUTCHER LTD.
Dog and Game Food Manufacturers
CLIMPSON & CO LTD.
Carpet Contractors
COCHRAN BOILERS LTD.
Boilermakers
JAMES COCKER & SONS
Suppliers of Roses
COLLINGWOOD & CO. LTD.
Jewellers & Silversmiths
COMPEL, COMPUTERS IN PERSONNEL LTD.
Supplier of Human Resource Information Systems

C. & G. CONCRETE LTD.
Supplier of Ready Mixed Concrete
COWNO LTD.
Suppliers of Dairy Cattle Identification Material
CPL DISTRIBUTION LTD.
Coal Merchants
CRANE SHEDS & SUMMERHOUSES
Manufacturer of Timber Buildings
ROBERT H. CRAWFORD & SON
Suppliers of Agricultural Machinery
CROWN BERGER LTD.
Manufacturers of Paint & Wallcoverings
CRYSTAL LITE CHANDELIERS
Chandelier Refurbishment & Maintenance
CYCLAX LTD.
Manufacturers of Beauty Preparations
DACRYLATE PAINTS LTD.
Manufacturers of Paints, Varnishes & Emulsions
DAKS LTD.
Outfitters
DALGETY ARABLE LTD.
Manufacturers of Arable Seed
DARBY NURSERY STOCK LTD.
Suppliers of Ornamental Shrubs and Trees
THOMAS DAY MOTORS LTD.
Motor Vehicle Suppliers
JOHN D. DEAS & CO LTD.
Suppliers of Kitchen Equipment
JOHN DEERE LTD.
Suppliers of Agricultural Equipment
R. DELAMORE LTD.
Suppliers of Chrysanthemum Stock
DERNIER & HAMLYN
Bespoke Lighting Manfs. & Restoration Specialists
STUART DEVLIN LTD.
Goldsmith & Jeweller
DOBBIES GARDEN CENTRES PLC
Seedsmen & Nurserymen
DODSON & HORRELL LTD.
Horse Feed Manufacturers
DOLLOND & AITCHISON LTD.
Dispensing Opticians
DOW AGROSCIENCES LTD.
Manufacturers of Crop Protection Products
DUDLEY GROUP T/A DUDLEY UK LTD.
Suppliers of Print and Stationery

DUFFIELDS OF EAST ANGLIA LTD.
Supplier & Repairer of Heavy Goods Vehicles
EASTERN ENERGY
Supplier of Gas and Electricity
EDMUNDSON ELECTRICAL LTD.
Suppliers of Electrical Products
ELSOMS SEEDS LTD.
Seedsmen
PETER ENRIONE
Tailor
ESTUARY ENGINEERING CO. LTD.
Suppliers of Power Transmission Equipment
FAIRHURST WARD ABBOTTS LTD.
Builders and Decorators
FARGRO LTD.
Horticultural Sundriesmen
FEN DITCHING CO. LTD.
Land Drainage Contractors
FINDLAY CLARK (ABERDEEN)
Seedsmen and Nurserymen
FIRE SAFETY EQUIPMENT LTD.
Suppliers of Fire Protection Equipment
JOHN FLEMING & CO. LTD.
Timber Merchants
W. FORBES
Taxidermist
FOSTER REFRIGERATOR (UK) LTD.
Suppliers of Commercial Refrigeration
FREDERICK FOX LTD.
Milliner
FRIMSTONE LTD.
Suppliers of Crushed & Graded Aggregates
FRISKIES PETCARE (U.K.) LTD.
Suppliers of Dog Foods
FULLWOOD LTD.
Dairy Equipment Manufacturers
GALLYON & SONS LTD.
Gunsmiths
THE GENERAL TRADING COMPANY
(MAYFAIR) LTD.
Suppliers of Fancy Goods
STANLEY GIBBONS LTD.
Philatelists
GIBSON SADDLERS LTD.
Suppliers of Racing Colours

GILBERT GILKES & GORDON LTD.
Water Turbine Engineers
GILBERTSON & PAGE LTD.
Manufacturers of Dog and Game Foods
MATTHEW GLOAG & SON LTD.
Scotch Whisky Blenders
GOODBRAND KNITWEAR
Knitwear Specialists
EDWARD GOODYEAR LTD.
Florist
GRUNDFOS PUMPS LTD.
Manufacturer of Pump Systems
GUARDIAN WINDOW DESIGN CO LTD.
Suppliers and Installers of Double Glazing
HALCYON DAYS LTD.
Suppliers of Objets d'Art
E.C. HALLAM ENGINEERING (LEICESTER) LTD.
Manufacturers of Construction Machinery
HALL & TAWSE LTD.
Building Contractors
HALL PLANK ROBINSON LTD.
Suppliers of Feed, Fertilizer and Agrochemicals
R.G. HARDIE & CO
Bagpipe Makers
HARDY AMIES LTD.
Dressmakers
HARDY BROTHERS JEWELLERS PTY LTD.
Silversmiths
HARDY MINNIS
Mercers of Woollen Cloth
HARE & HUMPHREYS LTD.
Decorators and Gilders
L.G. HARRIS & CO LTD.
Manufacturers of Paint Brushes and Painters Tools
HAVELOCK EUROPA PLC
Shopfitters
HAYTER LTD.
Manufacturers of Agricultural Machinery
HAYTHORNTHWAITE & SONS LTD.
Manufacturers of Grenfell Garments
HEAT CONNECTION
Heating and Ventilation Maintenance Engineers
HEYGATE & SONS LTD.
Manufacturer of Game Feeds
HILLIER NURSERIES LTD.
Nurserymen & Seedsmen

HILLING WOODSHAVINGS
Suppliers of Baled Woodshavings
HORSE REQUISITES NEWMARKET LTD.
Suppliers of Equine Products
HOUSE OF FRASER (STORES) LTD. T/A ARMY & NAVY STORE
Suppliers of Household & Fancy Goods
HOUSE OF FRASER (STORES) LTD. T/A FRASERS
Suppliers of Clothing and House Furnishing
HOVAL LTD.
Boiler Manufacturers & Engineers
HULL CARTRIDGE CO. LTD.
Manufacturers of Shotgun Cartridges
H.L. HUTCHINSON LTD.
Crop Protection and Spray Machinery Specialists
HYDRO AGRI (UK) LTD.
Manufacturer of Agricultural Fertilisers
INDESPENSION LTD.
Trailer Manufacturers
I.R.S. LTD.
Sign and Notice Manufacturer
RICHARD IRVIN - BUILDING SERVICES DIVISION
Building Services Contractors
CORNELIA JAMES LTD.
Glove Manufacturer
JAMES & SON (GRAIN MERCHANTS) LTD.
Suppliers of Animal Feed Stuffs
T.G.JEARY LTD. (T/A AGRICENTRE)
Suppliers of Animal Health and Hygiene Products
JISEX INTERNATIONAL
Suppliers of Cattle Breeding Services
C. JOHN (RARE RUGS) LTD.
Suppliers of Carpets
BOB JONES LTD.
Horse Transport Contractors
J. JOSLIN (CONTRACTORS) LTD.
Stonemasons
JUDGE'S CHOICE PET FOOD LTD.
Pet Food Supplier
KARL LUDWIG COUTURE
Dressmaker
KEMIRA FERTILISERS
Manufacturers of Agricultural Fertilisers
KEYLINE BUILDERS MERCHANTS LTD.
Suppliers of Building Materials

JOHN K. KING & SONS LTD.
Seedsmen
KING'S LYNN GLASS & TRIMMING LTD.
Glass Merchants and Glaziers
KINLOCH ANDERSON LTD.
Tailors and Kiltmakers
PETER KNIGHT (BEACONSFIELD) LTD.
Suppliers of Interior Furnishings
KODAK LTD.
Manufacturers of Photographic Supplies
KVERNELAND KIDD LTD.
Manufacturers of Farm Machinery
LAMBOURN RACEHORSE TRANSPORT LTD.
Horse Transport Contractors
LANGSTANE PRESS LTD.
Printers & Stationers
LAPORTE UK LTD.
Suppliers of Clay Pigeons and Equipment
JAMES LATHAM PLC
Wood Merchants
G.P. LATTER & CO. (ENGINEERS) LTD.
General Engineers
LAUNER LONDON LTD.
Manufacturers of Handbags and Leathergoods
LAWN-BOY FARM SERVICES
Suppliers of Chainsaws and Horticultural Equipment
MG LAWS, ELECTRICAL CONTRACTOR
Electrical Contractor
ANDREW LAWSON JOHNSTON
Artist in Glass
KEN LEECH TREES
Fruit Tree Nurserymen
LEYLAND TRUCKS LTD.
Manufacturers of Commercial Vehicles
LILLYWHITES LTD.
Outfitters
LINCOLNSHIRE DRAINAGE CO LTD.
Drainage Contractors
LINDISPOSABLES LTD.
Cleaning & Catering Disposable Products
S. LOCK LTD.
Embroiderers
PAUL LONGMIRE LTD.
Supplier of Jewellery & Leather Goods
LOWE & OLIVER LTD.
Electrical Contractors

W.S. LUSHER & SON LTD.
Building Contractors
LYRECO U.K. LTD.
Suppliers of Office Stationery & Equipment
JOHN MACKANESS
Maker and Supplier of Charcoal
P.D. MALLOCH
Suppliers of Shooting & Fishing Equipment
MANHATTAN FURNITURE
Manufacturers & Installers of Kitchen & Bathroom Furniture
MANN EGERTON & CO LTD.
Automobile Engineers
MARLEY BUILDING MATERIALS LTD.
Suppliers of Roof Tiles
HENRY MAXWELL & CO LTD.
Bootmakers
THE MAYFAIR CLEANING CO. LTD.
Cleaning Services
H. MAY (ASCOT) LTD.
Automobile Engineers
MCARTHUR GROUP LTD.
Suppliers of Fencing Ironmongery and Farriers Equipment
GUS MCBLAIN DISTRIBUTORS
Supplier of Paints and Wallcoverings
N & J MEADHAM LTD.
Builders
MERRYWEATHER & SONS LTD.
Fire Engineers
MEYER & MORTIMER LTD.
Military Outfitters
MINNS BROS LTD.
Builders
MOBIL OIL CO. LTD.
Suppliers of Petroleum Fuels & Lubricants
MODO MERCHANTS LTD.
Paper Merchants
MOORES FURNITURE GROUP LTD.
Furniture Manufacturers
MOSS AND CO (HAMMERSMITH) LTD.
Timber Merchants
JOHN MOWLEM & CO. PLC
Building Contractors
MR TYRE T/A FOSSITT & THORNE
Tyre Distributors and Service
A. NASH
Manufacturer of Besom Brooms and Pea Sticks

NATIONAL FOALING BANK
Supplier of Foster Mares for Orphan Foals
NCR LTD.
Suppliers of Computer Equipment and Services
NDS ANIMAL FEEDS
Supplier of Dog and Horse Feeds
NETLON LTD.
Manufacturers of Plastic Mesh
NEWEY & EYRE LTD.
Suppliers of Industrial & Domestic Electrical Equipment
NLS FABRICATIONS
Welding Fabricators and General Metal Workers
NORFOLK SEEDS LTD.
Seedsmen
NORTHERN HEATING
Suppliers of Central Heating Equipment
NOVARTIS SEEDS LTD.
Seed Suppliers
OES (LONDON) LTD.
Supplier of Office Furniture and Equipment
OSMONDS
Suppliers of Animal Nutrients and Health Products
OTIS LTD.
Manufacturers & Suppliers of Passenger Lifts
P & D RECORDING AND CONFERENCE
FACILITIES LTD.
Recording and Public Address Engineers
M.W. PAGE
Carpet Contractors
PAGE MONRO LTD.
Florist
PAPWORTH GROUP
Travel Goods Makers
PARKER PEN CO.
Manufacturers of Pens, Pencils & Ink
PARTCO LTD.
Suppliers of Vehicle Parts & Specialised Hand Tools
PATTRICK & THOMPSONS LTD.
Timber Merchants
PAYE STONEWORK & RESTORATION LTD.
Building Facade Restoration and Conservation
PEDIGREE MASTERFOODS (DIV. OF MARS UK
LTD.)
Manufacturer of Canned Dog Food
PETRON LOFTS
Pigeon Loft Manufacturer

THOMAS PETTIFER & CO LTD.
Suppliers of Horse Health and Nutritional Products
PILKINGTON PLC
Manufacturers and Suppliers of Glass
MALCOLM PLUMB
Central Heating Specialist
PRATT & LESLIE JONES LTD.
Suppliers of Fancy Goods
PRINGLE OF SCOTLAND LTD.
Manufacturers of Knitted Garments
JOHN PRINGLE
Motor Engineer
PROBIOTICS INTERNATIONAL LTD.
Suppliers of Animal Health Products
PROTIM SERVICES LTD.
Damp Proofing & Timber Treatment Specialists
PROTIM SOLIGNUM LTD.
Manufacturers of Wood Preservatives
PROTOCOL
Photographic Printer
JAMES PURDEY & SONS LTD.
Gun and Cartridge Makers
QUADTAG LTD.
Suppliers of Game Rearing Equipment
RADIO RENTALS LTD.
Suppliers of Television Receivers
RANSOMES JACOBSEN LTD.
Manufacturers of Horticultural Machinery
S. REDMAYNE LTD.
Tailors
REDPATH BUCHANAN
Lightning Protection Suppliers
BEN REID & CO LTD.
Nurserymen & Seedsmen
REMPLOY LTD.
Manufacturers of Knitwear
RIGBY & PELLER
Corsetieres
RIVERSIDE GARAGE
Automobile & Electrical Engineers
ROBERTS' RADIO LTD.
Suppliers and Manufacturers of Radio and Television
ROKILL LTD.
Pest Control Services
MAUREEN ROSE - COUTURE
Designer & Maker of Couture Dresses & Eve Wear

THE ROYAL ABERDEEN WORKSHOPS FOR THE
BLIND & DISABLED T/A GLENCRAFT
Manufacturers of Curtains and Beds
ROYAL ALBERT LTD.
Manufacturers of Paragon Fine Bone China
THE ROYAL BRITISH LEGION POPPY
FACTORY LTD.
Manufacturers of Poppies & Suppliers of Rosettes
R.S. BOILER SERVICES
Heating and Plumbing Engineers
ARTHUR SANDERSON & SONS LTD.
Suppliers of Wallpapers, Paints & Fabrics
SANFORD UK LTD.
Manufacturers of Writing Instruments
SCOTCH PREMIER MEAT LTD.
Suppliers of Beef & Lamb
JAMES SCOTT
Electrical Contractor
SCOTTISH COMMUNICATION SYSTEMS
Suppliers of Communication Equipment
SCOTTISH HYDRO-ELECTRIC PLC
Suppliers of Electricity
THE SCOTTS CO. (U.K.) LTD.
Manufacturers of Horticultural Products
SECURICOR OMEGA EXPRESS LTD.
Express Parcel Carriers
SEMEX (UK SALES) LTD.
Supplier of Cattle Breeding Services
SENATE ELECTRICAL WHOLESALERS LTD.
Suppliers of Electrical Goods
SHEEN DEVELOPMENTS LTD.
Manufacturer of Horticultural Labels
SLEETREE LTD.
Suppliers of Mechanical, Electrical & Cleaning Services
PETER J. SMITH
Supplier of Horticultural Plants
FRANK SMYTHSON
Stationers
SOLDIERS' SAILORS' AIRMENS' AND FAMILIES
ASSOCIATION FORCES - HELP
Manufacturers of Fancy Goods
PHILIP SOMERVILLE LTD.
Milliner
SOUTHERN BEARINGS LTD.
Mechanical Engineering Suppliers

SOVEREIGN CHEMICAL INDUSTRIES LTD.
Building Material Manufacturers
SPARKS OF ABERDEEN LTD.
Suppliers of Refrigeration Equipment
SPENCER COATINGS LTD.
Manufacturers of Paints & Putties
SPINK & SON LTD.
Medallists
SPINKS & SKERRY
General Builders
STANTON HOPE LTD.
Suppliers of Forestry Equipment
STEINER GROUP LTD.
Hairdressers
STEINWAY & SONS
Pianoforte Manufacturers
STONEHAM PLC
Furniture Manufacturer
STRAIGHTS DIRECT LTD.
Agricultural Merchants
SUTTONS CONSUMER PRODUCTS LTD.
Seedsmen
SYKES & SON LTD.
Building Contractors
TARRANT REFRIGERATION & AIR
CONDITIONING
Dairy Product Refrigeration
ANTHONY TATE
Chemist
O.A. TAYLOR & SONS BULBS LTD.
Bulb Growers
TIRLIN PIN DYKERS
Drystane Dykers
TOTALGAZ
Suppliers of Bulk (LPG) Propane and Gas Tanks
UNITED AGRI PRODUCTS LTD.
Suppliers of Horticultural Chemicals
VENT-AXIA LTD.
Suppliers of Unit Ventilation Equipment
VITAX LTD.
Manufacturers of Fertilisers & Insecticides
VOLTEK AUTOMATION LTD.
Lighting Design/Mf-Specialist Energy Conservation
WALLACE, CAMERON & CO. LTD.
Manufacturers & Suppliers of First Aid Dressings

WALLIS & WALLIS JOINERY
Building Contractor
WALTER DAVIDSON & SONS LTD.
Chemists
WALTHAM FOREST ENGINEERING LTD.
Metal Workers
WARTSKI LTD.
Jewellers
WATER AND GAS SERVICES
Water and Gas Engineers
WEAC LTD.
Safety Communications
BERNARD WEATHERILL LTD.
Riding Clothes Outfitters & Livery Tailors

P. WEBB ROOFING AND BUILDING SERVICES
Roofing Contractors
WEXHAM MOWER SERVICE
Maintenance of Grass Cutting Machinery
WILLIAM WILSON LTD.
Suppliers of Plumbing, Electrical & Building Materials
WILLIAM WOOD & SON LTD.
Garden Contractors
WITHAM OIL & PAINT LTD.
Lubricant Blenders and Paint Suppliers
WOLSELEY CENTERS LTD. T/A PLUMB CENTER
Suppliers of Plumbing and Heating Equipment
XEROX LTD.
Manufacturers and Suppliers of Xerographic Copying
Equipment

2001 Royal Warrant Holders

Grantor: HM The Queen - Master of the Household

3663
Grocery, Provision Products & Frozen Food
ABELS MOVING SERVICE T/A ABELS
Removals and Storage Contractor
ABOYNE & BALLATER FLOWERS
Greengrocer and Florist
AGMA PLC
Cleaning & Hygiene Products
ANGOSTURA LTD.
Manufacturers of Angostura Bitters
ROBERT ANTHONY CARPETS LTD.
Carpet Suppliers and Planners
ELIZABETH ARDEN LTD.
Manufacturers of Cosmetics
AUSTIN REED GROUP PLC
Outfitters
BACARDI-MARTINI LTD.
Suppliers of Martini Vermouth
G.P. & J. BAKER LTD.
Suppliers of Furnishing Fabrics & Wallcoverings
ALBERT BALLS (KING'S LYNN)
Wholesale Fish & Shellfish Merchant
BARNARD & WESTWOOD LTD.
Printers & Stationers
BARRADALE FARM LTD.
Egg Supplier
BASS BREWERS LTD.
Brewers
JAMES BAXTER & SON LTD.
T/A JAMES BAXTER & SON
Purveyors of Potted Shrimps
W.A. BAXTER & SONS LTD.
Purveyors of Scottish Specialities
BEHAR PROFEX LTD.
Restorers of Fine Antique Carpets and Tapestries

BENDICKS (MAYFAIR) LTD.
Manufacturers of Chocolates
V. BENOIST LTD.
Purveyors of Table Delicacies
BENRING CONSULTANTS
Supplier of Furniture Repair Products
BERRY BROS & RUDD LTD.
Wine & Spirit Merchants
BESTFOODS UK Ltd.
Manufacturers of Corn Oil, Cornflour and Mayonnaise
BLACK & EDGINGTON LTD.
Marquee Hirers and Flag Makers
BLOSSOM & BROWNE'S SYCAMORE
Launderers & Dry Cleaners
BLUEBIRD BUSES T/A STAGECOACH BLUEBIRD
Bus and Coach Services
CHAMPAGNE BOLLINGER S.A.
Purveyors of Champagne
J.W. BOLLOM & CO. LTD. T/A HENRY FLACK LTD.
Manufacturers of Polishes and Fire Protective Coatings
THE BOOTS COMPANY PLC
Manufacturing Chemists
BOOTS THE CHEMISTS LTD.
Chemists
BRINTONS LTD.
Carpet Manufacturers
BRITISH NOVA WORKS LTD.
Manufacturers of Floor Maintenance Products
BRITISH SUGAR PLC
Manufacturers of Sugar
BRITVIC SOFT DRINKS LTD.
Manufacturers of Fruit Juices and Soft Drinks
JOHN BROADWOOD & SONS LTD.
Pianoforte Manufacturers and Tuners
H. BRONNLEY & CO LTD.
Toilet Soap Makers

H.P. BULMER LTD.
Cider Makers
JOHN BURGESS & SON LTD.
Manufacturers of Pastes and Condiment Sauces
CADBURY LTD.
Cocoa & Chocolate Manufacturers
CAMPBELL & NEILL
Suppliers of Fresh and Smoked Fish
CAMPBELL BROTHERS
Purveyors of Meat & Poultry
CANNON HYGIENE LTD.
Suppliers of Hygiene Services
CARLSBERG - TETLEY BREWING LTD.
Suppliers of Ale and Lager
CARPETS INTERNATIONAL (UK) LTD.
Carpet Manufacturers
CARR'S OF CARLISLE
Manufacturers of Biscuits
CENTURA FOODS LTD.
Marmalade Manufacturers
CEREBOS
Suppliers of Table Salt & Pepper
CHALMERS BAKERY LTD.
Bakers & Confectioners
MATTHEW CLARK TAUNTON LTD.
Cider Manufacturers
CLYDE CANVAS HIRE LTD.
Manufacturer and Hirer of Marquees
COBB OF KNIGHTSBRIDGE
Butchers
COCA-COLA GREAT BRITAIN LTD.
Suppliers of Soft Drinks
COLE & SON (WALLPAPERS) LTD.
Suppliers of Wallpapers
COPE & TIMMINS LTD.
Brass Finishers & Spring Makers
CORNEY & BARROW LTD.
Wine Merchants
WM. CRAWFORD & SONS LTD.
Biscuit Manufacturers
ROBERT CRERAR
Maker of Highland Dress Accoutrements
DAIRY CREST LTD.
Suppliers of Fresh Milk and Dairy Products
DARVILLE & SON LTD.
Grocers

D.D.P. LTD.
Purveyors of Fruit and Vegetables
DEANS FOODS LTD.
Supplier of Eggs
JOHN DEWAR & SONS LTD.
Scotch Whisky Distillers
DEWHURST BUTCHERS LTD.
Butchers
DIVERSEYLEVER LTD.
Suppliers of Dishwashing Compounds and Controls
PEDRO DOMECQ S.A.
Suppliers of Domecq Sherry
DONATANTONIO PLC
Fine Food Ingredient Importers and Distributors
DORMA
Suppliers of Bedlinen and Household Products
EARLY'S OF WITNEY PLC
Manufacturers of Blankets
EXPRESS DAIRIES-DIVISION OF EXPRESS LTD.
Dairy Suppliers
FAIRFAX MEADOW
Specialist Butchers
FENLAND LAUNDRIES LTD.
Launderers
FINDLATER MACKIE TODD & CO LTD.
Wine & Spirit Merchants
J. FLORIS LTD.
Perfumers
FORTNUM & MASON PLC
Grocers & Provision Merchants
FOX'S BISCUITS
Biscuit Manufacturers
FREUDENBERG HOUSEHOLD PRODUCTS L.P.
Suppliers of Non-woven Cleaning Materials
THE GAINSBOROUGH SILK WEAVING CO. LTD.
Manufacturers of Furnishing Fabrics
GASKELL TEXTILES LTD.
Manufacturers of Carpet Underlays
J.R. GAUNT & SON LTD.
Ribbon Suppliers
GIVAN'S IRISH LINEN STORES LTD.
Linen Drapers
J. GODDARD & SONS LTD.
Manufacturers of Silver & Metal Polishes
THOMAS GOODE & CO. LTD.
Suppliers of China & Glass

GRAMPIAN COUNTRY PORK HALLS LTD.
Suppliers of Meat Products
JAMES GRAY & SON IRONMONGERS
& ELECTRICIANS LTD.
Suppliers of Cleaning Materials
GRIPPERRODS LTD.
Manufacturer of Flooring Installation Products
W HABBERLEY MEADOWS LTD.
Manufacturers of Gold Leaf
HAMILTON & INCHES LTD.
Silversmiths & Clock Specialists
HARRODS LTD.
Suppliers of Provisions & Household Goods
JOHN HARVEY & SONS LTD.
Wine Merchants
JAMES HAWKER & CO. LTD.
Purveyors of Sloe Gin
PETER F. HEERING
Purveyors of Cherry Heering
H.J. HEINZ CO. LTD.
Purveyors of Heinz Products
H.R. HIGGINS (COFFEE-MAN) LTD.
Coffee Merchants
THE HILL BRUSH COMPANY LTD.
Manufacturers of Household Brushware
HILL THOMSON & CO. LTD.
Scotch Whisky Distillers
THOMAS HINE & CO.
Suppliers of Cognac
THE HOBART MANUFACTURING COMPANY
LTD. T/A HOBART
Manufacturers of Kitchen Equipment
HOOVER LTD.
Suppliers of Vacuum Cleaners
HOWGATE DAIRY FOODS LTD.
Cheesemaker
HP FOODS LTD.
Manufacturers of HP Sauces
HUNTER & HYLAND LTD.
Suppliers of Curtain Rails and Upholstery Fittings
HYAMS & COCKERTON LTD.
Purveyors of Fruit and Vegetables
HYPNOS LTD.
Upholsterers & Bedding Manufacturers
INITIAL TEXTILE SERVICES
Launderers and Dry Cleaners

THE IRISH LINEN COMPANY
Supplier of Fine Linens
THE JACOB'S BAKERY LTD.
Biscuit Manufacturers
LEON JAEGGI & SONS LTD.
Suppliers of Catering Utensils & Equipment
L. JALLEY & CO LTD.
Fruit & Vegetable Supplier
JENNERS, PRINCES STREET, EDINBURGH LTD.
Suppliers of Furnishing Materials
SC JOHNSON PROFESSIONAL LTD.
Manufacturers of Wax Polishes,
Cleaners & Hygiene Products
JONES YARRELL & CO. LTD.
Newsagents
JUSTERINI & BROOKS LTD.
Wine Merchants
K.C.S. LTD.
Cleaning Contractor
KELLOGG MARKETING & SALES CO. (UK) LTD.
Purveyors of Cereals
KENSINGTON LIGHTING CO. LTD.
T/A ANN'S KENSINGTON LIGHTING CO.
Lampshade Makers and Lighting Suppliers
G.B. KENT & SONS PLC
Brush Makers
KIMBERLY CLARK LTD.
Manufacturers of Disposable Tissues
KIRKNESS & GORIE
Supplier of Honey
KLEEN-WAY (BERKSHIRE) CO.
Chimney Sweepers
JAMES KNIGHT OF MAYFAIR AND CECIL & CO.
Fishmonger
KNIGHT'S GALLERY
Mount Cutters & Picture Framers
KNOWLES & SONS (FRUITERERS) LTD.
Purveyors of Fruit and Vegetables
KRUG VINS FINS DE CHAMPAGNE S.A.
Purveyors of Champagne
LANSING LINDE LTD.
Manufacturers of Industrial Trucks
CHAMPAGNE LANSON PÉRE ET FILS
Purveyors of Champagne
LEA & PERRINS LTD.
Purveyors of Worcestershire Sauce

LEVER BROTHERS LTD.
Soap and Detergent Makers
H.S. LINWOOD & SONS LTD.
Fishmonger
HUGH MACKAY
Carpet Manufacturers
MALTON FOODS
Suppliers of Bacon and Hams
MANOR BAKERIES LTD.
Manufacturers of Cakes
MAPPIN & WEBB LTD.
Silversmiths
MARINE HARVEST (SCOTLAND) LTD.
Suppliers of Fresh Scottish Salmon
MARTIN & SON EDINBURGH LTD. (T/A MARTIN
& FROST)
Interior Furnishings Specialist
EFG MATTHEWS OFFICE FURNITURE LTD.
Office Furniture Supplier
D. & F. MCCARTHY LTD.
Fruit & Vegetable Merchants
MCCAW, ALLAN & CO. LTD.
Manufacturers of Fine Bed Linens
MCCORMICK (UK) LTD. T/A SCHWARTZ
Suppliers Herbs, Spices, Seasonings & Sauce Mixes
MCPHERSONS
Fruit and Vegetable Merchants
MCVITIE & PRICE LTD.
Biscuit Manufacturers
METAMEC
Manufacturers of Horological Products
MINTON LTD.
China Manufacturers
MITRE FURNISHING GROUP
Suppliers of Furnishing Fabrics and Bedding
CHAMPAGNE MOËT & CHANDON
Purveyors of Champagne
MORNY LTD.
Manufacturers of Soap
CHAMPAGNE GH MUMM & CIE
Purveyors of Champagne
JOHN MYLAND LTD.
Manufacturers of French Polishes, Stains & Wax Polishes
NAIROBI COFFEE & TEA CO. LTD.
Coffee Merchants

NASTIUKS
Supplier of Fruit and Vegetables
NESTLÉ UK LTD.
Manufacturers of Nestlé Products
HENRY NEWBERY & CO. LTD.
Suppliers of Furnishing Trimmings
OCS SUPPORT SERVICES LTD.
Cleaning Contractors
PARTRIDGES OF SLOANE STREET LTD.
Grocers
A. & F. PEARS LTD.
Soap Manufacturers
H.A. PERCHERON LTD.
Suppliers of Furnishing Fabrics
PHS TREADSMART
Suppliers of Mats & Matting Services
PICREATOR ENTERPRISES LTD.
Suppliers of Products for Restoration & Conservation
PILGRIM PAYNE & CO. LTD.
Cleaners of Soft Furnishings & Carpets
PINNEYS OF SCOTLAND
Purveyors of Smoked Salmon
PORTER NICHOLSON
Upholsterers' Warehouseman
J. PREEDY & SONS LTD.
Supplier of Glass Table Tops
PRESTAT LTD.
Purveyors of Chocolates
ARTHUR PRICE & CO. LTD.
Cutlers & Silversmiths
PRICE'S PATENT CANDLE CO. LTD.
Candlemakers
PROCTER & GAMBLE UK
Manufacturers of Soap & Detergents
QUAKER TRADING LTD.
Suppliers of Quaker Food Products
RANKS HOVIS MCDOUGALL LTD.
Manufacturers of Chutney & Oriental Sauces &
Purveyors of Indian Curries
RECKITT BENCKISER PLC
Manufacturers of Antiseptics, Air Fresheners, Polishes,
Cleaners
PETER REED GROUP LTD.
Manufacturers of Bed Linen
RENSHAW SCOTT LTD.
Purveyors of Almond Products

RIDGWAYS
Tea Merchants
JAMES ROBERTSON & SONS
Preserve Manufacturers
ROBINSON'S SOFT DRINKS LTD.
Manufacturers of Fruit Squashes and Barley Waters
CHAMPAGNE LOUIS ROEDERER
Purveyors of Champagne
L. ROSE & CO. LTD.
Suppliers of Lime Juice Cordial
JOHN ROSS JNR. (ABERDEEN) LTD.
Fish Merchants and Curers
ROYAL BRIERLEY CRYSTAL LTD.
Suppliers of Crystal Table Glassware
ROYAL DOULTON PLC
Manufacturers of China
H. & L. RUSSEL LTD.
Manufacturers of Garment Hangers
RUSSELL HUME LTD.
Suppliers of Meat & Poultry
DONALD RUSSELL LTD.
Supplier of Meat and Poultry
THE RYVITA CO. LTD.
Manufacturers of Crispbreads
GEOG. G. SANDEMAN SONS & CO. LTD.
Wine Merchants
WM. SANDERSON & SON LTD.
Scotch Whisky Distillers
THE SAVOY COFFEE DEPARTMENT
Suppliers of Coffee
SCHWEPPES LTD.
Soft Drink Manufacturers
R.F. & J. SCOLES
Butchers
SCOTTISH & NEWCASTLE PLC
Brewers
SEKERS FABRICS LTD.
Manufacturers of Furnishing Fabrics
SELFRIDGES PLC
Suppliers of Food, Gift Items and Household Goods
EDWARD SHARP & SONS LTD.
Confectioners
ELIZABETH SHAW LTD.
Manufacturers of Confectionery
H.M. SHERIDAN
Purveyor of Meat & Poultry

SKYMAN SACKS AND BAGS LTD.
Supplier of Sacks
SLEEPEEZEE LTD.
Bedding Manufacturers
SLUMBERLAND PLC
Bedding Manufacturers
TOM SMITH GROUP LTD.
Suppliers of Christmas Crackers
SMITHKLINE BEECHAM CONSUMER
HEALTHCARE
Suppliers of Lucozade
SMITHS THE BAKERS
Bakers
SODEXHO PRESTIGE LTD.
Caterers
R.R. SPINK & SONS (ARBROATH) LTD.
Fishmongers
SPODE
Manufacturers of China
STAPLES & CO. LTD.
Manufacturers of Bedsteads & Bedding
ST. JUDE'S LAUNDRY
Launderers
STODDARD INTERNATIONAL PLC
Carpet Manufacturers
J. STOPPS & SONS LTD.
Bakers & Confectioners
GEORGE STRACHAN LTD.
General Merchants
SWEDISH MATCH UK LTD.
Match Manufacturers
TANQUERAY GORDON & CO. LTD.
Gin Distillers
TATE & LYLE PLC
Sugar Refiners
JOSEPH TERRY & SONS
Confectionery Manufacturer
THERMOS LTD.
Manufacturers of Vacuum Flasks
THRESHER & GLENNY LTD.
Shirtmakers
TIDMARSH ESTATE LTD.
Suppliers of Window Blinds
G.J. TURNER & CO (TRIMMINGS) LTD.
Manufacturers of Furnishing Trimmings

R. TWINING & CO. LTD.
Tea and Coffee Merchants
ULSTER WEAVERS HOME FASHIONS LTD.
Suppliers of Kitchen Textiles
VAN DEN BERGH FOODS LTD.
Suppliers of Margarines, Low Fat Spreads, Mustards & Sauces
THE BRITISH VAN HEUSEN CO LTD.
Shirt Makers
VEUVE CLICQUOT-PONSARDIN
Purveyors of Champagne
JOHN WALKER & SONS LTD.
Scotch Whisky Distillers
H. & T. WALKER LTD.
Suppliers of Canned Foods
WALLEY LTD.
Suppliers of Crockery & Glassware
THE WAREHOUSE SOUND SERVICES LTD.
Sound Equipment Suppliers
WARNER FABRICS PLC
Suppliers of Silks and Furnishing Fabrics
JOSIAH WEDGWOOD & SONS LTD.
Manufacturers of Ceramic Tableware & Giftware
WEETABIX LTD.
Manufacturers of Breakfast Cereals

THE WENSUM COMPANY PLC
Livery Tailors
WHITWORTHS GROUP LTD.
Manufacturers of Provisions and Dried Fruits
WHYTOCK & REID
Decorators and Furnishers
WILKIN & SONS LTD.
Jam and Marmalade Manufacturers
WILKINSON PLC
Glass Restorer
ANDREW WILSON & SONS LTD.
Catering Equipment Hirers
WINDSOR GLASS COMPANY LTD.
Glass Merchants
ROBERT WISEMAN & SONS LTD.
Suppliers of Milk and Dairy Products
WOLSEY LTD.
Manufacturers of Hosiery & Knitwear
RICHARD WOODALL
Suppliers of Traditional Cumberland Sausages, Cumberland Hams & Bacon
THE WORCESTER ROYAL PORCELAIN CO
Manufacturers of China and Porcelain
YARDLEY & CO LTD.
Manufacturers of Soap

2001 Royal Warrant Holders

Grantor: HM The Queen - The Lord Chamberlain's Office

ALLIANCE ENGRAVING & LETTERING CO LTD.
Engravers
STEPHEN AUSTIN & SONS LTD.
Printers
BENTLEY & SKINNER (BOND STREET
JEWELLERS) LTD.
Jewellers and Silversmiths
BJS CO. LTD.
Electroplaters and Silversmiths
BOYD COOPER LTD.
Makers of Nursing Uniforms
DEGE & SKINNER
Tailors
EDE & RAVENSCROFT LTD.
Robe Makers
CHARLES FARRIS LTD.
Chandlers
FIRMIN & SONS PLC
Button Makers
GIEVES & HAWKES LTD.
Livery & Military Tailors
GREENAWAYS
Printers

JOEL & SON FABRICS
Supplier of Fabrics
KASHKET & PARTNERS LTD.
Coat & Uniform Makers
LAERDAL MEDICAL LTD.
Supplier of Medical Equipment
PLANET BOTANIC LTD.
Supplier of First Aid Products
TOYE, KENNING & SPENCER LTD.
Suppliers of Gold & Silver Laces, Insignia & Embroidery
UNISYS LTD.
Suppliers of Computer Systems
UNITECH COMPLETE COMPUTING
Software Developers
DENIS VERE COLLINGS
Calligrapher
J.W. WALKER & SONS LTD.
Pipe Organ Tuners and Builders
WATKINS & WATSON LTD.
Organ Blower Manufacturers
WILKINSON SWORD LTD.
Sword Cutlers
WILSON & SON
Piano and Harpsichord Tuners

2001 Royal Warrant Holders

Grantor: HM The Queen - The Royal Mews

ABBEY SADDLERY & CRAFTS LTD.
Supplier of Saddlery Workshop Materials
AKZO NOBEL COMMERCIAL TRANSPORT
COATINGS
Manufacturers of Coach Paints
ALEXANDRE OF ENGLAND 1988 LTD.
Tailors
ANSTEE (1994) LTD.
Forage Merchants
APPLIED SWEEPERS LTD.
Suppliers of Sweeping Machines
BUTTONS SADDLERY
Suppliers of Saddlery and Horse and Rider Clothing
CAR CARE PRODUCTS GROUP
Supplier of Vehicle Polishes and Cleaners
CARR & DAY & MARTIN LTD.
Manufacturers of Saddlery Care Products
CASTROL LTD.
Manufacturers of Motor Lubricants
CHAMPION AUTOMOTIVE PRODUCTS
Suppliers of Sparking Plugs
ALBERT E. CHAPMAN LTD.
Upholsterers and Soft Furnishers
A. COOPER T/A COOPERS OF MARBLE ARCH
LTD.
Gentlemen's Outfitters
COPPERMILL LTD.
Manufacturers of Industrial Cleaning Cloths
R.A. CREAMER AND SON LTD.
Automobile Engineers
CROFORD COACHBUILDERS LTD.
Wheelwright & Coachbuilder
G.E. CURZON
Forage Merchants
DAY SON & HEWITT LTD.
Manufacturers of Veterinary Products

DUNLOP TYRES LTD.
Motor Vehicle Tyre Suppliers
EASTERN COUNTIES LEATHER PLC
Manufacturers of Chamois Leather
EQUICENTRE
Farrier
ESSO PETROLEUM CO. LTD.
Purveyors of Motor Spirit
EUROPCAR UK LTD.
Motor Vehicle Hirers
FARMKEY
Horse Freeze Marking Security Service
FINELIST GROUP PLC
Manufacturers of Electrical Equipment
FORBO NAIRN LTD.
Manufacturers of Floor Covering
FORD MOTOR CO. LTD.
Motor Vehicle Manufacturers
FRAMES RICKARDS LTD.
Road Transport Contractors
W. & H. GIDDEN LTD.
Saddlers
GLIDDON'S GLOVES & LEATHERWEAR LTD.
Supplier of Gloves
GD GOLDING (TAILORS) LTD.
Tailors
E.H. HUTTON (COACHBUILDERS) LTD.
Manufacturers and Repairers of Horse Boxes
INITIAL METROPOLITAN WINDOW CLEANING
CO LTD.
Window Cleaners
JABEZ CLIFF & CO. LTD.
Saddler and Loriner
JAGUAR CARS LTD.
Manufacturers of Daimler & Jaguar Cars

JEYES GROUP LTD.
Manufacturers of Hygiene Products
K. SHOES
Bootmakers
JOHN T. KEEP & SONS LTD.
Paint Manufacturer
LAND ROVER
Manufacturers of Land Rover Vehicles
LDV LTD.
Manufacturers of Light Commercial Vehicles
SARA LEE - HOUSEHOLD & BODY CARE UK LTD.
Manufacturers of Shoe/Leather Care Products and
Insecticides
LISTER SHEARING EQUIPMENT LTD.
Manufacturers of Animal Care Products
JOHN LOBB LTD.
Bootmakers
M. & K. MECHANICAL HANDLING
Suppliers of Electric Vehicles
M & T ENGINEERING
Vehicle Servicing and Repairs
MG ROVER GROUP LTD.
Manufacturers of Rover and MG Motor Cars
MORDAX STUDS LTD.
Makers of Mordax Studs
NENE MILLING
Specialist Horse Feed Manufacturer
CHARLES OWEN & CO (BOW) LTD.
Protective Headwear Manufacturer
PATEY (LONDON) LTD.
Manufacturers of Hats
PHS GREENLEAF
Installers and Maintainers of Plant Displays
HENRY POOLE & CO (SAVILE ROW) LTD.
Livery Outfitters
JEFFERY A. PRATT
Suppliers of Animal Health & Veterinary Products

REDWOOD & FELLER
Tailors
REYNOLDS BOUGHTON LTD.
Manufacturers of Waste Handling & Transport Equipment
ROLLS-ROYCE AND BENTLEY MOTOR CARS LTD.
Motor Car Manufacturers
SANDICLIFFE GARAGE LTD.
Suppliers of Motor Horse Boxes and Automobile
Engineers
SEVEN SEAS LTD.
Manufacturers of Veterinary Products: Vitamins:
Minerals & Supplements
SHELL UK LTD.
Purveyor of Motor Spirit
SHEPPY FERTILISERS LTD.
Fertiliser Manufacturer
W.L. SLEIGH LTD.
Motor Vehicle Hirers
WALTER E. STURGESS & SONS LTD.
Suppliers of Horse and Carriage Conveyances
SWAINE ADENEY BRIGG LTD.
Whip & Glove Makers
UK SAFETY GROUP LTD.
Suppliers of Safety Footwear
VALE BROTHERS LTD.
Manufacturers of Horse Grooming Brushes
VALE MILL (ROCHDALE) LTD.
Manufacturers of Cleaning & Laundry Products
VAUXHALL MOTORS LTD.
Motor Vehicle Manufacturers
ERIK GEORGE WEST
Heraldic Artist
MARK WESTAWAY & SON
Manufacturers of Horse Forage
WHITE KNIGHT LAUNDRY SERVICES LTD.
Launderers and Dry Cleaners
WINDSORIAN COACHES LTD.
Coach Operator

2001 Royal Warrant Holders

Grantor: HM The Queen - Royal Collection Department

ALDEN & BLACKWELL
Booksellers
JC BATEMAN
Suppliers of Storage, Equipment & Display Products
CAIRS LTD.
Manufacturers of Computer Support and Systems
CARVERS & GILDERS
Carvers, Gilders and Restorers
CLASSIC PHOTOGRAPHIC SERVICES LTD.
Photographic Services
CONNOLLY LEATHER LTD.
Leather Tanners & Curriers
CONSERVATION BY DESIGN LTD.
Suppliers of Storage, Equipment & Display Products
CONSERVATION RESOURCES (UK) LTD.
Manufacturers of Archival Storage Materials
A.C. COOPER (COLOUR) LTD.
Colour Photographers
FINE ART SERVICES LTD.
Suppliers of Fine Art Services
FINE BINDING
Bookbinders
GARRARD & CO. LTD.
Jewellers, Goldsmiths and Silversmiths
W.L. HARRILD & PARTNERS LTD.
Suppliers of Bookbinding Equipment
HAZLITT, GOODEN & FOX LTD.
Fine Art Dealers
J. HEWIT & SONS LTD.
Manufacturers of Leather
JUST CASTINGS (UK) LTD.
Precious Metal Casters
KENT SERVICES LTD.
Suppliers of Specialist Packaging for Works of Art
THE LIGHTING SERVICES PARTNERSHIP
Designers & Suppliers of Special Lighting Equip.

MAGGS BROS LTD.
Purveyors of Rare Books and Manuscripts
MINIATURE AND FINE ART CONSERVATION
(JERSEY) LTD.
Miniature and Fine Art Conservator
MOMART LTD.
Transporter of Fine Arts
CHARLES PERRY RESTORATIONS LTD.
Antique Furniture Restorers
PETERSFIELD BOOKSHOP
Picture Framer & Supplier of Art Materials
PHOENIX FINE ART
Suppliers of Fine Art Services
PHOTOBITION SERVICE LTD.
Suppliers of Exhibition Graphics and Signs
PLAN CONSERVATION
Restorer of Drawings
PLASPAK SUPPLIES LTD.
Polyethylene Film and Bag Suppliers
PLOWDEN & SMITH LTD.
Restorers of Fine Art Objects
POLYBAGS LTD.
Polythene Bag Makers
RANKINS (GLASS) CO. LTD.
Suppliers of Non-Reflective Glass
T. ROGERS & CO. (PACKERS) LTD.
Packers & Transporters of Works of Art
G. RYDER & CO. LTD.
Specialist Box Makers
SECOL LTD.
Manufacturers of Archival & Photographic
Storage Systems
SKY PHOTOGRAPHIC SERVICES LTD.
Photographic Services
STUART R. STEVENSON
Suppliers of Artist and Gilding Materials

SWANN HEDDON-ON-THE-WALL
Cabinet Maker
TAYLOR PEARCE RESTORATION SERVICES LTD.
Conservators of Sculpture
RODNEY TODD-WHITE & SON
Fine Art Photographers
ARNOLD WIGGINS & SONS LTD.
Picture Frame Makers
WILLIAAM COX PLASTICS STOCKHOLDING LTD.
Suppliers of Plastic Sheet

2001 Royal Warrant Holders

Grantor: HRH The Duke of Edinburgh

ARTISTIC IRON PRODUCTS
Carriage Builder
AUTOSCAN LTD.
Manufacturers of Power Filing Systems
J. BARBOUR & SONS LTD.
Manufacturers of Waterproof & Protective Clothing
GRAHAM BEGG LTD.
Radio and Television Suppliers
BEKEN OF COWES LTD.
Marine Photographers
BENNEY
Gold and Silversmiths
BLOSSOM & BROWNE'S SYCAMORE
Launderers and Dry Cleaners
ANTHONY BUCKLEY & CONSTANTINE LTD.
Photographer
HAROLD COX & SONS JEWELLERS LTD.
Clockmakers and Silversmiths
DAKS LTD.
Outfitters
DOLLOND & AITCHISON LTD.
Dispensing Opticians
DUDLEY GROUP T/A DUDLEY UK LTD.
Suppliers of Office Automation, Furniture Print & Stationery
EDE & RAVENSCROFT LTD.
Robe Makers
THE GATES RUBBER COMPANY LTD.
Manufacturers of Waterproof Rubber Footwear
THE GENERAL TRADING COMPANY (MAYFAIR) LTD.
Suppliers of Fancy Goods
GIEVES & HAWKES LTD.
Naval Tailors and Outfitters
EDWARD GOODYEAR LTD.
Florist

PAT GRANT
Hairdresser
HALCYON DAYS LTD.
Suppliers of Objets d'Art
HATCHARDS
Booksellers
HOLLAND & HOLLAND LTD.
Rifle Makers
JOHNS & PEGG LTD.
Military Tailors
JONES YARRELL & CO LTD.
Newsagents
JOHN N. KENT
Tailor
KINLOCH ANDERSON LTD.
Tailors and Kiltmakers
LAND ROVER
Manufacturers of Land Rover Vehicles
JOHN LOBB LTD.
Bootmakers
JAMES LOCK & CO LTD.
Hatters
PAUL LONGMIRE LTD.
Supplier of Jewellery & Presentation Gifts
LYLE & SCOTT LTD.
Manufacturers of Underwear and Knitwear
MG ROVER GROUP LTD.
Manufacturers of Rover and MG Motor Cars
PENHALIGON'S LTD.
Manufacturers of Toilet Requisites
JAMES PURDEY & SONS LTD.
Gun Makers
SPINK & SON LTD.
Medallists
STEPHENS BROTHERS LTD.
Shirt Maker & Hosier

TIS SOFTWARE LTD.
Computer Software Manufacturers
TRUEFITT & HILL
Hairdressers
UNITECH COMPLETE COMPUTING
I.T. Providers
WILKINSON SWORD LTD.
Sword Cutlers

2001 Royal Warrant Holders

Grantor: HM Queen Elizabeth The Queen Mother

ABOYNE & BALLATER FLOWERS
Greengrocer and Florist
ACKERMANS CHOCOLATES LTD.
Confectioners
AINSWORTHS HOMOEOPATHIC PHARMACY
Chemists
ALEXANDRE OF ENGLAND 1988 LTD.
Tailors
AMBASSADOR SERVICES
Hygiene Specialist - Kitchen Deep Cleaning
AMEC FACILITIES LTD.
Building Services Engineers
ALBERT AMOR LTD.
Suppliers of Fine Porcelain
KEVIN ANDREWS, UPHOLSTERERS & INTERIORS
Upholsterers
ANELLO & DAVIDE (BESPOKE AND
THEATRICAL) LTD.
Bespoke Shoe Manufacturers
AQUASCUTUM LTD.
Makers of Weatherproof Garments
THE "AT-A-GLANCE" CALENDAR CO LTD.
Calendar Manufacturers
ELIZABETH ARDEN LTD.
Manufacturers of Cosmetics
ASPREY LONDON LTD.
Jewellers, Goldsmiths and Silversmiths
AUTOGLYM
Supplier of Car Care Products
BACARDI-MARTINI LTD.
Suppliers of Brandy and Martini Vermouth
BANDAVILLE LTD.
Conveyors of Motor Vehicles
BARRADALE FARM LTD.
Egg Supplier

BASS BREWERS LTD.
Brewers
JAMES BAXTER & SON LTD.
T/A JAMES BAXTER & SON
Purveyors of Potted Shrimps
W.A. BAXTER & SONS LTD.
Purveyors of Scottish Specialities
BEHAR PROFEX LTD.
Restorers of Fine Antique Carpets and Tapestries
JOHN BELL & CROYDEN LTD.
Chemists
BENNEY
Gold and Silversmiths
V. BENOIST LTD.
Purveyors of General Groceries
BEWS BUTCHERS
Butchers and Poulterers
BLACK & EDGINGTON LTD.
Marquee Hirers and Flag Makers
BLOSSOM & BROWNE'S SYCAMORE
Launderers & Dry Cleaners
J. W. BOYCE
Seedsmen
BP OIL UK LTD.
Purveyors of Motor Spirit
C.H. BRANNAM LTD.
Pottery Makers
F. & J. BREMNER
Haulage Contractors
BRITVIC SOFT DRINKS LTD.
Manufacturers of Fruit Juices and Soft Drinks
JOHN BROADWOOD & SONS LTD.
Pianoforte Tuners
H. BRONNLEY & CO. LTD.
Toilet Soap Makers

BURLEY'S NEWSAGENTS
Newsagent and Tobacconist
CADBURY LTD.
Cocoa & Chocolate Manufacturers
CAITHNESS GLASS LTD.
Glassmaker
CALEYS (WINDSOR)
Suppliers of Household & Fancy Goods
CALOR GAS LTD.
Suppliers of Liquefied Petroleum Gas
CAMPBELL & CO.
Suppliers of Highland Tweeds
CARRINGTON & CO. LTD.
Jewellers & Silversmiths
CARTERS (J. & A.) LTD.
Manufacturers of Invalid Furniture
CARTERS TESTED SEEDS LTD.
Seedsmen
CARTIER LTD.
Jewellers and Goldsmiths
ALISTAIR CASSIE
Television Supplier & Engineer
CASTROL LTD.
Purveyors of Motor Lubricants
CHALMERS BAKERY LTD.
Bakers & Confectioners
COLLINGWOOD & CO. LTD.
Jewellers
COOPER -AVON TYRES LTD.
Tyre Manufacturers
CORNEY & BARROW LTD.
Wine Merchants
COUNTRYWEAR
Field Sports Outfitter
R.A. CREAMER AND SON LTD.
Automobile Engineers
CROMESSOL CO. LTD.
Manufacturers & Suppliers of Disinfectants & Detergents
D.D.P. LTD.
Purveyor of Fruit and Vegetables
D.I.S. WATER
Suppliers of Water Softening Equipment
DAIRY CREST LTD.
Suppliers of Fresh Milk and Dairy Products
WALTER DAVIDSON & SONS LTD.
Chemists

DETTLYN LTD. T/A EGHAM MOWER SERVICE
Suppliers of Horticultural Machinery
DOLLOND & AITCHISON LTD.
Dispensing Opticians
DORMA
Suppliers of Linen and Household Products
DOVETAIL ENTERPRISES(1993)INC ROYAL
DUNDEE BLINDCRAFT PRODUCTS & LORD
ROBERTS WORKSHOP
Furniture Makers
DREAMLAND APPLIANCES LTD.
Manufacturers of Electric Blankets
JOHN DUN & CO LTD.
Seed Merchant
JOHN DUNNET
Agricultural Contractor
EDE & RAVENSCROFT LTD.
Robe makers
EGHAM ANIMAL FOOD SUPPLIES
Corn and Animal Feed Merchants
EHRMANNS
Wine Merchants
ELDRIDGE POPE & CO PLC
Wine Merchants
EMMETTS STORE
Curers & Suppliers of Sweet Pickled Hams
FAIRFAX MEADOW
Suppliers of Pork Sausages
CHARLES FARRIS LTD.
Candlemakers
FIRMIN & SONS PLC
Button Makers
FORD MOTOR CO. LTD.
Motor Vehicle Manufacturers
FORTNUM & MASON PLC
Suppliers of Leather & Fancy Goods
JAMES J FOX & ROBERT LEWIS
Cigar Merchant
FOX'S BISCUITS
Biscuit Manufacturers
JOHN FREDERICK LTD.
Carpet Cleaners
A. FULTON CO. LTD.
Umbrella Manufacturers
GARRARD & CO. LTD.
Jewellers & Silversmiths

THE GENERAL TRADING COMPANY (MAYFAIR) LTD.
Suppliers of Fancy Goods
GIBSON SADDLERS LTD.
Suppliers of Racing Colours
J. GODDARD & SONS LTD.
Suppliers of Silver & Metal Polishes
GOODCHILDS THE MASTER BAKERS
Bakers
THOMAS GOODE & CO. LTD.
Suppliers of China & Glass
EDWARD GOODYEAR LTD.
Florist
GREENAWAYS
Printers
P. & J. HAGGART LTD.
Tartan and Woollen Manufacturers
HALCYON DAYS LTD.
Suppliers of Objets d'Art
HANCOCKS & CO. (JEWELLERS) LTD.
Goldsmiths & Silversmiths
HARDY MINNIS
Mercers of Woollen Cloth
D.R. HARRIS & CO. LTD.
Chemists
HARRODS LTD.
Suppliers of China, Glass & Fancy Goods
HARVEY NICHOLS & CO. LTD.
Drapers
C.H. HAYGARTH & SONS
Gunmaker and Cartridge Manufacturer
HEAT CENTRE
Gas Supplier and Servicing Gas Appliances
WALLACE HEATON LTD.
Suppliers of Photographic Equipment
HILLIER NURSERIES LTD.
Nurserymen & Seedsmen
HOOVER LTD.
Suppliers of Vacuum Cleaners
HOUSE OF FRASER (STORES) LTD. T/A ARMY & NAVY STORE
Suppliers of Household & Fancy Goods
HOWARD CHAIRS LTD.
Upholsterers and Soft Furnishers
HP FOODS LTD.
Manufacturers of HP Sauces

HYPNOS LTD.
Furnishers and Upholsterers
INITIAL TEXTILE SERVICES
Launderers and Dry Cleaners
THE JACOB'S BAKERY LTD.
Biscuit Manufacturers
JAGUAR CARS LTD.
Manufacturers of Daimler & Jaguar Cars
JEEVES OF BELGRAVIA
Dry Cleaners
JEYES GROUP LTD.
Manufacturers of Hygiene Products
G.M. & M. JOHNS, FAMILY BUTCHERS
Butcher
JOHNSON BROTHERS
Manufacturers of Ceramic Tableware
SC JOHNSON PROFESSIONAL LTD.
Manufacturers of Wax Polishes, Cleaners & Hygiene Products
PETER JONES
Draper & Furnisher
JONES YARRELL & CO. LTD.
Newsagents
JUSTERINI & BROOKS LTD.
Wine and Spirit Merchants
K. SHOES
Bootmakers
KARL LUDWIG COUTURE
Dressmaker
KIMBERLY CLARK LTD.
Manufacturers of Disposable Tissues
KLEEN-WAY (BERKSHIRE) CO.
Chimney Sweeps
KNIGHTS
Fishmongers
KNOWLES & SONS (FRUITERERS) LTD.
Purveyors of Fruit and Vegetables
LAND ROVER
Manufacturers of Land Rover Vehicles
LANG BROTHERS LTD.
Scotch Whisky Distillers
LDV LTD.
Manufacturers of Light Commercial Vehicles
W. LEE
Decorators and Building Contractors

LENTHERIC LTD.
Manufacturers of Perfumery Products
LEVER BROTHERS LTD.
Soap and Detergent Makers
LIBERTY PLC
Silk Mercers
H.S. LINWOOD & SONS LTD.
Fishmonger
PAUL LONGMIRE LTD.
Supplier of Silver & Presentation Gifts
ROGER LOWE SERVICES
Suppliers and Repairers of Domestic Appliances
A. MACKAY & SONS
Fishmonger
MAURICE & ROBERT
Hairdressers
THE MAYFAIR CLEANING CO. LTD.
Window Cleaners
MCCALLUM & CRAIGIE LTD.
Suppliers of Lan-Air-Cel Blankets
D. & F. MCCARTHY LTD.
Fruit & Vegetable Merchants
D & J MCCARTHY
Joinery Contractors
METAMEC
Manufacturers of Horological Products
METRO CABLE TV LTD.
Suppliers of Cable Services
MG ROVER GROUP LTD.
Manufacturers of Rover and MG Motor Cars
MITRE FURNISHING GROUP
Suppliers of Furnishing Fabrics and Bedding
MORNY LTD.
Manufacturers of Soap
MOYSES STEVENS LTD.
Florists
MUSKS LTD.
Suppliers of Musks Sausages
NAIROBI COFFEE & TEA CO. LTD.
Coffee Merchants
NESTLÉ UK LTD.
Manufacturers of Nestlé Products
NRG GROUP LTD.
Suppliers of Reprographic Office Equipment
OSMONDS
Suppliers of Animal Nutrients and Health Products

PAPWORTH GROUP
Trunk & Cabinet Makers
PARKERS
Saddlers
BERNARD PARKIN
Racing Photographer
PAXTON & WHITFIELD LTD.
Cheesemongers
A. & F. PEARS LTD.
Soap Manufacturers
E. PETRIE
Painters & Decorators
S.J. PHILLIPS LTD.
Antique Dealers
JOHN PLAYER & SONS
Tobacco Manufacturers
PLOWDEN & SMITH LTD.
Restorers of Fine Art Objects
KATHY POW BEAUTY CARE
Manicurist
PRATT & LESLIE JONES LTD.
Suppliers of China, Glass & Fancy Goods
PREMIER BRANDS UK LTD.
Manufacturers of Christmas Puddings
PRESTAT LTD.
Purveyors of Chocolate
JOHN PRINGLE
Supplier of Motor Spirit, Oil & Accessories
PRINGLE OF SCOTLAND LTD.
Manufacturers of Knitted Garments
PROCTER & GAMBLE UK
Manufacturers of Soap & Detergents & Shortening
RADIO RENTALS LTD.
Suppliers of Television Receivers
RAY HOLT (LAND DRAINAGE) LTD.
Land Drainage Contractors
C.J. REID (ETON)
Chemist
G. & A. REID
Suppliers of Cleaning Materials
RENSHAW SCOTT LTD.
Purveyors of Almond Products
RIDGWAYS
Tea Merchants
RIGBY & PELLER
Corsetieres

ROBERTS' RADIO LTD.
Radio Manufacturers
ROBERTSONS OF TAIN LTD.
Supplier of Agricultural & Horticultural Machinery
ROLLS-ROYCE AND BENTLEY MOTOR CARS LTD.
Motor Car Manufacturers
ROYAL ALBERT LTD.
Manufacturers of Paragon Fine Bone China
ROYAL BRITISH LEGION INDUSTRIES LTD.
Makers of Leather & Fancy Goods
THE ROYAL CROWN DERBY PORCELAIN
CO. LTD.
Manufacturers of Fine Bone China
RUDOLF
Milliner
RUSSELL HUME LTD.
Suppliers of Meat & Poultry
GORDON RUSSELL LTD.
Manufacturers of Furniture
WILLIAM SANDERSON & SON LTD.
Scotch Whisky Distillers
SCHWEPPES LTD.
Soft Drink Manufacturers
ALAN J. SCOTT LTD.
Livestock Hauliers
SEMEX (UK SALES) LTD.
Supplier of Cattle Breeding Services
EDWARD SHARP & SONS LTD.
Confectioners
SHEPHERD NEWSAGENTS
Newsagent
H.M. SHERIDAN
Purveyor of Meat & Poultry
W.L. SLEIGH LTD.
Motor Vehicle Hirers
SLUMBERLAND PLC
Bedding Manufacturers
TOM SMITH GROUP LTD.
Suppliers of Christmas Crackers
FRANK SMYTHSON
Suppliers of Stationery & Office Equipment
SOLLEYS FARMS LTD.
Suppliers of Dairy Products
WILLIAM SOUTER LTD.
Suppliers of Hardware and China

R.R. SPINK & SONS (ARBROATH) LTD.
Fishmongers
STEINER GROUP LTD.
Cosmeticians
J. STOPPS & SONS LTD.
Bakers & Confectioners
STOWELLS OF CHELSEA LTD.
Wine & Spirit Merchants
GEORGE STRACHAN LTD.
General Merchants
SUTTONS CONSUMER PRODUCTS LTD.
Seedsmen
SWAINE ADENEY BRIGG LTD.
Umbrella Makers
TANQUERAY GORDON & CO. LTD.
Gin Distillers
O.A. TAYLOR & SONS BULBS LTD.
Bulb Growers
DONALD THOMSON
Grocer
THRESHER & GLENNY LTD.
Shirtmakers
LINDA THURSTON
Beautician
TRIANCO REDFYRE LTD.
Manufacturers of Domestic Boilers
R. TWINING & CO. LTD.
Tea and Coffee Merchants
THE UNIVERSITY OF OXFORD SHOP
Suppliers of Official University of Oxford Collection
Products
VAN DEN BERGH FOODS LTD.
Suppliers of Dairy Products
VAUXHALL MOTORS LTD.
Motor Vehicle Manufacturers
VERNONS ELECTRICAL LTD.
Electrical Engineers
VEUVE CLICQUOT-PONSARDIN
Purveyors of Champagne
W F ELECTRICAL PLC
Suppliers of Electrical Equipment
WAITROSE LTD.
Grocers
WALLACE, CAMERON & CO LTD.
Manufacturers & Suppliers of First Aid Dressings

ALBERT WANT & CO. LTD.
Suppliers of Household Hardware & Garden Sundries
WARES WINDOW CLEANING
Window Cleaner
WARTSKI LTD.
Jewellers
KEN WATMOUGH
Fishmongers
JOHN WATSON SEEDS
Supplier of Agricultural Seeds
BERNARD WEATHERILL LTD.
Livery Tailors
WEETABIX LTD.
Manufacturers of Breakfast Cereals

WHITBREAD FREMLINS
Brewers
WHITWORTHS GROUP LTD.
Manufacturers of Provisions and Dried Fruits
E.J. WICKS
Saddler
ARNOLD WIGGINS & SONS LTD.
Picture Frame Makers
WINDSORIAN COACHES LTD.
Coach Operator
WOLSEY LTD.
Manufacturers of Hosiery & Knitwear
YARDLEY & CO LTD.
Perfumers & Manufacturers of Soap

2001 Royal Warrant Holders

Grantor: HRH The Prince of Wales

ABBEY MOTORS (HEMEL HEMPSTEAD) LTD.
Servicing & Repairs of Motor Vehicles
AINSWORTHS HOMOEOPATHIC PHARMACY
Chemists
AMBERLEY VALE FOODS LTD.
Master Butchers
ANDERSON & SHEPPARD LTD.
Tailors
ANTON LAUNDRY LTD.
Launderer
MICHELINE ARCIER AROMATHERAPY
Manufacturer & Supplier of Aromatherapy Bath Oils
ASPREY LONDON LTD.
Jewellers, Goldsmiths & Silversmiths
ASTON MARTIN LAGONDA LTD.
Motor Car Manufacturer and Repairer
ATCO-QUALCAST LTD.
Manufacturers of Motor Mowers
AUSTIN REED GROUP PLC
Outfitters
AUSTRALIAN DRIED FRUITS (EUROPE) LTD.
Purveyors of Dried Fruits
AUTOGLYM
Supplier of Car Care Products
J. BARBOUR & SONS LTD.
Manufacturers of Waterproof & Protective Clothing
BENNEY
Gold and Silversmiths
V. BENOIST LTD.
Purveyors of Table Delicacies
BENSON & CLEGG LTD.
Suppliers of Button & Badges
BENTLEY & SKINNER
(BOND STREET JEWELLERS) LTD.
Jewellers and Silversmiths

BERRY BROS & RUDD LTD.
Wine and Spirit Merchants
BILLINGS & EDMONDS LTD.
Tailors and Outfitters
BLOSSOM & BROWNE'S SYCAMORE
Launderers and Dry Cleaners
BRICKELL SWIMMING POOLS
Swimming Pool Construction & Suppliers
H. BRONNLEY & CO. LTD.
Toilet Soap Makers
BURBERRY LTD.
Outfitters
PAUL BURNS PHOTOGRAPHY
Social Photographer
CANDLE MAKERS SUPPLIES
Candle Makers Supplies
CARLUCCIO'S LTD.
Supplier of Italian Food and Truffles
CARTIER LTD.
Jewellers and Goldsmiths
CASH'S (UK) LTD.
Manufacturers of Woven Name Tapes
CHALMERS BAKERY LTD.
Bakers & Confectioners
THE CHINA REPAIRERS
China Restorer
CHRISTY COSMETICS LTD.
Suppliers of Skincare Products
CLAN FISHING RODS LTD.
Manufacturer & Repairer of Fishing Tackle
COLSTON GRAPHICS LTD. T/A LEIGHTON
PRINTING CO.
Printers & Stationers
A.C. COOPER (COLOUR) LTD.
Fine Art Photographers

COPELLA FRUIT JUICES LTD.
Suppliers of English Apple Juice & Juice Blends
CORGI HOSIERY LTD.
Knitwear & Hosiery Manufacturers
CORNEY & BARROW LTD.
Wine Merchants
COUNTRYWEAR
Field Sports Outfitter
COVER TO COVER CASSETTES LTD.
Producer and Publisher of Audio Books
CRABTREE & EVELYN (OVERSEAS) LTD.
Suppliers of Fine Toiletries
R.A. CREAMER AND SON LTD.
Automobile Engineers
ROBERT CRERAR
Gold and Silversmith
J. & J. CROMBIE LTD.
Outfitters
DAKS LTD.
Outfitters
WALTER DAVIDSON & SONS LTD.
Chemists
THOMAS DAY MOTORS LTD.
Supplier of Motor Vehicles
DORMA
Suppliers of Bed & Table Linen
DUDLEY GROUP T/A DUDLEY UK LTD.
Suppliers of Office Automation, Furniture Print &
Stationery
EDE & RAVENSCROFT LTD.
Robe Makers
ELITE CLEANING & HOMECARE SERVICES LTD.
Interior Cleaning Specialists
EQUICENTRE
Farrier
G. ETTINGER LTD.
Manufacturers of Leathergoods
EXIMIOUS LTD.
Manufacturer of Monogrammed Accessories
C. FARLOW & CO. LTD.
Suppliers of Fishing Tackle & Waterproof Clothing
FINDUS LTD.
Supplier of Frozen Food
FISHER PRODUCTIONS LTD.
Suppliers of Lighting and Production Services

STEPHEN FLORENCE
Furniture Maker and Designer
J. FLORIS LTD.
Manufacturers of Toilet Preparations
FORD MOTOR CO. LTD.
Motor Vehicle Manufacturers
FORTNUM & MASON PLC
Tea Merchants and Grocers
GINO FRANCHI
Conservation Mount and Picture Framer
GARRARD & CO. LTD.
Jewellers, Goldsmiths and Silversmiths
GENERAL DOMESTIC APPLIANCES LTD.
Manufacturers of Domestic Appliances
THE GENERAL TRADING COMPANY (MAYFAIR)
LTD.
Suppliers of Fancy Goods
GIEVES & HAWKES LTD.
Tailors and Outfitters
THOMAS GOODE & CO. LTD.
Suppliers of China & Glass
HALCYON DAYS LTD.
Suppliers of Objets d'Art
FRANK HALL
Tailors
HAMPSHIRE RADIO-PHONES LTD.
Supplier of Cellular Communications Equipment
HARRODS LTD.
Outfitters & Saddlers
HATCHARDS
Booksellers
HOLLAND & HOLLAND LTD.
Suppliers of Bespoke Guns, Shooting Accessories &
Country Clothing
HOUSE OF CHEESE
Suppliers of Cheese
HOUSE OF HARDY LTD.
Manufacturers of Fishing Tackle
HYAMS & COCKERTON LTD.
Purveyors of Fruit and Vegetables
IBM UNITED KINGDOM LTD.
Suppliers of Information Systems
JAGUAR CARS LTD.
Manufacturers of Daimler & Jaguar Cars
JEEVES OF BELGRAVIA
Dry Cleaners

JEROBOAMS
Cheesemongers
D. JOHNSTON & CO. (LAPHROAIG)
Distiller & Supplier of Single Malt Whisky
PETER JONES
Draper & Furnisher
JONES YARRELL & CO. LTD.
Newsagents
KENT SERVICES LTD.
Suppliers of Specialist Packaging for Works of Art
ROBERT KIME
Supplier of Antiques & Interior Decoration
KINLOCH ANDERSON LTD.
Tailors and Kiltmakers
JAMES KNIGHT OF MAYFAIR AND CECIL & CO.
Fishmongers
LAERDAL MEDICAL LTD.
Supplier of Medical Equipment
LAND ROVER
Manufacturers of Land Rover Vehicles
LANSING LINDE LTD.
Manufacturers of Fork Lift Trucks
CHAMPAGNE LAURENT-PERRIER
Purveyors of Champagne
JOHN LOBB LTD.
Bootmakers
JAMES LOCK & CO. LTD.
Hatters
MAPPIN & WEBB LTD.
Silversmiths
TONY MARENGHI SPECIALIST INTERIOR
CLEANING
Interior Cleaning Specialist
EFG MATTHEWS OFFICE FURNITURE LTD.
Office Furniture Supplier
THE MAYFAIR CLEANING CO. LTD.
Window Cleaners
DENISE MCADAM LTD.
Hairdresser
D. & F. MCCARTHY LTD.
Fruit & Vegetable Merchants
MCPHERSONS ATLANTIC LTD.
Supplier of Exotic Mushrooms
MG ROVER GROUP LTD.
Manufacturers Land Rovers, Rover Group Ltd. Warwick

JOHN MILLER (CORSHAM) LTD.
Suppliers of Garden Machinery & Chain Saws
MOSIMANN'S LTD.
Caterers
MOYSES STEVENS LTD.
Florists
NAIROBI COFFEE & TEA CO. LTD.
Coffee Merchants
NATURE SPRINGS WATER CO. LTD.
Suppliers of Natural Mineral Water
NORFOLK LAVENDER LTD.
Growers and Distillers of English Essential Oils
OLIVER & LANG BROWN
Forestry Contractors
PALMBROKERS
Supplier of Greenery and Interior Plants
DAVID PALMER BUILDING CONTRACTORS LTD.
Building Contractors
PARKER PEN CO.
Manufacturers of Writing Instruments & Inks
YEO PAULL LTD.
Suppliers of Marquees and Equipment
PAXTON & WHITFIELD LTD.
Cheesemongers
PENHALIGON'S LTD.
Manufacturers of Toilet Requisites
PETERSFIELD BOOKSHOP
Picture Framer
E. & J. PHILLIPS LTD.
Bakers and Confectioners
PHOENIX FINE ART
Suppliers of Fine Art Services
PINNEYS OF SCOTLAND
Purveyors of Smoked Salmon
POTS AND PITHOI
Supplier of Terracotta Pots
MICHAEL POWLES LTD.
Suppliers of Bentley Motor Cars & Automobile Engineers
JEFFERY A. PRATT
Suppliers of Animal Health & Veterinary Products
ARTHUR PRICE & CO. LTD.
Cutlers & Silversmiths
PRICE'S PATENT CANDLE CO. LTD.
Candlemakers

JOHN PRINGLE
Motor Engineer

JAMES PURDEY & SONS LTD.
Gun and Cartridge Makers

RADIO RENTALS LTD.
Suppliers of Television Receivers

FIONA RAE
Goldsmith, Silversmith and Jeweller

ROBERTS' RADIO LTD.
Manufacturers and Suppliers of Radio Receivers

ROLLS-ROYCE AND BENTLEY MOTOR CARS LTD.
Motor Car Manufacturers

ROYAL BRIERLEY CRYSTAL LTD.
Suppliers of Crystal Table Glassware

ROYAL DOULTON PLC
Manufacturers of China

ROYAL NATIONAL COLLEGE FOR THE BLIND
Pianoforte Tuners

RSL COM
Supplier of Cellular Airtime

RUSSELL HUME LTD.
Suppliers of Meat & Poultry

RUSSELLS OF TETBURY
Dry Cleaners

THE SCOTCH HOUSE LTD.
Outfitters

SEARCY TANSLEY & CO. LTD.
Caterers

KEVIN SHEEHAN
Clockmaker and Repairer

SHEPHERD NEAME LTD.
Supplier of Cherry Brandy & Specialist Orders

H.M. SHERIDAN
Purveyor of Meat & Poultry

SHIPTON MILL LTD.
Flour Miller

SLEEPEEZEE LTD.
Bedding Manufacturers

W.L. SLEIGH LTD.
Motor Vehicle Hirers

SMITHKLINE BEECHAM CONSUMER HEALTHCARE
Suppliers of Toothpaste

FRANK SMYTHSON
Suppliers of Stationery & Office Equipment

SONY UNITED KINGDOM LTD.
Supplier of Consumer Electronic Products

ANDREW SOOS T/A BENEDEK LTD.
Leather Goods Manufacturer

SPINK & SON LTD.
Medallists

START-RITE SHOES LTD.
Shoemakers

STEPHENS BROTHERS LTD.
Shirt Maker & Hosier

GEORGE STRACHAN LTD.
General Merchants

STUART & SONS LTD.
Purveyors of Fine Crystal Tableware and Gifts

SWAINE ADENEY BRIGG LTD.
Suppliers of Umbrellas

ANTHONY TATE
Chemist

THAMES & COTSWOLD
Cycle Suppliers

THE TOLSEY
Suppliers of Books and Stationery

TOTAL BUTLER LTD.
Suppliers of Fuel Oils

R.E. TRICKER LTD.
Shoe Manufacturers

ROBIN TUKE
Supplier of Mobile Communication Equipment

TURNBULL & ASSER LTD.
Shirtmakers

KENNETH TURNER LTD.
Suppliers of Perfumed Candles, Room Fragrances & Toiletries

R. TWINING & CO. LTD.
Tea and Coffee Merchants

VAUXHALL MOTORS LTD.
Motor Vehicle Manufacturers

VODAPAGE LTD.
Supplier of National Radio Paging Services

WALLACE, CAMERON & CO. LTD.
Manufacturers & Suppliers of First Aid Dressings

WARTSKI LTD.
Jewellers

KEN WATMOUGH
Fishmongers

WEETABIX LTD.
Manufacturers of Breakfast Cereals
WELSH & JEFFERIES LTD.
Military Tailors
ROLLO WHATELY LTD.
Picture Framer
WINTERBORNE ZELSTON FENCING
Mf. of Trad. Cleft Estate Fencing and Gates
XEROX LTD.
Manufacturers and Suppliers of Xerographic Copying Equipment
YARDLEY & CO. LTD.
Manufacturers of Toilet Preparations

OFFICERS OF THE LOCAL ASSOCIATIONS

2001

	Name	Company
WINDSOR		
President	David May	H. May (Ascot) Ltd..
Secretary	K. Douglas Hill	C.J. Reid (Eton)
London Representative	Fred Newman	Abbey Rose Gardens
Treasurer	Jeremy Clark	A.A. Clark
ABERDEEN		
President	Colin Campbell	Langstane Press
Secretary	George Alpine	–
London Representative	Mark Fleming	John Fleming & Co. Ltd.
EDINBURGH		
President	Jim Mackie	Wilson & Son
Secretary	Willie Munro	–
London Representative	Brian Smellie	James Grey & Son
SANDRINGHAM		
President	Alec McKee	John Deere Ltd..
Secretary	Frank Morris	–
London Representative	Nicholas Copeman	BBC Fire Protection Ltd..
Treasurer	Shaun Tusting	W. J. Boddy & Sons Ltd..

COMPANIES HOLDING FOUR ROYAL WARRANTS

2001

Company	Legend	Grantee
Ede & Ravenscroft Ltd..	Robe Makers	Michael Middleton
The General Trading Company (Mayfair) Ltd..	Suppliers of Fancy Goods	David Part, OBE, TD, DL
Blossom & Browne's Sycamore	Launderers and Dry Cleaners	Daniel Browne
Jones Yarrell & Co. Ltd..	Newsagents	David Mackay
Land Rover	Manufacturer of Land Rover Vehicles	Robert Dover
Halcyon Days Ltd..	Suppliers of Objets d'Art	Peter Norman, LVO
Benney	Gold and Silversmiths	Prof Gerald Benney, CBE

A

Abbey Rose Gardens 105
Aberconway, Lord *55*
Aberdeen, Trinity Hall 114, *114*
Aberdeen Association of Royal Warrant Holders 38, 109-17
    Braemar Gathering 115-16
    joined membership with London 110
    officers 235
    subscription 111
Airlie, Earl of, Lord Chamberlain *60*, 86
Aitken, Rt Revd Aubrey 125, 127
    Aubrey Aitken Memorial Trophy 128
Albert, Prince 109
Albion Tavern 29
Alden & Blackwell, booksellers 107
Allen, Katherine, lace draper 17
Allied Domecq 71, 122
Alpine, George, Secretary Aberdeen Association 111, 115
Amies, Hardy 11
Anderson, Lieutenant-Colonel David 122
Anne, The Princess Royal 22, 69, 92-3, *93*, 115
annual banquets, *see* banquets
Archibald, Alan 114
Archibald, Michael, President Aberdeen Association 114, 115
Archibald's, cabinet makers 113
Ardath, cigarette manufacturers 64
Arlington, Earl of, Lord Chamberlain 17
Army & Navy Stores, suppliers of household and fancy goods 59
Arnold, Jane 16
Ashley-Smith, Dr Jonathan 84
Association of Royal Tradesmen 28-9, *28*
Atholl, Duke of, President 43
Athow, Sean *89*
Atkinson, Rupert, royal portraits 90, *90*
Austin Reed, men's outfitters 72

B

Bacon Marketing Board 59
G.P. & J. Baker, curtains 54
Balmoral Castle *108*
Bankes, Juliet 92
bankruptcy of Warrant Holders 33-5
banquets 22, 28-31, *29, 40, 43*, 53, *53*, 63, *78*, 95
    150th anniversary celebrations 76, *76*
    Banquet of 2000, 22, *93*
    Caledonian Banquet 79, *79*
    Coronation of George IV *101*
    invitation *52*
    menu cards *30-1, 33, 79*
    Millennium Banquet 92, *93*
    programmes *30-1, 33, 126*
J. Barbour & Son, rainwear 73
Barbour, Margaret, President 73, 79, 82
Barnard & Westwood, printers 14
Barnes, David, President Edinburgh Association 121
Bass, brewers 47, 73
Baxter, Gordon, President Aberdeen Association *104*, 115

Beauchamp, Sir John 13
Bedborough, Mr 102
Belgium, Royal Warrants 132, 135
Benson & Hedges 73
Beresford Marshall, C. 54
Berry Bros, wine merchant 21, *21*
Berthelet, Thomas, printer and binder 14
Bidney, Jane, lace maker 26-7
Bidwell, Sir Hugh, Lord Mayor of London 75
Billings & Edmunds, school outfitters 88
Birkhall Castle 114
Bishop, Derek 106-7
Black, William, locksmith 17
Blythwood, Lord, President 43
Board of Green Cloth 16, 29, 32, 37
BOCM Silcock 73
Bodinnar, Sir John, President 59
Boilerine Ltd, manufacturer of radiator tablets 43
Bond Street *42*
Boots the Chemist 11
Bottom, Geoffrey, President Sandringham Association 127
Bovril, hot drinks 43
Bowman, Jonathan, President Sandringham Association 127, *128*
Braemar Gathering 115-16, *116*
Braid, H.M., President 5
Brazil, Warrant Holders 134
Brett-Smith, Adam, President 59, 93, *93, 128*
Brideman, George 16
Brighton Pavilion stables *19*
Royal Yacht Britannia 115, *117*, 123
Britten, Alan
    President 83-5, 128
    Chairman QEST 90-1, *93, 94*
John Broadwood & Sons, piano makers 25, *25*
Brookhouse, Major, Secretary 48, 55, *55*
Brotherton, Thomas 11
Brough, Peter, and Archie Andrews 103
Browett, Taylor & Cordery 43
Buchanan, James 134
Buckingham Gate offices 59, *65*, 68, *77*, 84-5
Buckingham Palace *82*, 95
Buckingham Palace Garden Party 75
Buckingham Place offices *80*, 85, *92*
Burbidge, Sir Richard, President 59, 68
Burgess, John 20
Burgoyne, Mr 47
Burgoyne's, wine merchants 47
Burns, Paul, photographer 88
'By Appointment' roses 74-5, *74*
Byass, William, President 44

C

Cadbury Brothers, chocolate makers 25
Caley, Mrs, milliner and dressmaker 20, 102
Caley & Son 102
Caley Brothers, advertisement *102*
Callard, Steward & Watt, bakers 42, 49

Callard, Ernest, President 42
Callard, T.B., President 49
Calor Gas 115, 122, 128
Campbell, Mr, President 42
Campbell, Iain
    President Edinburgh Association *82,* 122-3
    centenary reception 122
    Hugh Faulkner Putter Competition *122*
Canada, use of Royal Arms 50
Carr & Co., biscuit makers 25
Carr, Rupert, President 59, 63
Carrington & Co., jewellers and silversmiths 42
Carrington Smith, W., President 42
Cassie, television shop 113
Castle of Mey 111-12, *112*
Caxton, William, printer 14, *15*
Chalmers, bakers 113
Chamberlayne, Dr Edward, *The Present State of England* 17, 18
Chapman, Davina, calligrapher 90
Paul E. Chappuis, manufacturers of daylight reflectors 43
Charles II 17, *17*
Charles, Prince of Wales *78, 129*
    environmental policy 77-8, *78,* 88, 93
    portrait *90*
    Prince's Trust 88
    socialising with Warrant Holders 84, 86, 87, 88
    Warrants granted 64-5, 77, 87-8
Charlotte, Queen, Warrant Holders 20
Charrington, Jack, 68-9
Charringtons, brewers 68
Cheyne, John, Master of the Horse 14
Chivas, James, President Aberdeen Association 109
Chivas Whisky 109
Chivers & Sons, purveyors of jams 59
Chivers, William, President 59
Chubb & Sons, locks and safe makers 25
Chubb, Charles, locksmith 20, 62
Clarke, Lieutenant-General Sir Travers, President 43, *55*
Clerk of the Stables 19-20
Cobbold, Lord, Lord Chamberlain 62
Cobden, Mr 102
Cole, Sir Henry 26
Coleclough, Peter, President 63
Coleman, James, Secretary 49
Companies Act 48
Connell, John, President 64,
Coombes, William, sadler 35
Frank Cooper, marmalade makers 42
Cooper, Captain William, President 42
Copeman, Nick *129*
Corney & Barrow, wine merchants 59, 61, 93, 122
Courage, Brigadier, President 56
Harold Cox & Sons Jewellers 105
Thomas Crapper, sanitary engineers 44
Crawford, Crawfie 16
Crawford, Geoffrey 84
Crichton, Colonel the Hon. Sir George 102

cricket matches 128-9, *129*
Cromwell, Oliver 16, *17*
Cullimore, Colin 74

D
Daily Mail 45-6, *46,* 47
Daily Mirror 60-1
Davidson's, chemist 113
Davies, T.E., President 64
Day, Son & Hewitt, suppliers of animal medicine 59
Day & Martin, boot polish manufacturers 59
Day, Tom *103,* 106, 112-13
Thomas de la Rue 70
de Thunderley, Reginald, purveyor of cloth 11-12
de Vogüé, Comte Alain, President 71, *121*
Debenham & Freebody, furriers and silk mercers 42
John Deere, agricultural machinery 128, *128*
Dege & Skinner, tailors and shirt makers 14, 28, *28,* 74, 83, 92, 135
Denmark, Royal Warrants 132, 135
Dent, Mrs, chronometer maker 25
DER 73
Dewar, John 47
John Dewar and Sons, whisky distiller 47, 59, 122
Dewar-Durie, Andrew 122
Dewhurst, butchers 74
Dickson-Wright, Sir Arthur 60
Dillon, Mrs, worker of bookmarkers 25
dinners
    see also banquets
    Citizens' dinner in Aberdeen 109
    Royal Tradesmen 30-1, *30-1*
    Windsor Tradesmen 100, 103, 104
Distillers Company 64, *72, 79*
Dobbies, garden centre 121
Douglas, Bill, President Edinburgh Association 119, 122
Douglas, Major R.E., President Edinburgh Association 119, *119,* 121
Douglas, Robert A., Secretary Edinburgh Association 119
Douglas, William, President 64
Douglas-Home, Sir Alec *see* Lord Home of the Hirshel
Dowdell, Jim 128
Dowell's Rooms 119, *120*
Drapers Company 7
du Cros, A.P. 47
Dunlop, tyre company 47
Dutton, Pippa *125*
Dyce, William 26-7, *26*

E
Eaton, Katherine, lace draper 17
Benjamin Edgington, marquee and tent manufacturers 55
Edinburgh Association of Royal Warrant Holders 27, 38, 119-23
    annual lunch/dinner 120-1, 123
    officers 235
Edinburgh, Duke of 60, *61,* 76, *76, 90*
    and Edinburgh Association 22
    portrait *90*
    and Windsor Association 103

Edinburgh Royal Tradesmen 119-23
Edward I
  Great Wardrobe 13
  investing his son *11*
  Queen Eleanor's Cross *11*
Edward II 11
Edward III
  Great Wardrobe 13
  Royal Charter 7
Edward IV *13,* 14
Edward VII
  funeral *103*
  warrants granted 44, 53
Edward VIII *56,* 64
  King's House 55, *55*
Edwards, Fleetwood, Keeper of the Privy Purse 37
Edwards' Hair Restorer advertisement *36*
Eleanor, Queen, cross *11*
Elizabeth I 15-16, *16*
Elizabeth II 26, 75, 95
  150th anniversary banquet *72*
  Buckingham Palace Garden Party 75
  Golden Jubilee 83, 95
  as Princess 59
    housing for pensioners 63-4
    Warrants granted 59
  Royal Charter celebrations 62, *62*
Elizabeth, The Queen Mother *68, 72,* 91-2, *92, 106-7, 113, 116, 119*
  80th birthday 69, 95
  90th birthday 73
  100th birthday 92-3
  Castle of Mey 112
  Coat of Arms *105*
  portrait 76, *77*
  The Queen Elizabeth Scholarship Trust 69, 72-3, 76, 78, 84, 86, 89, 95, 116
  Queen Elizabeth Scholarships 27, 89-91, 95
    Scholars 89-91, *89, 94,* 95, 148-50
    Scholars reception 92-3, *94*
  Sandringham Flower Show 128-9
  sculpture *92*
P. Erard, harp and pianoforte makers 42
Eustons, Nicholas, button maker 17
Express Dairy, milk 43

F
Faletti, John 49-50
Farrers 73, 95
Faulkner, Hugh
  Secretary 52, 67, 72-3, 79, 81, 84, 86, *121*
  150th anniversary celebrations 74, 95
  Hugh Faulkner Putter competition 122, *122*
  Scholarship Trust 72-3
Fayed, Mohammed 59
fees levied on Warrant Holders 19, 32-3
female Warrant Holders 28-9
Ferens, Rt Hon. T.H. 47

Findlater, Mackie, Todd, wine and spirit merchant 90, 91, 112
Finn, Holly 91
Firmin, Philip Douglas, buttonmaker 20
Firmin, Samuel, buttonmaker 20
Firmins, buttonmakers 20
Fleming, Mark, President Aberdeen Association 115
Floris, smooth pointed comb makers *8, 20*
foreign Presidents 71
foreign trade mark applications 50-1
foreign Warrant Holders 37
foreign warrants 132-5
Forteviot, Lord, President 59, *59*
France, Imperial Warrants 133
Franchi, Gino 88
François I of France 12
Freemasons Hall *27,* 28
Freemasons Tavern 29, 75
J.S. Fry, chocolatier 54, 133
Fry, Donovan, President Sandringham Association *104,* 128-9
Fyshe, Walter, tailor 16

G
Gamble, John, chimney sweep 107
Gannex mackintosh 60
Garrard & Co. Ltd, Crown Jewellers 59, 74
Garrard, Robert, goldsmith 20
Gassiers, David, golf club maker 18
General Accident, insurance provider 43
General Trading Company, fancy goods *70,* 83
George III, Warrants granted 20
George IV *20*
  coronation banquet *101*
  Royal Coat of Arms *20*
  Warrants granted *8,* 20
  Windsor Castle 100
George V *25*
  coronation robe *47*
  jubilee 120
  Kings House 53-5, *54-5*
  marriage *26,* 27
  Warrants granted 92
George VI *119, 107*
  Warrants granted 53, 56, 92
George, Sir Richard
  President 73, 78-9, *78,* 91, 112
  Treasurer 85, *94*
German Needle Manufacturers' Association 50
Germany, Imperial Warrants 133
Gibbs, Haynes, Secretary 37, *37, 40*
Gibbs, Walter, Secretary *40*
Gieve, Robert, President 14, 82-3, *82*
Gieves & Hawkes, naval and military tailors 14, 82
gifts to Royal Family 95, 104
Gilbert, Col. D.K.M., President Sandringham Association 126, 128
Glave's shop 45
Glenny, Charles, Treasurer 55
golf *18,* 122

Gonzalez Byass, sherry producers 44
Thomas Goode 90
Graf, Roy 107
Henry Graves & Co.Ltd, printsellers and publishers 42
Graves, Algernon
    President 42
    Secretary 46
James Gray & Son, ironmongers 64, 119, 121, 122
Great Spicery 13
The Great Wardrobe 13
    Wardrobe of Robes 15
Gretton, Colonel 47
Guinness and Son 53
Gumley, Louis S. *119*
Guy, William John 134

H
Hacking, Major Sir Douglas 48
Haggart, Captain James 42
Haggarts, tartan manufacturers 42
Hague, Sir Harry, President 59
Hall & Tawse, building contractors 111, 116, *116*
Hamill, James *89*
Hamilton & Inches, jewellers 120
Hamptons 54
Hanover Square offices 43, 57
Hardy-Roberts, Sir Geoffrey 62, 86
Hargood, John, sword cutter 18
Harkness, Peter 74
Harmsworth 47
Harris, Anne, laundress 14-15
Harris, James, plush manufacturer 21
Harris, Jonathan *92*
Harrods, outfitters 59, 68
Harvey Jones, Sir John 72
Hayter, Lord George, President 62
Hazel, Jeff 128
Hazel, Mike *129*
Heald, Tim, *By Appointment* 74
Henriquet, J.M. 52
Henry II 7
    Charter *9*
Henry VIII 12, *12,* 14
Herbert, Mr, clockmaker 18
Heseltine, Sir William 127
Hewytt, Thomas, poulterer 14
Highgrove *88*
Hill, Douglas, Secretary Windsor Association 105, *105*
Hine, Sidney, President 59, 61, 63
Holder, Mr, locksmith 17
Holland & Holland, gunmakers *61,* 83
Holman, Samuel, Secretary 45
Holyroodhouse *118*
Home of the Hirsel, Lord 60, 123
Honiton lace makers 26-7, 87
Hoover Ltd, electric cleaners 54
Hope, R.H.W., Secretary 57, 60

House of Windsor company 86
Howard Rotovator Co. Ltd, agricultural equipment 63
Alfred Hughes & Sons, cake and biscuit manufacturers 56
Hughes, Howard 56
Hunter, John
    Chairman Association of Royal Tradesmen 28-9
    work book *28*
Huntley & Palmers, biscuit and cake manufacturers 59, 64
Hurdman, Jill *128*
Hussey, Mr 103

I
Inches, jewellers 120
The Incorporated Association of Her Majesty's and Other Royal Warrant Holders Limited 41
India
    use of Royal Arms 49-50
    Warrant Holders 135
Isaac, J.W., President 59
Isaacs, Rufus *49*
Italy, Warrants 135
Iveagh, Lord 53, *55*

J
James II 18
Jamieson, Henry, fishing rod manufacturer 113, 115, *115*
Jamieson, William, Secretary Aberdeen Association 109
Janvrin, Sir Robin 60
Jasper, Stephen 14
Jay, Tom Simpson, President 37, 41-2, *41,* 96
Jay's, silk mercers 41
Jenkins, Sir Brian 22, 92
Jenner, Mr, joiner 99-100
Jenners, department store 120
Jeyes' White Porcelain Toilet Box 54
Edwin John & Co., bidet manufacturers 54
Johnny Walker, Scotch whisky distillers 59
Johnson and Justerini, cordial merchants 20
Johnston, Andrew Lawson, glass engraver 113
Joint Silver Anniversary Trust 63-4
Jones, Captain Garrow 48
Jones, William, tailor 16
Justerini & Brooks, wine merchants 20, 122

K
Kagan, Joseph 60
Keen's Mustard advertisement *50*
Kelly, Rod 89
Kent, Duchess of 20
G.B. Kent & Sons, hairbrush makers 25
Keown-Boyd, Colonel Bill 61-2, 64, 67, 68, 71, 81, 93, 125
King Edward VII Hospital for Officers 69, 95
King's Armoury at the Tower 13
King's House 53-4, *54,* 60, 69, 95, 103
Kinloch Anderson, kilt makers 79, 120
Kinloch Anderson, Douglas
    President Edinburgh Association 79, *104,* 121, 123

Caledonian Banquet 79, *79*
Kinnard, Mr, joiner 17
kitchens *18, 19*
Knight, Charles, printer 99
John Knight Ltd, soap manufacturers 43
Kopley, Austen, printer 14, *14*
Kumagai Gummi 76

L
Lace Drapers 17
Laing, Anthea *89*
Charles Lancaster & Co.Ltd, gunsmiths 42
Langs Biscuits 120
Lanson, champagne producers 44
Laphroaig 122
Leicester, Earl of 127
Leslie, Martin 111-12
Lever Bros, soap and detergent manufacturers 43, 44, 53
Leverhulme, Lord, President 43, 53, *53*
Levey, Santina M. 27
Lewinski, Jorge 74
Limmer & Trinidad Lake Asphalt Co., asphalt 54
Liptons, tea and provision dealers 133
Livingston, Boynton P. 60
London Reception 82-3, 95
Lord Chamberlain *60*, 62, 96
    abolition of fees 33
    policing role 36
    and Royal Tradesmen 62
    rules 85, 95
    signs Warrants 8
    tradesmen 18
    Tradesmen's Warrants Committee 7, 85
Lord Chamberlain's department 7, 18
'Lord Chamberlain's Rules' 85, 95
Lord Steward
    annual dinner 29
    fees levied 19, 32
    purveyors 18, 32-3
Lord Steward's department 18
Lovekyn, Arthur 14
Lovekyn, George [father], serjeant tailor 13-14
Lovekyn, George [son] 14
Lowein, John *68*
Loyd, Sir Julian 125, *127*
Lusher, Bill, President Sandringham Association 125-6, *126*, 128
Lusher, Mark, President Sandringham Association 127-9, *129*

M
A.& J. McBain 110
McCarthy, John 129, *129*
D.& F. McCarthy Ltd 129
McGregor, Mrs, lapidiary 25
McGregor, Marie 76, *77*
McHardy, Colonel 112, 114
McKee, Alec, President Sandringham Association 128, *128*
Mackie, Jim 121

Maclean, Lord, Lord Chamberlain 64-5, *64*, 69, 125
Macready, Sir Nevil, President 67-9, *68*, 83, 125
Magnus, Mayott 74
Manchester, Earl of, Lord Chamberlain 17
Mancroft, Lord 60
Marbery, Mrs 15
Margaret, Queen 11
Marks, John, President 71-2, 83
Marriott, Bex 92
Marshall and Rose, pianos 54
Martin & Company 51
Martin & Frost, interior furnishers 121
Martin, Robert *121*
Mary, Queen *25, 26,* 62-3, 92
Master of the Horse 14, 33-5
Maude, Colonel Sir George 34, 35
Maudslay, Sir Rennie 61, 125
Mawe, Mrs, minerologist 25
May & Baker 126
Mayer, Daniel, President 42
Mercers Company 7
Merchandise Marks Act 36, 44, 48
Merchant Taylors Company 7, 92
Merryweather, fire extinguishers 54
Meyer & Mortimer Ltd., military outfitters 135
Michael of Kent, Prince 86
Millennium Banquet 92, *93*
Miller, Morris 122
Miller, Robert Douglas, President Edinburgh Association 120, 121
Mitchell, Roger, President 83, *85*
Mobil Oil Company Ltd 68, 75
Montgomery Wilson, W., President 42
Moore, Peter 21
The Morning Post 22
Morrison, Brigadier, Secretary 60-1
Morshead, Owen 102
Munro, Willie, Secretary Edinburgh Association 123
Murray, Ian
    at Highgrove *88*
    President Aberdeen Association 113, 115

N
Nastiuk, Bohdan 121
National Assurance Company 120
National Benzole, motor spirit 69
Neighbour, Mrs, tailoress 32
Netherlands, Royal Warrants 132, 135
Newbegin, Charles, President *55*
Newman, Fred 105-6, *106, 128*
Newton & Co., barometers 54
Nicholays, furriers *47*
Norsworthy, Patricia 81

O
Ogilvie, Julia 120
Olan Conservation, drawing restoration 107

Old England 52
Ord, Peter 113, 116
Osborne House *34*
Ovaltine 59

P
Palengat, David, President 71
Palmer, Reginald, President 59
Palmer, William, President 60, 64-5
Parkers, writing implements 92
Parry, Ray 107
Part, David, President 69-70, 83
Patel, Uma, President Windsor Association 104-6
Patents, Designs and Trade Marks Act 36
Patey's Trade Mark application *49*
Pawne, William 14
Peachey, Mrs, modeller of wax flowers 25
A. & F. Pears, soap manufacturers 43, *44*
Pears, Robert
    President 43, *57, 57*
    Secretary 56, *57*
Peat, Sir Gerrard 85
Peat, Sir Michael 85-6
modernising of Royal Warrants 86-7
Pembroke, Earl of 37
Penhaligon's 83
Perrier, mineral water 47
Perry & Co., trade mark application *46*
Philipps, Hon.R.Hanning, President 59
Pickles, Sheila 83
Pickup, Col. Christopher, Secretary 81-2, *81, 82,* 85, 91, 94-7, 112
Piercy, Jeremy 107
plate 75, *75*
Plowden & Smith 74, 84
Plowden, The Hon. Anna 74, 84, *84,* 91
Plowden Medal 69, 84, 95
policing the warrant 36, 44-51
Henry Poole and Co. 133, 134, 135
Portland, Duke of 33
Thomas Potterton, gas water heaters 54
Pow, Kathy, manicurist 107
Prince's Trust 88
Pringle, Robert, motor engineer 113
Procter & Gamble 79
Protim Services, timber treatment 107, 126
James Purdey & Sons, shotguns 25
purveyors 18, 32-3

Q
Queen Elizabeth, The Queen Mother, *see* Elizabeth, The Queen Mother
The Queen Elizabeth Scholarship Trust 69, 72-3, 76, 78, 84, 86, 89, 95, 116
    100th birthday of Queen Mother 92, *94*
    as freeholder of Buckingham Place 85
    Trustees 145-7
Queen Elizabeth Scholarships 27, 89-91, 95
    Scholars *48,* 89-91, *89, 94,* 95, 148-50

R
RAC Club 82
    badge *83*
Rae, Fiona, enamellist 88
Ratcliff, Lieutenant-Colonel 47
H.D. Rawlings, mineral water manufacturers 42
H.& M. Rayne, shoemakers and handbag manufacturers 59
Rayne, Sir Edward
    President 59, *66,* 82
    Treasurer 67-8, 71-2, 72
    150th anniversary celebrations 74, *76*
Reading, Bishop of 72
Reckitt's 'Blue', dye manufacturers 47
Reed, Barry Austin 74, *78*
    President 53
    150th anniversary celebrations 73, *76*
    Chairman QEST 72-3, *77*
Regent Street *42*
Reid, Campbell, President Edinburgh Association 123
Reid, David, President Edinburgh Association 121, 123, *128*
Richard II 7, *10*
Richard III 13-14, *14*
Riddell-Webster, John, President 69, 125, *126*
Rideout, Emily 43
Roberts, Dick, President 67
Roberts Radios 67
Robertson, David 109
Rolls-Royce Ltd, motor cars 43, 44
rose 74-5, *74*
Ross, Ian 79
Ross, Sir Malcolm 85, 96-7
Rossiter, Ann *94*
Rossleigh, motor engineers 121, *121*
Rowe, Christopher
    President 90-2, 112
    Chairman QEST 90-1, *92*
Rowntree, chocolatiers 47
Rowntree, A.S. 47
Royal Brierley 79
Royal Coats of Arms 6, 8, 20, 36-7, *70, 120*
    abuse of use 45-9
    George IV *20*
    imitators 51
    legal position of use of 86
    National Assurance Company 120
    Peascod Street Arms 103
    Prince of Wales (1901) *36*
    Scottish and English 120, *120*
    use abroad 49-51
Royal Doulton, anniversary plate 75, *75*
Royal Household
    accounts 13
    annual drinks party 68
    Great Spicery 13
    independence of departments 19
    modernising systems 86, 105-6
    relationship with RWHA 32, 37-8, 62, 70, 92, 96

Tradesmen's Warrants Committee 96, 131
Warrant-granting policy 87
The Royal Tradesmen's Association 41
Royal Warrant Holders Association 8, 13, 41, 83-4, 95
    see also Warrant Holders; Queen Elizabeth Scholarship Trust
    150th anniversary of formation 72-6
    aims 84
    annual dinners see banquets
    archive 57
    Association formed 23
    Association incorporated 36-8, 62, 73
    charitable enterprises 69-70
    Council members 136-7
    gifts to Royal Family 95, 104
    Hon Treasurers 144
    Honours Board 41
    Joint Silver Anniversary Trust 63-4
    London Reception 82-3
    membership 46, 65, 95
    Plowden Medal 69, 84, 95
    premises
        Beaconsfield 57
        Buckingham Gate 59, 65, 68, 77, 84-5
        Buckingham Place 85, 92
        Hanover Square 43, 57
    Presidents 41-3, 81-3, 138-42
    President's Badge 58
    relationship with Royal Household 32, 37-8, 62, 70, 92, 96
    Royal Charter of Incorporation 36-8, 62, 73
    Secretaries 81, 143
    subscriptions 95
    use of Royal Coat of Arms 45-51
    Way Ahead Committee 83-4, 89, 93
The Royal Warrant Holders Association Limited 41
Royal Warrants of Appointment 16-17, 86
Russia, Imperial Warrants 134
Rutland, William, lace draper 17

S
Sandeman, wine merchants 71
Sandeman, Tim, President 71
Sanderson, wall paper manufacturers 54
Sandicliffe Garage, motor horse boxes 74
Sandringham Association of Royal Warrant Holders 69, 125-9, 127
    cricket matches 128-9, 129
    dinner programme 126
    inauguration 125-6
    officers 235
Sandringham Flower Show 128-9
Sandringham House 124
Sanitas & Co. 59, 68
Satchell & Son, Glengarry Caps 35
Scarman, Mr, Steward 29
scholarships 27, 67, 89-91, 95
J. Schweppes & Co, soda water manufacturers 20, 51, 59
Scott, Lord Herbert, President 43, 44, 55
Scotts, hatters 42

Securicor 73
Seignor, Robert, watchmaker 18
Seven Incorporated Trades of Aberdeen 114, 114
Sharp's toffees 71
Shepherd, Brian 111
Sheridan, Michael, President Aberdeen Association 113, 115
Sheridans, butchers 113, 115
Sherwood, Roy, 'The Court of Oliver Cromwell' 16
Shirras, Laing, Purveyors of Brazier 110, 110
Shirras, George, President Aberdeen Association 38, 39, 110
H. & G. Simonds, brewers 56, 59
Simonds, E.D., President 59
Simonds, F.A. Vice-President 55, 56
Skinner, Michael
    President 83, 92, 94
    Millennium Banquet 92, 93
    QEST 92, 94
    tailor 14, 28, 74
Slade's advertisement 45
Sleigh, Lowrie, Edinburgh Association President 72, 121, 121
Sleigh, Sir William 121
Smellie, Brian 82, 121, 122
C. Smith & Son, gold lace men 33
Smith, Peter, President 73
Smith, Sharon 48
Smith's, clocks 54
Spain, Warrants 135
stables 19, 19
Stamfordham, Lord 102
Staniland, Kay 12, 27
Staples Brothers 29
Start-rite, children's shoes manufacturer 78, 78
Staybrite Rustless Steel Equipment 54
Stephens Brothers, shirt makers 73, 74
Stevens, Keith, President 59, 61, 62, 93
Stoddart, Sandy 95
Stone, E.Baldock 33-5
Storrs, John, Secretary Sandringham Association 125, 125-6, 128-9
Strachan, George, general merchant 113
subscriptions 95
Sutherland, Colin, President Aberdeen Association 111, 115, 116, 116
Swaine, James, whipmaker 20
Sweden, Royal Warrants 133, 135
Symes, Lai 89

T
Taylor & Henderson 110
Taylor, David 110
Tebbott, Robert, builder 99-100, 99, 100
Thatched House tavern 22, 28
Thatcher, Mrs 16
Thomson, Garry 85
Thomson, George, history of Aberdeen Association 38, 109
Thomson, John 35
Thorn, Mr, President 42
Tillett, Louis J. 43, 48-9
The Times 45, 46, 47

Tims, Sir Michael 62
Tipton, Thomas, President 42
Toye, Kenning & Spencer, gold and silver lace and embroidery 25, 74
Toye, Bryan, President 74, 78, *115*
Trade Mark Act 44, 47, 48
trade mark applications 50-1
Tradesmen's dinners in Windsor 100, 103, 104
Tradesmen's Warrants Committee 7, 85
Trebor mints 71
Trefgarne, Baron 48
Trenchard, Lord and Lady 60
Tupper, Admiral Sir Reginald 55, *55*, 60
Twining & Sons, tea merchants 25, *64*, 73-4
Twining, Sam
    President 59, 63-4, *63*, 73-4, 125
    150th anniversary celebrations 74
    and Prince Charles as Grantor 64
    Treasurer 84, 95
Twining, Stephen, President 59, 60

U
Unite, James, President 42
John Unite Ltd, tentmakers 42
United States, use of Royal Arms 50
Upton, Henry, sadler 35

V
Vanity Fair 37
Vauxhall 73
Veuve Clicquot, champagne 71
Victoria, Queen 22-3, *23, 109*
    Diamond Jubilee 38-9, 38
    as Princess 20
    statues 109-110, *110-11*
    viewing the llama *32*
    Warrants granted 25, 92
    wedding dress lace 26-7, *24, 26, 39*, 87
    and Windsor tradesmen 101-2
Vincent, W.R. 92
Vincent's of Reading 92

W
Waddington Games 83
Waddingtons, playing cards 68, *71*
Wall, Richard, pork butcher 20
Walls, pork-in-ordinary 59
Walls, Thomas 59
A. Wander Ltd 59
The Wardrobe 13
Wareing, Mr, haberdasher of hats 17
Warrant 8, *8*
Warrant Holder, definition 7
Warrant Holders 19-23, 70
    see also Royal Warrant Holders Association
    applications 77-8
    bankruptcy 33-5
    fees levied 19, 32-3

female holders 28-9, 54
foreign 37
individuals 33-4
losing a Warrant 35
membership of Association 46, 65
oath of loyalty 25
obligations and duties 8-9
policing the warrant 36, 44-51
qualifications required for membership 87
surrender of Warrants 59
unauthorised holders 35-6
Warrant Holders Trust 27
Warrants of Appointment 135
Watney Mann, brewers 59
Watney, Oliver, President 59
Watson, Sir Duncan, President 44, *55*, 83-4
Duncan Watson Ltd, electrical engineers 44
Watson, Victor, President 68, 70-1, *71*
Way Ahead Committee 83-4, 89, 93
Bernard Weatherill Ltd., livery tailors 48
Weatherill, Sir Bernard 48, *48*
Weavers Company 7
    Charter *9*
Webster, James, President 43
Weetabix, breakfast cereals 73, 78
Welford & Son, dairymen 42
Welford, John, President 42
Wellman Bros 103, *104*
Wells, Sir Frederick, President 59, 68
Westall, Bernard 70
Westmorland, Earl of 19-20
Wharam, Robert, President 44, 48
Whately–Rollo 88
Whitbreads 73
White, David 78
White Horse Distillers 56
Whitfield, Miss, envelope maker 25
Whittington, Betty 14, 17, 56
Whytock & Reid, furnishing company 119, 123
Wilkinson & Son 92
Wilkinson, James, gun maker 20
William IV 21, 22
warrants granted 20, 92
William and Mary 18
Williams-Thomas, David 79
Williamson, J., President 59
William Wilson & Co., building materials 104, 114
Wilson, Graeme
    President 71-2, 104, *104*, 114-15
    Windsor, Eton & District Association affiliation with national
    Association 104-5
Wilson, Jim 128
Wilson, Sir Harold 60
Wilson's, piano tuners 121
Wilton Royal Carpet Company, carpets 54
Windsor Castle *98*
Windsor, Eton & District Association of Royal Warrant Holders 21, 32,

38, 72, 99-107
    affiliation with London Association 104
    dinners 100, 103, 104
    officers 235
    Peascod Street Arms 103
Wise, William, President 43
Witham Oil & Paint 127
William Wood & Son 106, *106, 107*
Wood, Louis 89
Woodhouse, Richard, President 74
Woodman, A.M. 55
Wycherley, Annie 68, 81, 85, *128*
Wysing, Stephen, corn cutter 18

Y
Youdale, Roy 89, *89*